STOLEN BASES

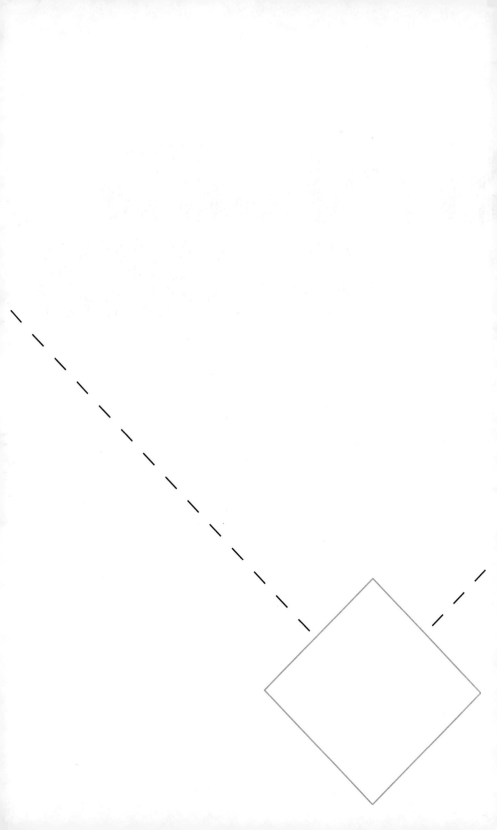

STOLEN BASES

Why
American
Girls
Don't
Play
Baseball

JENNIFER RING

UNIVERSITY OF ILLINOIS PRESS
Urbana and Chicago

Library of Congress Cataloging-in-Publication Data
Ring, Jennifer, 1948-
Stolen bases : why American girls don't play baseball /
Jennifer Ring.
p.   cm.
Includes bibliographical references and index.
ISBN 978-0-252-03282-0 (cloth : alk. paper)
1. Baseball for women—United States.
2. Baseball—Social aspects—United States.
I. Title.
GV880.7.R56   2009
796.357082—dc22   2008040129

For the girls

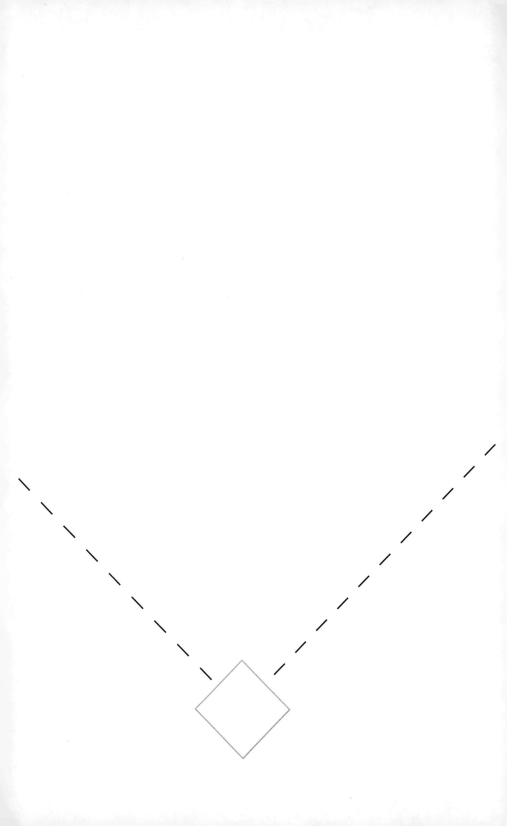

Contents

Acknowledgments

Love of baseball is not an acquired taste: it's a genetic inheritance that must be accepted as a part of one's life. If you have the gene, you'd think it would be easy to write a book about baseball. For me it was not. Writing *Stolen Bases* has been one of the most intellectually and emotionally challenging experiences of my life. The support of many people has sustained me in what has proven to be an extra-inning game.

My mother Frances Ring, a Yankee fan (which can't be helped . . . she was born in New York), is responsible for whatever part of my genetic inheritance is a writer and has believed for years now that this book would finally be published. My father George Ring was a Brooklyn Dodgers fan who stayed loyal when they showed up in L.A., took me to my first ball game at the Los Angeles Coliseum and bought me a baseball glove when it became clear I needed one. All the varieties of childhood baseball I played with my brother Guy Ring and Jeffrey Freiberg (Dodgers fans) filled my summers even when Little League wasn't for girls.

The baseball gene was distributed unevenly to the next generation. My daughter Johanna Jacobson has graciously tolerated her parents' and sister's baseball obsessions throughout her life (and is a loyal A's fan nonetheless). Her gift with language revitalized this project one winter afternoon when she read a very rough draft while I bundled up on her couch and waited for her verdict. Lillian Jacobson (A's fan) was still in Little League when I began writing the book. I did not plan on the length of the intervening years, so it was an unanticipated joy to be able to ask her to read and help me revise the nearly completed manuscript last winter when she was home from college. Her willingness to help, her critical eye for both baseball and literary errors, and the hours we spent together on the manuscript made the home stretch precious.

My closest friends and colleagues encouraged this project even as it drew me across disciplinary boundaries and away from the political theory that brought us together. Arlene Saxonhouse (Yankees fan) remarked to me at a political science conference years ago, "I think you should write your baseball book," which got me started. Mary Dietz's reassurances that the project was significant, even as I wandered away from the security of the scholarship we had learned together as graduate students, gave me confidence to continue. Joan Burton created the earliest opportunity for me to speak about baseball to a scholarly audience at Trinity University. She and her husband Dave Stinchcomb (White Sox fan) have shared their warmth and support of this project since the beginning, watching baseball with me on both coasts as well as in Texas (even though Dave and I had to explain to Joan that *full house* was a term from poker that could not be used to describe *bases loaded*). Victor Wolfenstein, always my teacher, urged me to be patient with this project at a critical moment when frustration threatened to overwhelm me. Celia Roblin and Roz Tritton of the Oxford Women's Cricket Club graciously taught me everything I know about cricket during a memorable summer visit. Jim Glennie of the American Women's Baseball Federation opened my eyes to the world of organized women's baseball in the United States. Shirley Burkovich and Karen Kunkel took time in the sweltering Scottsdale heat at Team USA trials to regale me with stories of their baseball careers. Michael Messner and Ann Travers introduced me to new colleagues and a new discipline as I explored the cutting edges of sports sociology.

Farsighted and open-minded members of the Reno athletic community contributed to the baseball story that fueled the writing of this book. Coach Jay Uhlman of the University of Nevada baseball team showed unwavering belief and confidence in his batting and fielding student Lilly, even when it seemed as though everyone else was trying to push her out of her beloved game. His warmth, humor, and optimism helped us tolerate discouraging times and celebrate the good moments. Speed and strength trainer Rob Conatser found the right formula to prepare a teenage girl to play baseball with teenage boys while maintaining a balanced and healthy perspective. His knowledge and spirit are themselves a source of energy. Coach Ron Malcolm of Wooster High School welcomed the first girl to play high school baseball in northern Nevada onto his team and allowed her career to continue. The support of the coaches, players, and parents of the Wooster Colts made the 2004–2006 seasons special. The coaches at WB Baseball in Reno provided baseball expertise and a home for training that was filled with warmth, good humor, and as little stress as possible. Thank you to Nick Kuster, Pat Flurry, Aaron Demosthenes, Jody Schwartz, and Kyle Bateson.

Completion of the book also took the support and assistance of friends at the University of Nevada. Eric Herzik (Cubs fan), in his capacity as both dean of the College of Liberal Arts and chair of the Department of Political Science, found ways to fund aspects of the project and enabled me to find time to work on it. He offered the creative support that every faculty member hopes for. President Joe Crowley of the University of Nevada generously granted an interview in which he shared his knowledge of the NCAA, Title IX, and gender equity. Nevada Athletic Director Cary Groth provided invaluable perspective on college athletics. Ann Ronald read an early version and offered helpful suggestions. Leah Lin Jones and James Read were invaluable research and editorial assistants. Kristen Kabrin (Yankees fan), administrative assistant for the political science department at Nevada, stepped in at the last moment, mobilized her extraordinary skill, and with breathtaking efficiency prepared the manuscript for submission.

I am beholden to Joan Catapano of the University of Illinois Press for her sustained belief in this project even when it was a mess. Her astute choice of readers provided me with the advice and perspective I needed to mold the manuscript into a book. I deeply appreciate the insights of Adrian Burgos Jr. and an anonymous reader for their detailed and perceptive suggestions. Breanne Ertmer, Jennifer Clark, and Copenhaver Cumpston of the University of Illinois Press, and photographer Richard Hopkins provided expertise that made the book's production a joy for me. Finally, I thank Judy Gruber of the University of California at Berkeley for putting me in contact with the University of Illinois Press when this book was not much more than an idea. She was an extraordinary colleague and friend.

STOLEN BASES

Prologue
Entitlement and Its Absence

An athletic little girl, four years old, watches baseball on television with me. She is my daughter. She plays ball games with her friends but favors what her sister refers to as "small ball-stick" games rather than "big ball-goal" games. One day in a sporting goods store, on a rack low enough for her to see, she spies a baseball glove. It's her size and exactly like the bigger gloves: black leather, beautiful lacing, brand name embossed on the leather in shiny gold script, satiny cloth label sewn into the strap that fits over her hand. She loves it. She wants it. I take it off the rack and show her which hand it goes on, her right hand. She tries it on and it's perfect. It's the only glove in the store small enough and made for a southpaw. "It's just right for you, isn't it?" I say, and buy the glove. A ballplayer is born.

She'd be happy playing catch in the front yard all the time if she could get someone to throw to her, and she shows remarkable patience swinging a small bat at a pitched rubber ball until she makes solid contact. She begins hitting it regularly, and the game becomes even more irresistible to her. When we throw the ball back and forth in the yard, I take care not to throw hard and to avoid throwing it at her face. I "feed" her the ball so she'll be able to catch it easily. Then one day, very soon after she begins playing, well before she's five years old, I realize I don't have to be so careful; she can catch the ball. And throw it back. We have a real game going.

Two years later, Lilly is old enough to participate in Little League. I sign her up and she joins the Mariners, gets her yellow and blue uniform, and picks the number 2. The coach is a friend of mine who asks me to be his assistant coach. I'm happy to help; "inside baseball" skills are at a minimum at this level and I feel qualified enough to help the kids learn to catch and bat and to tell them which way to run when they make contact with the ball. The team, by some miracle, is undefeated during the season. One of the highlights of the year is Lilly's game-saving catch of a pop-up, running all the way around the pitching machine without tripping over the cord. Coach Ted gives her the game ball that day.

The next year our family moves from the California Bay Area to northern Nevada. Lilly signs up for one of the "farm" teams in her new town's Little League. Whole games are pitched with a pitching machine. The coach is a gentle, paternal man, and when we arrive at his house for the first team meeting, he enthusiastically introduces Lilly to her new teammates, "Look fellows! We have a girl on our team!" They are the Cubs. She soon proves herself the most reliable hitter on the team and bats fourth in the batting order. Since there are no called third strikes, she really has an opportunity to hit cleanup. A parent watching one game observes to another, "Whoever made out the lineup is a genius. Every time the bases are loaded Lilly gets up to bat!" In spite of its cleanup hitter, this team is not successful at winning. But the season is a good one: nice kids, having fun playing ball.

Lilly encounters her first batting slump when she begins facing live pitching the following year. She is frozen at the plate, as are many of the boys. This response seems the better part of wisdom, and athletically appropriate, since the pitchers are eight-year-olds with little idea about how to get the ball in the vicinity of home plate while avoiding the batter. The smartest way to face pitches is indeed to stand warily in the batter's box and wait until it's time to duck or hit the dirt. Not a problem; we find her a batting coach at a local sporting goods store, and she soon snaps out of her slump and starts swinging the bat again. She bats at the top of the order, and as a lefty she has found her favorite position at first base. Her new coach is also an easygoing man who thinks she's "the best pure hitter in the league," and picks her first in the draft the following year, bragging to her parents that she was the first player drafted in the league, as well as on his team, in spite of the fact she is the only girl.

She has another standout season, which ends on a slightly sour note. Lilly is the first child in our family to play organized sports. Since her dad and I are Little League novices, we don't realize the tournament scheduled at the end of the season is as important as the regular season, and we have planned the family vacation before the end of the tournament. The Cubs are undefeated in the first part of the tournament, but when Lilly departs the team promptly loses and is eliminated. When we return from vacation, the coach jokes with her about this and mentions that there was also a nine- to ten-year-old all-star team picked, which did not include the "best pure hitter in the league." I sense storm clouds gathering but try to ignore it.

The following year, Lilly tries out for the "majors," the highest level of play in her league. She is one of the youngest players in her year because her birthday falls just before the cutoff date of July 31. She is ten but playing as an eleven-year-old. If she had been born in August, she would have qualified for an additional year in Little League before having to move on to a full-sized baseball diamond in Babe Ruth baseball. Parents with more extensive Little League experience know when to conceive to best complement a baseball career. Several have tampered with birth certificates to enable their sons to have an extra year of Little League. I find myself wondering how such forgery can be accomplished and realize I am beginning to take the game as seriously as the parents I have come to despise.

Lilly is, as usual, the only girl in the league, and also one of the youngest and smallest players trying out for the majors. She doesn't get picked. She's back in the minors, with her good old coach from the previous year. She is puzzled and looks to her dad and me for cues. Should she feel humiliated? But she loves her old coach and teammates. We tell her she'll get more playing time and probably develop more as a ballplayer staying in the minors for an additional year. She's fine with it. I am less fine, wary and hypersensitive for any signs of unfair treatment. I am a mama bear, my ears pricked up and my nostrils twitching, alert to any possible threat to my cub's love of baseball.

Next spring, Lilly is eleven trying out as a twelve-year-old once again for the majors. This time she makes one of the teams with a new coach and teammates. The coach is welcoming and shows enthusiasm about having a girl on his team. She has a good season: plays every game all game long at first base and bats sixth, rather than her usual second or third. I'm not crazy about that since Lilly is "a hittin' machine," a fact acknowledged by all. She's not a home run hitter, but she has a remarkable batting average and on-base percentage. "There are runners in scoring position and here comes Little Miss RBI," parents often remark to each other as Lilly stands in the on-deck circle. She should be batting higher in the order, I think. But I'm learning the coaches do not seek my advice about such matters.

This is her last season in Little League, and she has no intention of playing softball next year. At the end of the season, the coaches have a meeting to decide who will play on the all-star team. I am learning that for the families of these stars, the entire regular season is not much more than a prelude to the season that counts: all-stars and summer ball. Lilly knows what day the all-star selections will be made, knows she is one of the best players in the league, and trusts her coach as only an eleven-year-old can do. Finally, after no phone call all day, she musters her nerve and calls him after dinner. "Coach, did you nominate me for all-stars? No. Oh . . . Okay, bye." Tears fill her eyes as she quietly puts down the phone. It is the first major adult betrayal of her life.

Indeed, it is an astonishing act of injustice, and I am flabbergasted. It is difficult for me to understand. Other coaches in the league see me around town and volunteer, "Tell Lilly she had my vote. I don't know why she wasn't nominated." It was her own coach who had not even put her name up to be voted on for all-stars selection. He had kept her out of the running. Each coach in the league could nominate four players. Lilly's coach nominated his son, the two assistant coaches' sons, and a fourth boy who was a decent player who had not had anywhere near the season Lilly had and whose real passion was for hockey. He dropped baseball after that summer. There was also a second-seed all-star team. The coach of that team requested to the league president that Lilly be allowed to play on the second-seed team, since she was passed up for the first team and obviously deserved to play in the "postseason." His request was denied by the league president without an explanation.

The league president happened to be the wife of Lilly's coach. I wrote her a letter requesting a description of the selection process and asking why Lilly had not been nominated. I cited Lilly's season stats, which I had roughly kept track of on a piece of paper torn out of a notebook. The league president wrote me a defensive letter, copied to an attorney, stating that the coaches have complete choice about the all-stars and the league does not keep or consult statistics when choosing them. This is completely false; stats are indeed kept in extraordinary detail on the Palm Pilots of every coach in the league. The official denial only confirmed that the players had been chosen for political rather than athletic reasons. The storm clouds I'd been sensing for years now burst. I was drenched in rage, much angrier than Lilly was. I tried to work off my anger as we went to the ball fields early each summer morning, ahead of the Nevada heat, to practice "long toss," trying to strengthen her arm for fall ball on a full-sized baseball diamond. I would stand at home plate, she would stand in the outfield, I would hit the ball to her, and she would throw it back to the plate. Twelve years old and already her arm was so strong I couldn't keep up with her.

Her experience with youth baseball did not improve the following year or for the next three years. Lilly was in Babe Ruth baseball with twelve- to fifteen-year-olds (in youth baseball birthday math). The men who coach at this level are foolishly serious about the consequences of their sons' play. The boys are still boys and capable of having a girl on their team without noticing anything amiss in the universe. The coaching fathers had for the most part moved up from Little League with their sons, with the exception of the gentler, easier-going men who quit, wisely avoiding the silly drama of men coaching their sons at this stage while believing they are preparing them for a chance at baseball glory. This is where the fathers' lost dreams come to dominate the baseball diamond. Many of the men had played high level baseball in their younger days; a few even played in the minor leagues or very briefly in the majors. None had achieved their goals completely, and all were determined that their sons would get at least as far as they did. With breathtaking stupidity, even the most knowledgeable baseball fathers stood behind the backstop during their sons' at bats, screaming with each pitch, "Keep your shoulders level!" "Keep your head down!" "Bat speed! Bat speed!" "What did you swing at that one for?" "Oh, for Chrissake!" as their sons pop up or ground out or strike out. How could they do otherwise with that sort of distraction interrupting all possibility of concentration?

Lilly is hitting better than ever, but she plays only the minimum required by league bylaws, late in each seven-inning game, for an inning or two if the score is lopsided. She has a new coach who admits, "She does have a way of always getting on base." But he prefers to stick with the starters he has selected who are all headed for the same high school team. He will keep them in the lineup, waiting until they hit, rather than change the batting order in response to persistent slumps or the eagerness of the players on the bench. When Lilly does have a chance to play, she still plays first base because of her quick hands, in spite of the fact that taller players are now preferred at this position. She is not given the option of pitching, but she's not too interested in adding the pressure of standing in the middle of the diamond with parents screaming about every pitch to the burden of proving that girls can play baseball every time she steps onto the field.

One day, when she is playing first base, the third base coach of the team at bat signals a hit and run with a runner on first. But the batter pops up the ball to first base, Lilly catches it, and the runner on his way to second wheels around and tries to return to first. He is tall and fast, and Lilly, who has had her eye on the ball she was catching, turns to try to tag him as he scrambles back to the bag. He does not dive back to the bag as he should have, but runs. Because she is now blocking his path with the ball in her hand, they collide, landing in a tangled heap on the base path. Nobody is hurt. Lilly had done the right thing: she caught the ball for the first out and was ready to tag the runner caught off base to make the double play herself. The pitcher, standing on the mound watching this, had failed to cover first. But Lilly's coach decides that it's too dangerous for her to play first base and moves her to right field for the rest of the season. He pays no heed to her father's or my insistence that we do not believe she is in excessive danger; she is a ballplayer and knows the risks. She would be in greater danger at any number of other positions: catcher, middle infield on a double play, even outfield, where calling another fielder off a fly ball is still a rare event.

She would probably also be in greater danger of injury in a ballet or gymnastics class, and everybody in the league is aware that earlier that year a twelve-year-old *softball* player had been hit in the face with a pitch, requiring extensive cosmetic and orthodontic repairs. Lilly's response, beyond horror and sympathy for the injured girl, was, "Who wants to stand that close to a pitcher when you're batting?" Softball does not seem a safer game to her. Nor is she anxious to try sliding into base wearing shorts. Lilly is a baseball player, and she is being penalized for having done the right thing at her position. The one time the coach considers putting her back at first base and putting his son in right field, the boy is enraged: "Are you kidding? Right field?" he screams at his father. Lilly is sent back to the outfield. I know of this exchange only because it took place in Lilly's presence, and she mentioned it to me, recognizing full well the lack of respect for her that it unmasked. Of course, none of the coaches think of teaching her how to pitch, even though they could use a lefty. Pitching is an honor reserved for coaches' sons. In spite of all this, she works her way into the starting lineup by the end of the season, by dint of sheer numbers: her RBIs. Even when she is sent in to bat late in a game, cold from sitting in the dugout for nearly two hours, she delivers what is needed: a clutch single and an RBI. In the end, she could not be denied.

The next season, she moves up to the fourteen- and fifteen-year-old teams with yet another coach. But it is the same story of marginalization, lack of playing time, and getting blamed for the mistakes of the other players and the coaches themselves. I sit in the outfield bleachers now, along with a few other disgruntled parents, because I worry that my constant sense of outrage will lead to indecorous behavior if I sit near the coaches and their families behind home plate. After one cold weeknight game in which Lilly waits for hours to play for the last half inning, she takes a little longer than usual to emerge from the dugout with her gear bag after the game. As she gets into the car, she says, "I told him I'm done. I quit the team." I am silent for a moment. I am not really surprised, but the news chills me. I finally say, "Good for you. What did he say?" She replies, "He said, 'I'm sorry you feel that way. Was it the playing time? Because that's not going to change. It's not in my plans to start you.'" She quit in the middle of the third season of being treated like a mediocre ballplayer.

I was convinced that her treatment had nothing to do with her playing ability and desperate to prevent her from internalizing the message that she isn't good at baseball. Still, even I, a profoundly biased mother, cannot turn off the coaches' voices in my head. I know how difficult it must be for her to resist the insidiousness of their message as I find myself wondering, "*Is* she as good as I think she is?" I try to look objectively at the boys she has played with. I replay tapes of them in my mind over and over again. They're all decent ballplayers. They have to be at this increasingly sophisticated level of baseball. The bigger boys are certainly stronger than Lilly. But I don't see any future superstars among them or even any future major leaguers. There are one or two standouts, kids who will probably play some Division 1 college sport. Not all of them are totally committed to baseball; some will go on to play football or basketball. Even with the talented few, however, injuries and the capriciousness of growth rates will enable some and disable others before a college—much less a professional—career will be possible. Some throw farther. Some hit farther and run faster. Few have Lilly's quickness of hands or consistency at bat, or her graceful swing. Nobody denies that her mechanics are as good as they need to be. As I replay these comparisons over in my mind, I come to the conclusion that they're all just kids playing baseball and she's as good as she needs to be to compete. When David Eckstein, the highly respected major league shortstop, was playing in the World Series with the Angels, the television commentators noted that his teammates had nicknamed him "Just Enough." A few years later, Eckstein was again in the World Series, and this time he was the World Series MVP for the St. Louis Cardinals. Two World Series rings for a man who is 5 feet, 7 inches tall and weighs 165 pounds. He has "just enough" size and more than enough heart to be a champion. Lilly certainly has "enough" to play baseball with adolescent boys in a recreational league. Why was she being treated so badly by the men who were coaching her?

The answer, I came to understand, was that *I* was playing the wrong game. I naively thought I was playing a game called "Kids Play Baseball" or something like that. The game these men were playing was completely different. The game they were playing, even in Little League, was called, "My son has a great future in baseball and whatever helps him get there is the reason I'm here. The league exists in order to showcase him." I was looking for fairness; they were looking to win at all costs, because that is the current, corrupted name of the American game.

— — —

In a recent issue of *Elysian Fields Quarterly*, author Doug Bukowski describes the similar experience of his own extremely talented daughter on a twelve-year-old boys' baseball team. "She went to a team where the coach screamed and the players froze her out. My All Star was judged no better than the boy with prosthesis; they shared playing time. Clare was humbled without being given a chance at redemption."[1] Bukowski's daughter was willing to play softball when she was shunted out of baseball, in spite of the fact that her father writes, "The thought of her playing softball bothers me greatly. The game is both separate and unequal. At least with the Negro leagues, the rules and equipment stayed the same. But shorter distances and a larger ball are deemed appropriate for girls. Why, exactly, given that women athletes aren't relegated to smaller swimming pools or basketball courts? Every difference between baseball and softball implies weakness compounded by inferiority."[2]

Lilly and Clare are contemporary girls. In the thirty-five years that girls have been legally permitted to play organized Little League baseball, not much has changed. In a 1973 *New York Times* article entitled "In the Suburbs, Little League Is More Than Just a Game," David A. Andelman describes the pressures put on eight- to twelve-year-old boys in one representative suburban community in Long Island to play baseball and play it seriously. Andelman describes twelve-year-old Joyce DePasquale watching the game from behind the chain-link fence behind the backstop. She is watching her eleven-year-old brother Louis batting at a critical moment in a close game. "Joyce . . . grasps the chain links tightly, her large brown eyes peering through the grating. 'I play ball with my brother and my father,' she says wistfully. 'And I play softball. But I don't like softball. I'd like to play baseball.' Louis singles to first, steals second and third, then scores the first run of the game for Oceanside Laundry. Outside the fence, Joyce grins and claps her hands, then turns sadly and walks down the street toward home."[3]

— — —

Lilly won't quit. In fact, the more they try to drive her out of the game, the more she digs in. She finds an independent local team to play with for the rest of spring season and takes private lessons to prepare for high school fall practice season. She has a private hitting and fielding coach who truly believes she has the talent to play baseball and shares her belief that softball is not the game for her. When she is treated disgracefully, as she has been for the past few years, he gets a puzzled look on his face, not believing the talent he sees in her can be denied by anyone in their right mind. At her batting lessons, Lilly, "Coach Jay," and I share our incredulity and conclude that indeed, the coaches must not be in their right minds. But it all takes a toll on Lilly. I know she is beginning to doubt herself.

She goes out for the high school baseball team freshman year. After four months of winter conditioning and performing well enough by her own exacting standards (as well as that of the boys she was trying out with) to make the team, she is unceremoniously cut. "This has nothing whatsoever to do with gender," insists the high school coach, a wealthy volunteer coach/parent, not a teacher or an employee of the school district. He is a prominent member of the business community and accountable to nobody for his actions with the team. He is also an alumnus of the school and its baseball team, and his two sons are poised to follow in his footsteps and play ball for their father. "You'll just have to get bigger, faster, and stronger." While she knows she will have to get bigger, faster, and stronger to keep playing baseball at this level, as will all the boys, she also knows that was not the reason she was cut.

As she leaves the field this time, tears streaming down her face once again, her expression is of shock and betrayal for the second time in her fourteen years. She does not want to return to school. She has played baseball all her life with the same boys who made the team. They know and she knows she was not cut for lack of ability. To acquiesce in that injustice is intolerable. She is an honor student, the school she is at is a good one, and her parents are academics. But we know we need to find another school or we will have taught her to accept insult, injustice, and humiliation. It is too important a lesson to overlook, both for Lilly and the other students who know full well why she was cut. Passivity in the face of it would not only crush Lilly's spirit, but send the message to all the other students that girls do not have to be treated respectfully and taken seriously. Indeed that lesson may have been the one intended by the coach: no girl should have the audacity to believe she can keep up with the boys on a high school baseball diamond.

I doubt the coach consciously sees things this way; I am certain he believes his decision is justified by sheer baseball criteria. He has evaluated the five "tools" of baseball for all the kids who tried out for his team. He has given them a score of one to five on each of the tools: batting for power, batting for percentage, running, throwing, fielding. It all sounds scientific and objective. Except that there are no actual numbers used to measure the tools. It's completely subjective, and the coach makes it clear that he can pick whomever he wants. It is unclear to me how one could make the case that there was any discrimination involved, whether it be against a girl, a member of a racial or religious minority, or a member of a poorer economic class. It just so happens that all of the players selected for the team are light-skinned, Christian, and from fairly wealthy parents. The one Asian-American and the one Hispanic boy who tried out for the team with Lilly have also been cut. But the coach would probably insist to his dying day that he chose his players solely on the basis of baseball acumen and his ability to evaluate their skills.

It had never occurred to me that I would consider removing a child of mine from a decent academic school for a sport. Not even for baseball. Bukowski describes himself and his wife, as his daughter is poised on the verge of high school: "Despite five college degrees between them, he and his wife do not know if they will send their daughter to a high school based on its academics or sports program."[4] I find myself, surprisingly, in the same position. We go shopping for another school. There are no guarantees Lilly will be able to play baseball, but at least she won't have to live in the toxic atmosphere of the school she has been in.

We find a high school much less privileged than the first. It has a good academic magnet program and it feels friendly, less like a country club. Unlike the parents at her first high school, the parents at the new one are not in a position to be able to ensure their children's athletic success with generous financial donations to the school. At the first school, field lights, a scoreboard, a new weight room, and even a new baseball stadium with a state-of-the-art field and grooming equipment were acquired with parental contributions. This is the American public school system at its most inequitable: cut taxes to win elections and allow the parents in the wealthy schools to fund their children's education with tax-deductible donations. Then attract the best athletes who aren't zoned for that school with your superior facilities, and get the school board to grant them "variances." This sort of recruiting buys state championships for the rich and paves the way for intercollegiate recruiting violations and the dominance of the wealthiest teams in professional sports. We may talk to our children about the importance of being "good sports" and "playing fair," but that lip service pales in comparison to the experience of "how it's done" in the real world. The lessons are learned well by our adolescent athletes: win at all costs, democracy be damned, private enterprise rules, and the wealthy deserve their victories.

Varsity and junior varsity sports at Lilly's new school are accessible to all students with a modicum of ability and a desire to learn, although some cannot participate because they hold down jobs after school or must care for younger siblings while their parents work. The parents are predominantly working class and less available to meddle with school athletic programs. Men show up at their children's' afternoon games at about 5 o'clock, still wearing mechanics', carpenters', and plumbers' clothing. There are very few business suits to be seen in the stands and very few coiffed, well-dressed women. The parents are of diverse racial and ethnic backgrounds. One of my favorite moments when our baseball team does well against a richer school is a mother yelling out, "Yeah! Good job, guys! White Trash Rules!" There are no field lights at all, and the kids paint their own bleachers. In fact, a traditional prank played on the varsity baseball rookies is to tell one of them to go turn off the field lights after a practice ends at dusk. The veteran players watch and laugh as their young teammate runs around the field looking for the light box before remembering there is none. It is expected that the young athletes at this school will learn more about and improve at the sports of their choice by playing, rather than being selected for the quality of their private coaches, their off-season traveling teams, or the size of their parents' bank accounts. The school's coaches are actually teachers, in the business of educating young athletes in the classroom as well as on athletic fields. The coach, along with his assistants, watch her hit and throw, decide they need a lefty in the rotation and teach her to pitch, too.

So there is a breathing space: a successful sophomore year on junior varsity, and preseason conditioning and tryouts for varsity in her junior year. Lilly knows, once again, that she did well in the preseason and that she had a good tryout. She also knows the varsity roster is almost full with last year's juniors, including several pitchers who are being wooed by Division 1 college teams and the pros. She prepares herself for not making the varsity squad. "At least I know I'll be playing baseball this year," she says repeatedly. "I don't care whether it's JV or varsity." She trusts the coaches (it's hard to destroy the resilience of an open-hearted kid), genuinely likes the other boys who are trying out, and hopes for the best. And she makes the team.

This may read like a success story, and indeed it is. But consider what it took to get one talented athlete to the point of being able to play her favorite sport in high school. How many young people could endure so much discouragement, so much marginalization and deceit from adults, without deciding long before their goal was achieved that staying the course is not worth the trouble? Of those who persevere, how many would be able to keep intact the self-confidence and faith in themselves to enable them to perform at their competitive best? How much better might they be with a solid foundation of support from their environment? How many of us could hear an otherwise revered high school coach tell us we are mediocre, not big, strong, or fast enough, and not be damaged as athletes and as people?

In American high schools, the best players hope to continue with their sport, earning college scholarships and professional careers. They travel to "showcases" throughout the nation where audiences of coaches and scouts sift through their needs and evaluate the players. The very best are drafted by the pros or sign letters of intent in the fall of their senior years to play for a particular college or university the following year. In contrast, Lilly assumes nothing about her future in baseball. It's one season at a time, and it always has been. She visits prospective colleges during the summer between her junior and senior years and cautiously asks several athletic directors of Division 3 schools about the possibility of baseball. Several direct her politely to other varsity sports, specifically softball, or to intramural or club sports in which she may be interested. Two are very discouraging: "The NCAA won't let women play baseball. We have a softball team here, and that's what the women play." She assumes that high school baseball will mark the end of her baseball career and tries to prepare.

It is true, of course, that only a small percentage of high school athletes take the next step of playing at the collegiate or professional level. For the vast majority of fine athletes, high school is as far as they expect to go with their sport. What is problematic about girls and baseball is that only the exceptions battle their way even to high school ball, and beyond that none has a realistic hope of continuing. For girls, baseball has a glass ceiling to be collided with at twelve, or at most, seventeen, discouraging all but the most determined to take up the sport at all.

— — —

This book attempts to follow the history of the women's game in order to understand why American women have had such a difficult time playing a game that they so clearly love. It questions the historical, cultural, and economic forces that try to keep Lilly and all the girls who want to play baseball away from the game. Organized around an historical narrative that, unfortunately, repeats itself, it describes the circumstances and dynamics that twice stole baseball from American girls: once at the turn of the twentieth century and again in the late twentieth century, after it was no longer legal to exclude girls who wanted to play.

Woven through these two narratives is a theoretical and historical exploration of the intersection of race and class exclusion, along with gender exclusion, from the national pastime. At the very beginning of the twentieth century, Albert Goodwill Spalding, sporting goods magnate, baseball player, and promoter, declared baseball off limits for women and envisioned global baseball on a colonialist model. The exclusion of girls and the subordination of nonwhite men were both part of Spalding's American baseball vision. He articulated a mission for American baseball men: use the American sport to teach men from nonwhite races and non-European cultures to become civilized and rational on a white American middle-class male model. The vision was prophetic or, at least, a self-fulfilling prophesy. This book explores the prophecy and seeks ways to dismantle it, to rescue baseball from its arrogance and sense of exclusionary entitlement. It hopes to restore its more optimistic nickname: the people's game.

Chapters 1 through 4 describe the history of baseball, tracing its roots from girls' and boys' games in England to the creation of the myth that Abner Doubleday invented the game in Cooperstown, New York, in 1839. These first chapters trace the unacknowledged history of girls' and women's participation in the game from early versions in England until it arrived in the United States. American women have played organized baseball at the amateur, collegiate, and semiprofessional levels from the middle of the nineteenth century onward. Their history of play can be read as comedy or tragedy, as they were regularly chased from the field and just as persistently returned, time and again. Meanwhile, softball was invented by men who wanted to keep playing baseball indoors, through cold winter months. Chapters 5 and 6 offer a theoretical and historical perspective on emerging ideas about gender, race, and class in the late nineteenth and early twentieth centuries, exploring the evolution of baseball as the "national pastime" during those years. As baseball developed, the sport became a battleground for contesting the nature and place of gender, race, and class in American society.

Chapter 7 is an interlude: a discussion, for comparative perspective, of the history of English women's cricket. Englishwomen have also had to battle to play their national bat and ball game, and although they have had a longer struggle by several centuries, they have had more success than their American sisters in gaining access to their game of choice. The story of English women and cricket is an inspiring story of perseverance that is still in progress.

Chapters 8, 9, and 10 return to twentieth-century America to find history repeating itself. They explore contemporary baseball on the youth, collegiate, and professional levels as American girls' and women's attempts to participate in the national sport are beaten back again and again. These three chapters discuss the 1970s Little League lawsuits and ensuing substitution of softball as "girls' baseball," Title IX and the culture of college sports, and continued racial problems in the context of the current globalization of baseball's labor supply. Throughout the book, the incredulous question is raised: where are all the girls and women who have demonstrated over and over again that they just want to play?

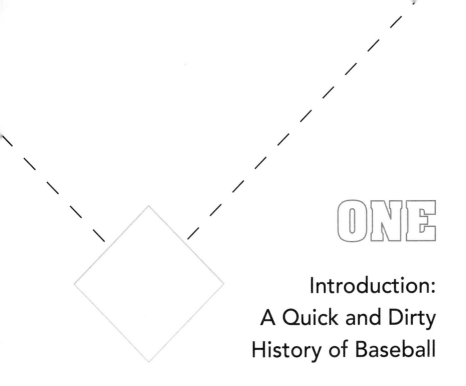

ONE

Introduction: A Quick and Dirty History of Baseball

Motives

Girls *can't* play baseball and American folklore has the rhetoric to prove it. From the ubiquitous declaration "Girls can't play baseball!" to the taunt "You throw like a girl" to Pete Rose's remarkably honest assertion that he was grateful he was born a boy because otherwise he couldn't have played baseball, the national pastime has been declared the domain of only half the nation. By the time I was nine years old, it was clear I fell among the excluded half. Before then, I was always among the first picked in games with the boys on my street because I was the neighborhood slugger who could also pitch. Then, in the fourth grade, the boys went off to organized Little League play, and I went from first picked to entirely excluded. I was left throwing a ball at my garage wall or tossing it in the air with one hand, batting it down the street, trotting after it, and then hitting it back to where I started. For hours. Still, it was the thing that occupied nearly all of my spare time, when I wasn't reading about the Dodgers in the *Los Angeles Times*. As a woman, I am thus doing what I can, writing about baseball instead of playing it.

The Boys' Game

Baseball has been likened to a civic religion, a sacred part of American culture. Venerable major league stadiums are its cathedrals; the World Series and the all-star games are the game's holy days; the Hall of Fame is the Vatican where saints are enshrined. Baseball's religious overtones may contribute to women's exclusion from the national pastime. As with most of the world's major religions, women are welcome in the pews but must not touch the sacred core of worship nor set foot in the pulpit. Televised crowd shots during the playoffs and World Series frequently show female fans at tense moments with hands clasped in prayer and eyes closed in devotion. But it requires an effort to conjure up an image of an American woman in a baseball uniform, strolling to the plate, bat in hand, or standing on a pitcher's mound rubbing up a new baseball. In fact, it is difficult to imagine a woman setting foot anywhere between the foul lines of a major league ballpark.

American popular culture reinforces the taboo against women's access to the national pastime. Even when the girls and women are portrayed in film or fiction as intelligent, attractive, three-dimensional characters, their hands never touch a baseball and their feet never set foot on a baseball diamond, save perhaps the occasional very young girl on a Little League team in a children's movie. Albert Spalding insisted over a century ago that a woman's place remains in the stands. Mass media's portrayal of women and baseball has confirmed that belief. This is perhaps to be expected in the early part of the twentieth century. For example, in a 1929 article titled "Grandstand Girls," former player Al Demaree examined the role of women in baseball, arguing that women were capable of wrecking the game even from the stands. He claimed that when women "intruded into the game there was usually trouble, which could take the form of cliques of wives, jealousy over salaries, or simply a comment by one wife about seeing one of the other's husbands with a good-looking girl. In addition, family affairs could be a distraction for a player and hinder his performance. Getting married during the season was considered bad luck."[1] The only possible benefit this former major leaguer could see to allowing women into ballparks was as spies. The girls were to date one of the opposing teams' pitchers the night before he was scheduled to pitch, making sure he had a late night with plenty to drink at a cabaret in order to impair the ballplayer's performance during the next day's game. The evil temptress, along with the nagging wife, became stock figures in twentieth-century baseball films, the counterpart of the angelically supportive girlfriend with no needs of her own.

Even more persistent than the sentiment that women and baseball are incompatible is the denial of women's actual history of play. Girls and women have been on baseball diamonds from the very start, in spite of having their presence erased time and again. In Ken Burns's highly regarded 1986 documentary *Baseball*, women barely make an appearance, although the sheer quantity of baseball history in the twenty-five-hour documentary would seem to leave room for some account of their role in the game. The few minutes Burns devotes to women and baseball are brief and inaccurate. In the first 119–minute "inning" of Ken Burns' nine-inning video tome, 86 seconds are devoted to women's baseball in the nineteenth century. The national anthem is played in full more times than can be easily counted, and in the first volume, Burns lauds boyhood baseball as the foundation of the national pastime. The army of slow-talking baseball intellectuals interviewed by Burns describe the centrality of the game to the "American system" (system of what remains undefined, but it is clearly intended to signify something deeper and more functional than mere "culture") with a sense of ponderous self-importance that belies the sheer fun of playing ball; the experts' insistence that baseball is fun lacks credibility. The one woman who does make an appearance is historian Doris Kearns Goodwin talking about the importance in her childhood of Jackie Robinson and the Brooklyn Dodgers.

There is no mention of the fact that women played professional baseball on all-women and mixed teams, against all-women's teams, men's teams, and mixed teams in the nineteenth century. There is no acknowledgment that future hall-of-famers Rogers Hornsby and Smoky Joe Wood drew their first paychecks as professional baseball players on "mixed" teams (with women), nor of the fact that the first professional women's baseball team in the United States was the African American Dolly Vardens in the 1880s in Pennsylvania. Burns dismisses the nineteenth-century female baseball phenomenon as a passing fad: "They did not play for long. The teams were soon forced to disband because the game was considered far too violent for young ladies."[2] In fact, women have attempted to gain access to America's diamonds for as long as baseball has been played here.

In Burns's documentary, the racial integration of major league baseball in 1947 is rightly regarded as a major national event, and Branch Rickey and Jackie Robinson are portrayed as two of the greatest men in American history. But the America that benefits from the courage of both men does not include women, and women's efforts to play baseball are slighted as a footnote to baseball. It's true that Robinson's entree began the process of rectifying decades of unconscionable racism, including that of Commissioner Kennesaw Mountain Landis, who had to die before Branch Rickey could sign Jackie Robinson with the Dodgers. Jackie Robinson suffered unspeakable abuses for years at the hands of white ballplayers and fans, and it is widely acknowledged that his life was cut short by a heart attack brought on by the stress he had endured. His determination, bravery, and athletic brilliance symbolically and actually opened many doors for men of color in American sports and other walks of life. However, it is not true, as Burns asserts, that when Robinson broke the color line, "Major league baseball became in truth what it claimed to be, the national pastime." The documentary does not mention that another of Commissioner Landis's achievements was to void the contract of minor league pitcher Jackie Mitchell on the grounds that "professional baseball was too strenuous a game to be played by women."[3]

Jackie Mitchell, a white seventeen-year-old left-handed pitcher with the Chattanooga Lookouts, was banned from professional baseball for the offense of being successful in an outing against the New York Yankees. In April 1931, the Yankees had come to Chattanooga to play the Lookouts in an exhibition game. Young Mitchell took the mound with two outs in the top of the first inning, with one run already scored and a man on first. Babe Ruth walked to the plate, tipped his hat to Miss Mitchell, and dug in. He swung at the first pitch and caught nothing but air. He let the next two pitches go by; the count was two balls and a strike. He swung at another sinker and missed again. He let one ball go by, and then, with a full count on him, took the next pitch. It ripped across the middle of the plate; Jackie Mitchell had just struck out the most powerful and celebrated hitter in major league baseball. Ruth was not gracious about it. He kicked the dirt in the batter's box, chewed out the umpire, threw his bat down in disgust, and returned to the visitor's bench.

Mitchell stayed in the game and struck out American League batting champion Lou Gehrig on three straight pitches. Gehrig, always more of a gentleman than Ruth, walked back to the dugout, shaking his head and smiling. The hometown crowd of some four thousand fans cheered wildly for their young hurler. The next man up was Tony Lazzeri. He fouled off several pitches and then took four for a walk. The national press was quick to pounce upon Ruth's strikeouts as faked, in which case it was probably the best acting he had ever done. (He had appeared in several movies in which his thespian abilities had been the butt of humor from his teammates and the general public.) Many commentators have claimed that the performance was staged for publicity, but that possibility was not a part of Landis's rationale for banning Mitchell nor were any promoters who might have been responsible for the event punished or rebuked for setting up a fraudulent publicity stunt.

The event was dismissed as "bawdy publicity" by the *Sporting News*, which scolded that the national game must be "treated with respect."[4] A writer for the *New York Evening Post* joked that the pitcher couldn't throw a curve ball, adding, "It takes curves to pitch baseball and Miss Mitchell's aren't that kind."[5] One fan from Missouri was unable to see the humor in the event, writing a letter in which he claimed the "stunt at Chattanooga" would have a bad effect on baseball. He said the game was already "too feminine" and ventured the opinion that men like Rogers Hornsby would never have been responsible for bringing females into the game. (Apparently this particular defender of baseball's dignity was unfamiliar with the fact that females brought Hornsby into the game—at least the professional game.) The writer went on to opine, "It's a he-man's game, and it seems like we even have to have red-blooded he-men to even promote it, as well as play it." In a fit of "there goes the neighborhood" logic, the fan predicted that women all over the country would now be signing baseball contracts, and he reminded the readership that women would "do anything from shaving their heads to shooting their husbands, just for the thrill of getting their names in the paper."[6]

No shaved heads were noted, no wounded husbands of women ballplayers were reported at emergency rooms, and women continued to show up on baseball diamonds as they had in the United States since the 1850s. For the most part, they were racially segregated. In the twentieth century, white women were permitted to play when men went to war, and black women were allowed to play when the integration of major league baseball drained the Negro Leagues of their best players. Satchell Paige coached a diminutive woman named Mamie "Peanut" Johnson, who became a ninety-eight-pound pitching sensation in the (all-male) Negro Leagues for several years in the late 1940s and early 1950s. Of her experience, she has noted that nearly all the men treated her with the respect she deserved after she established she could play ball and help them win. The few "dummies" she encountered weren't worth worrying about, and in terms of the discretion and modesty that might concern detractors, she and her teammates simply took turns using the dressing room. She knew she couldn't play in the "White girls' leagues," and so she had to play with the black men, and she quickly found that "striking out the fellas made me happy."[7] But ballplayers like Mamie Johnson are not recognized as a legitimate part of baseball history. Needless to say, the "integration" of major league baseball is as incomplete as the integration of all levels of baseball in America: it does not include America's girls and women, either in their own leagues or, like Mamie Johnson, in a league with the "fellas."

Twenty-one years later, on June 21, 1952, Commissioner Ford Frick was prompted to ban women from playing either minor or major league baseball after a woman signed a minor league contract with the Class B Harrisburg Senators. If baseball is the national pastime, the implication is that women are not part of the nation.

Foundation Stories

The efforts to identify the origins of baseball as entirely male read like a series of "Just So" stories. American boys invented baseball, the story goes. Baseball is the product of the genius of American boyhood. Baseball was invented by any number of young country lads with time on their hands, a ball, a stick, the side of a barn, and eventually a few companions. They amused themselves with stick and ball games called "One Old Cat" and "Two Old Cat." Albert Goodwill Spalding, the first professional baseball promoter, former Boston Red Stockings and Chicago White Stockings pitcher, sporting goods magnate, and inventor of the first sporting goods catalogue, offers up the boy, ball, and barn scenario as the natural history of baseball.[8] In order to institutionalize that history, he created a "commission" in 1907 comprised of friends and professional baseball insiders. Spalding's explicit agenda was to establish "once and for all" that baseball was indigenous to America and inherently masculine. His hand-picked baseball experts attributed the game to the Civil War hero General Abner Doubleday and placed its moment of birth in Cooperstown, New York, in 1839. Doubleday was a West Point cadet in 1839, and in order to have been in Cooperstown on that date, he would have had to have been AWOL, undoubtedly resulting in a negative impact on his future military career, but never mind that detail. The "evidence" that Doubleday was baseball's founding father was a letter written by a mentally unstable man named Albert Graves, who claimed to remember the moment when Doubleday drew a diamond with a stick in a dirt field in Cooperstown. Graves might have been in Cooperstown in 1839, but he would have been five years old, rendering his ability to recall the name of the cadet with the stick a little dubious. Later in life he was incarcerated in an asylum for the criminally insane for the murder of his wife. Nonetheless, neither his credibility nor recall was questioned by the Spalding commission.

Although the Doubleday-Cooperstown story was refuted almost immediately by historians, it is the version of baseball history that stuck, much like George Washington's cherry tree is embedded in the American imagination. It doesn't

seem to matter that the inventor of the baseball myth was a men
murderer. What was attractive about his story was that the Americ.
invented by an American military man whose masculinity was unin

> The Doubleday Myth . . . was promulgated by the Spalding Commission
> shot down immediately and convincingly by the journalist Will Irwin the following
> year. It was again debunked in 1939 by Robert W. Henderson of the New York Public
> Library, even as the baseball industry celebrated, with great pomp and circumstance,
> its "Centennial," the centerpiece of which was the grand opening of the National
> Baseball Hall of Fame and Museum in Cooperstown. Despite irrefutable evidence
> to the contrary, the media and the public, encouraged by the flag-waving bluster of
> the baseball industry, clung to the Doubleday Myth. It seemed they simply preferred
> the "immaculate conception" of baseball by the war hero Abner Doubleday to the
> messy evolution that the historical evidence clearly indicated. The Doubleday Myth,
> it seemed, would prevail regardless of the evidence.[9]

David Block, author of the most intelligent recent scholarly research on the
origins of baseball, dismisses much of the speculation about baseball's origins
as jingoistic fiction. "The age-old debate over baseball's ancestry has always
been long on bluster and short on facts. Since the earliest days of the game's
prominence in America, writers have been eager to expound upon its origins.
That they generally had no clue of what they were talking about never seemed
to slow them down."[10] Speculation about its origins arrived with the game itself.
The furor that culminated in Spalding's commission began when nineteenth-
century baseball expert Henry Chadwick remarked that baseball had evolved
from the English children's game of rounders, which he had played in England
as a boy. Chadwick emigrated from England to the United States as a child, fell
in love with baseball, and was so influential in the game's early development
that he was referred to as "Father Baseball." He was a baseball writer and reformer, and made many improvements on the game (including invention of the
box score) that modernized it considerably. He was so widely respected that his
insistence that baseball was related to an English game could not go unanswered.
American baseball men of the late nineteenth century would not tolerate having
the game's origins contaminated by anything English. Even more offensive than
association with England was the ignominious fact that English rounders was
played by both girls and boys.

Chadwick's remarks provoked a furor to defend the honor of the "American"
sport. The earliest defense against the blasphemous observation that baseball
came from England was recorded decades before Spalding called for a definitive
answer. A. H. Sedgwick, in the August 26, 1869, issue of the *Nation* claimed

that baseball was *not* derived from cricket, rather than *not* being derived from rounders. Since cricket was regarded as a respectable English sport, although less "manly" than any American sport, Sedgwick defended baseball against the influence of cricket rather than stooping to defend it against possible association with the juvenile and girly sport of rounders. The logic of his argument was convoluted.[11]

In the 1880s, baseball journalist William M. Rankin claimed that baseball had sprung up spontaneously in rural New York in the 1830s. His evidence for this claim was that the New York Knickerbockers, arguably America's first baseball team, must have had teams to play against in the 1840s—another case of inverted logic. Next, John Montgomery Ward, ballplayer and lawyer, published a book in 1888, *Base-ball: How to Become a Player*. He too asserted that baseball was of American origins. Block notes, "Unlike Rankin, who appeared to be motivated purely by the desire to defend baseball's originality, Ward was driven by extreme jingoism. He was so incensed by Chadwick's notion that baseball was of foreign derivation that in 1888 he devoted the first fifteen pages of his book to 'proving' that the sport was, in fact, of American birth." Ward was adamant that baseball could not be descended from rounders precisely because girls also played rounders: "Moreover, he sneered, this English baseball had been a game for women and girls, and therefore, by definition, could not have been a prelude to the 'robust' American sport."[12] Ward offered the theory that baseball was the spontaneous invention of American boys. "In the field of out-door sports the American boy is easily capable of devising his own amusements, and until some proof is adduced that base-ball is not his invention I protest against this systematic effort to rob him of his dues."[13]

Spalding became involved in the issue after his return from a world tour of baseball in 1889. Subjects of the British colonial empire had not been impressed by the "new" American sport paraded before them with so much American swagger. They scoffed that baseball was merely a dressed-up version of rounders, the game they had all played with girls when they were young. The disparaging remark was repeated at a banquet held at Delmonico's New York restaurant to honor the returning ballplayers and attended by dignitaries including Theodore Roosevelt and Mark Twain. In response to the insinuation that baseball was originally English, the guests, filled with food, spirits, and raucous good cheer, took up the chant "No Rounders! No Rounders!" and Spalding determined to form a commission to formally investigate and dispel the slanderous theory once and for all. Not until 1907 did he actually get around to doing it, but he was quite explicit about what he expected the commission to find. Block reports:

Acting with little pretense of objectivity, Spalding's commission solicited testimony from dozens of baseball old-timers, asking them to recall their earliest memories of the game. The following excerpt from a letter Spalding wrote to the Massachusetts baseball pioneer John Lowell typified the tone of his inquiries: "I have become weary of listening to my friend Chadwick's talk about base ball having been handed down from the old English game of 'Rounders,' and am trying to convince myself and others that the American game of base ball is purely of American origin, and I want to get all the facts I can to support that theory. My patriotism naturally makes me desirous of establishing it as of American origin, if possible, and as the same spirit will probably prompt you, I would like your ideas about it."[14]

The Spalding commission obligingly produced the Doubleday story, which was quickly dismissed by all who knew baseball. Nonetheless, the story stuck in the American popular imagination, and no amount of serious scholarship has succeeded in dislodging it. Spalding was clearly a public relations genius.

The accepted mythology about baseball's origins was created at the dawn of an era of American economic hegemony, when wealth and success measured standards of masculine dominance. The United States at the cusp of its century of manhood would not suffer the insinuation that anything associated with America was in any way feminine. That defensive attitude about American masculinity continues to undermine the beauty of the national game, as well as our reputation in the world as honorable and compassionate people. The home run has limited ability to shock and awe, especially when the masculinity it is supposed to display is chemically enhanced. During the major league postseason, the male television viewing audience is offered commercials for Viagra while many of the wealthy heroes on the field believe they can't get their jobs done without performance-enhancing substances. The event has been twisted into an exhibition of artificial rather than genuine masculinity.

Block investigates the origins of baseball with the humor, insight, and attention to detail of a well-told mystery. By the time he finishes, there is little doubt about where baseball came from. But before we turn to his account, it is important to note even this fine historian of the game introduces his investigation with an unwarranted assumption. The title of the first chapter of *Baseball Before We Knew It* is "Uncertainty as to the Paternity." While the paternity of the American game may indeed be more of a mystery than is generally assumed, the truly overlooked aspect of the game is baseball's *maternity*. Indeed, the American game is usually assumed to have no mother. It sprung, fully-formed, from the head of either Abner Doubleday or some cluster of American boys, resembling the birth of Athena, motherless, from the head of Zeus. But along with its fathers, baseball had many mothers, for the most part English girls and women. The game was invented by English girls and boys, and when it immigrated to the United States, American boys and men tried to shove girls off the diamonds and sandlots, telling them the game was too manly for them. Girls have been fighting to get back in the game ever since.

Girls and the Childish Game

If the story of its masculine American origins is inaccurate, does that mean it was a feminine English game? Not necessarily. Overly simplified dichotomies and the tendency to believe that pure masculinity is contaminated by any femininity at all have a venerable, if ignorant, history. In the nineteenth century, race law proclaimed that a person was "white" only if completely free of "black" blood. One African American relative somewhere in a person's distant genealogy was sufficient to disqualify one as a Caucasian in the minds of racists. The implication was that white is pure and black is a contaminant. There was an equally deadly equivalent a century later in the Nuremberg laws where Nazis defined the level of Jewish heritage needed to contaminate one's Aryan racial purity. Similar fears are at work as nineteenth- and twentieth-century American men appeared to proclaim that one drop of femininity in baseball's history was enough to undermine the game's masculine pedigree. The implication, again, is that manliness is pure and femininity is a contaminant. But rather than recognize that what they really feared was femininity, American men first went after anything English. Fear of femininity was submerged in the proclamation that anything English was prissy and effeminate compared to the activities of robust, masculine American men.

Block identifies only one American researcher in the early twentieth century who came close to revealing baseball's origins: "A determined New York librarian, Robert W. Henderson, was quietly pursuing a novel approach to the question of baseball's ancestry: serious historical research."[15] Henderson began his investigation in the years following publication of Spalding's findings. He found that people in the United States had been playing baseball long before 1839, when Doubleday was supposed to have invented it, and that a set of rules for a game called "rounders" was published in 1828. While America anticipated the nationwide celebration of baseball's phony centennial, Henderson published a book that established there was no evidence that Abner Doubleday or any other single individual was entitled to exclusive credit for the invention of the game.[16]

Block believes Henderson's research demonstrates that rounders was one regional variety of an English game that had more widely been called base-ball

from the start. It was indeed played by both boys and girls, and had many different variations in England, including stool ball, which was originally played by
English milkmaids with their stools, using rocks for balls. Putting a runner out by
throwing a ball at a stool appears to be a simplified version of cricket's rule that
a runner may be retired if a fielded ball is thrown to the wicket before the runner
arrives. Throwing the rock at a base runner to retire her was another rough and
tumble aspect of girls' stoolball that could hardly be described as "sissified."

When, in the late nineteenth century, Americans began to make an international hoopla about their new national game, the British immediately recognized
it and began their own investigations into origins. They found several versions
that had been played for centuries on British soil and were unsure which had
come first, rounders, base-ball, or stool ball: "The British public's confusion was
due to the same memory gap that had misled Chadwick. The term 'rounders'
had begun replacing the term 'base-ball' in England in the 1820s, and by 1874
most Englishmen had forgotten, or had never known, the game's original name.
This amnesia was surprisingly abrupt, given that as late as 1840 the authoritative
Encyclopedia of Rural Sports was observing: 'There are few of us of either sex
but have engaged in base-ball since our majority.'"[17]

According to this research, an English game called base-ball preceded English
rounders as well as American baseball, and was played by both boys and girls.
Rounders was a variation of base-ball, played in some regions of England, and
based upon the earlier and more widely played version:

> The facts speak for themselves. While the name "rounders" cannot be found any-
> where in the historical annals of England or the United States before 1828, the term
> "base-ball" shows up at least seven times in the eighteenth-century writings. The
> convincing proof that this eighteenth-century base-ball was the predecessor to mod-
> ern baseball emanates from the first published rules for "English base-ball" in 1796.
> These rules describe a bat-and-ball game in which a pitcher served to a batter, who
> had three attempts to put the ball in play. Once striking the ball, the base runner ran
> counterclockwise around the bases with the object of returning home. This familiar
> pastime, named "base-ball" and resembling baseball entered the historical record
> more than thirty years before the first known appearance of rounders.[18]

In sum, baseball evolved from a matrix of early English ball games, involving "unknowable numbers of children and youths experimenting in fields and
churchyards and village greens over a period of centuries, with the resulting
wisdom passing unobtrusively from one generation to the next."[19]

Rounders is still a staple of British childhood, and every adult who has ever
played it regards it as baseball's antecedent. An English rounders ball today

looks exactly like a small American baseball: hard, with a white leather cover and red stitching. In keeping with its folk origins, rounders was originally rougher and less refined than baseball, with runners being taken out by being thrown at. The fact that girls invented a game that involved throwing rocks at each other as they ran between stations, whether stools or bases, appears to have taught us nothing about the seriousness of girls' play, or about the penchant for physical roughness toward which girls have been inclined, at least until society teaches them it is unnatural and unfeminine. As the contemporary English journalist Lesley Hazelton remarked, after attending her first American baseball game at Yankee Stadium in 1979:

> Three hot dogs, two bags of peanuts, three glasses of beer and nine innings later, I was amazed to find out how much I already knew about baseball. In fact, I'd played a simpler form of it as a schoolgirl in England, where it was called rounders and was played exclusively by rather upper class young ladies in the best public schools, which in England of course means the best private schools. Yet though we played on asphalt and used hard cricket balls, and played with all the savagery that enforced good breeding can create, we never dreamed of such refinements as I saw in that afternoon. The exhilaration of sliding into base! That giant paw of the glove! The whole principle of hustle! A world awaits the well-bred young Englishwoman in the ballpark. But for me the most splendid of these splendors was to watch the American language being acted out.[20]

Women and the Manly Game

Baseball was declared both manly and American at the same time it was becoming professionalized. When profit is involved and people are to be paid and hero-worshiped for playing a game, it is important to explain the rationale for the output of cash and adoration. Baseball was presented as serious business for American *men*. Not just anybody could play—certainly not women, certainly not men of "inferior" races or cultures. The manliness of professional baseball also contrasted with boys' play. Professional baseball was hard work, not a game. Excellence demanded discipline rather than effortless talent. Team practices were the phenomenon of the professional era of baseball, and the best players were referred to as disciplined workers more than natural talents. Only grown men were capable of the requisite strength and effort and therefore worthy of the subsequent rewards: fame and fortune, or at least a paycheck for playing ball.

The American men who qualified for the calling were assumed to be entirely of white and of northwestern European Christian descent. The exclusion of all men of color was not regarded as an issue, and it was taken for granted that "national" did not include the nation's women. A. G. Spalding proclaimed, "A woman may take part in the grandstand, with applause for the brilliant play, with waving kerchief to the hero . . . loyal partisan of the home team, with smiles of derision for the umpire when he gives us the worst of it . . . But neither our wives, our sisters, our daughters, nor our sweethearts, may play Base Ball on the field . . . Base Ball is too strenuous for womankind."[21]

Those delicate fans, waving kerchiefs at their heroes, were encouraged to attend baseball games by means of commercial gimmicks such as "Ladies' Days" to discourage, it was hoped, working-class men from drinking, using foul language, gambling, and brawling at baseball games. The ladies were quick to grab reduced-price tickets and occasional free admission and soon proved the equals of men at drinking, swearing, shouting, and exhibiting all the aspects of devotees of the game. In fact, violence ensued when they inundated the ballparks in such numbers that the men, who paid higher prices, had to crowd into the few remaining seats. The fantasy that women would play nursemaid, mother, or moral guardian to the men was short-circuited by their indecorous behavior. They developed a reputation for rooting "as vociferously as the men," and the local newspapers were moved to comment on what happened to ladies at ballparks:

> The ladies are regular and numerous attendants at the grounds. The hundreds of them who stood on the seats and screamed and waved their handkerchiefs and brandished their fans in ecstasies of applause yesterday knew enough to come early and avoid the crush. How much they knew of the game . . . was to be seen by the way they behaved. As they took their seats in the grand stand they brought out their scorecards and pencils, argued over the merits of the coming players, and consulted little diaries, in which they had entered records of past League games.[22]

The New York reporter also noted that all classes of women were represented: "The rough and blackened finger tips of some of them showed them to be working girls; others, by unmistakable signs, even when they had not their children with them, showed that they were housewives and mothers; others still, by their costly dresses and the carriages they came in, were seen to be well-to-do women and young girls; and a few were of the class of female gamblers and sporting women that has grown so considerable in this city of late."[23]

At another Ladies' Day game women rioted when the umpire put a home-team player out of the game. Nineteenth-century sports writer Fred Lieb once described the "Ladies Auxiliary" of the Philadelphia Athletics of the 1880s as having some members with "slightly tainted" reputations. They called themselves the "Big Bosom 'A' Gals." Seymour wryly notes, "Without disparaging by faint praise, therefore, it may be said that the female fans equaled the male in intelligence and deportment."[24]

So immersed in the sport were nineteenth- and early twentieth-century women, that baseball's unofficial theme song, "Take Me Out to the Ball Game" was written in 1908 about a young Irish working girl, Kitty Casey (or in some versions "Nelly Kelly") by composers Jack Norworth and Albert von Tilzer. The verses of the song, in contrast to the chorus that is now sung during the seventh inning stretch at every major league baseball game and probably every other ballpark in America with a loudspeaker system, tells of Nelly, whose beau, Joe, makes the mistake of asking her on a date to Coney Island. The song in full goes:

> Nelly Kelly loved Base Ball games
> Knew the players, knew all their names,
> You could see her there every day,
> Shout "hurray" when they'd play.
> Her boy friend by the name of Joe
> Said to Coney Isle, dear, let's go,
> Then Nelly started to fret and pout,
> And to him I heard her shout:
> Take me out to the Ball game,
> Take me out with the crowd.
> Buy me some peanuts and crack-er-jack,
> I don't care if I never get back.
> Let me root, root, root for the home team,
> If they don't win it's a shame,
> For it's one, two, three strikes
> You're out at the old Ball game.

American insistence that baseball has always been for men only is an outright theft from American women, both white and black, who have been playing the game since it came to American soil. The manliness of baseball as well as the early whiteness of the game was limited to major league baseball. On a more earthly level, Americans of all classes, races, and genders have played the game since it became popular in the 1830s. Some barnstorming players were paid, much like traveling entertainers, musicians, circus performers, and so forth who earn salaries, even though they were neither white nor male. One local guidebook of 1883 described two "artistically dressed" baseball teams of "ladies of color" from Philadelphia and Chester, Pennsylvania. The Chester team, named the Dolly Vardens, sported red and white calico dresses "of remarkable shortness" with matching caps.[25]

White women also played. As early as 1868, a woman reported a baseball game for a Cincinnati newspaper between the Muffins and the Biscuits. Another woman, Mrs. Elisha Green Williams, used her maiden name and secretly served as official scorer for the home games of the Chicago White Stockings from 1882 to 1891. She sat among the wives of the players, but neither the women nor Mrs. Williams's son, who mailed in the scores after each game, knew what she was doing. To resort to going underground to keep score at a baseball game shows dedication to the sport and reveals equally the dedication of American society to avoid recognition of that dedication!

During the nineteenth and early twentieth centuries, there were baseball teams in men's and women's colleges, traveling women's "Bloomer Girl" teams, teams of men and women playing together, some including men wearing bloomers and wigs "in drag," and some with men dressed in conventional baseball outfits. Historian Harold Seymour also documents, to the extent that there are historical traces, the play of young women who were not college students and could not rely on that limited venue for access to baseball. "Those non-college women, who ventured to play baseball in public, like the poor and unsung, often left only faint traces of their passage. A few women's teams are said to have existed as early as the late sixties. One team documented is a group of high school girls who played in Los Angeles in 1874. . . . the first Washington, D.C., women's game reputedly took place in 1879."[26] American women's early involvement in baseball is not surprising when it is viewed as a continuation of centuries of play by English girls and women.

Genetic Endowment

By the middle of the twentieth century, baseball made efforts to address the most glaring affront to its reputation as "The People's Game": the exclusion from the major leagues until 1947 of men of color. In fact, there had been a handful of Native Americans, who were all given the patronizing nickname "Chief" by their helpful teammates and the sporting press. There had also been Latin American ballplayers in the early days, for the most part light-skinned Cubans who were referred to as "Spaniards."[27] Baseball has acknowledged the inaccuracies of the stereotypes that had been used as excuses for racism: African American men, or Asian men, or men of Latin American origin, or, for that matter, Italians and Jews could not possibly play baseball because they lacked the requisite physical and psychological characteristics. They were "too small," or "too bookish," or "reeked of garlic," or "had an aversion to war." They were too individualistic, or not competitive enough, came from an undemocratic culture that prevented them from understanding team spirit and the American way. They were, the subtext suggested, insufficiently masculine, or at least, masculine in the wrong way: not *American* men. Bob Feller, who regularly barnstormed against black ballplayers in the off seasons in the early twentieth century, had seen Jackie Robinson play many times and declared him too muscular to be good enough to play major league baseball with white men. "He has football shoulders and couldn't hit an inside pitch to save his neck. If he were a white man I doubt they would consider him big league material."[28] It should present no challenge to read this statement as the stereotypically racist thinking that regards black men as not human: more brutish than a "refined" white man. Yet women of any race are deemed not strong enough to play baseball. If they show that they are, and are also good ballplayers, they are not "real women."

The only consistency in this thinking is that the victim cannot win, cannot be "right" for whatever he or she is to be excluded from. The falseness of scientific pretense is demonstrated when the exceptional Italian (Joe DiMaggio), Jew (Hank Greenberg), African American (Jackie Robinson), Hispanic (Roberto Clemente or Felipe Alou), or Asian (Ichiro Suzuki) finally makes it into the lineup, and it is acknowledged that men of non-Aryan descent and body type can indeed play baseball. The fact that the same contradictory taunts that plague girls who want to play baseball were used to exclude the men of color who now dominate the game is overlooked: men with brown skin were too small and slow, men with black skin were too strong and fast (they would ruin the dignified game of baseball), men who weren't Christians weren't men at all. Also overlooked, or forgotten so regularly as to constitute the most blatant form of denial, is the fact that girls have been playing the "American game" ever since it came to this country. Avoiding these facts goes beyond the usual historical amnesia about women's contributions. Rather, it resembles a nationwide phobia about girls and women setting foot on hallowed baseball ground or touching the sacred hardball. Women are still not Americans if playing baseball is what it takes to be one.

TWO

The Girls' Game

Early Women's Baseball

Baseball achieved instant and widespread popularity in the United States when it was introduced in the early nineteenth century. The New York Knickerbockers were the nation's first organized baseball club, and they were just that, a club comprised primarily of young professional men who arranged baseball matches with other clubs. The matches were played in the spirit of upper-class amateur sports, where dignified comportment, good sportsmanship, and a gentlemanly sense of fairness were more important than winning or losing. After a match, the losing club would host the winners for dinner and provide food, drink, smoke, and boisterous good cheer. The Knickerbockers' version of baseball was called the New York game. Variations were a New England version known as the Massachusetts game, and Olympic town ball from Philadelphia, whose club had been organized in 1833 to play "a kind of rounders known as town ball."

Early nineteenth-century baseball thus came in many varieties, some of which more closely resembled what we would now call softball than modern-day baseball. The diamond was smaller than the modern infield. The balls were pitched to the batters underhand. There were no fielders' or catchers' gloves, no masks and no shin guards. The absence of gloves meant the ball was somewhat bigger than a modern baseball, the size of a modern-day softball or sometimes even bigger. At first the teams played until one side scored twenty-one "aces," or runs. In 1857 the game was changed to last nine innings. David Block writes that there were so many different varieties of the game, choosing one as the genuine predecessor to baseball is utterly impossible. "Given that uniform standards for playing baseball were nonexistent during those early years, the tiny pool of descriptive examples that have survived may be compared to nine snowflakes plucked from a blizzard, perhaps representative of the whole, but hardly comprehensive."[1] The game gradually coalesced into fewer and fewer varieties, a development that was mightily assisted by the rules adopted by the mid-nineteenth-century New York Knickerbockers. However, the adoption of official rules did not eliminate spontaneous adaptations of the game to fit informal conditions, whether on a school playground or to suit weekend outings at the local park for amateur players of all ages.

The first formalized rules of baseball were published on December 6, 1856, in *Porter's Spirit of the Times*, and reflected the rules established by the Knickerbockers. The baselines at that time were forty-two paces, or about seventy-five feet; the ball was to be pitched underhand (rule 9); the game was to be played to twenty-one "counts" or "aces" (rule 8), which were only later referred to as "runs," the same term used to score cricket. A batter was out if his hit was caught either on the fly or on one bounce (rule 12). The most important development eliminated the vicious rule of throwing the ball at the base runner. The Knickerbockers' more civilized substitutes were the tag and the force out: "A player running the bases shall be out, if the ball is in the hands of an adversary on the base, or the runner is touched with it before he makes his base; it being understood, however, that in no instance is a ball to be thrown at him" (rule 13). Prior to the adoption of this rule, a runner could be put out by "plugging" him with a ball thrown by a fielder, just like the old rounders and stool ball rules in England. Block concludes his discussion of these revolutionary changes in the American game with a reminder that this does not imply the New York Knickerbockers or any other Americans "invented" the game. "Were these rules an important contribution to the progress of baseball? Undoubtedly. Did they signify the birth of our modern game and constitute its lasting foundation? Not quite."[2]

Evidence for the link between American baseball and English rounders was first established in 1939 by New York librarian Robert W. Henderson. His examination of early game books for children demonstrated that the rules for rounders and baseball were at first identical. Henderson found the rules for rounders printed in *The Boy's Own Book*, a collection of children's games written by William Clark, published in London in 1829 and reprinted in America the same year. The rules were published by a Boston press in a little volume called *The Book of Sports* by Robin Carver, and again in 1835 in Providence, Rhode Island, in a volume entitled *The Boys and Girls Book of Sports*. The name *baseball* was known in both England and America even before 1829. In 1744 John Newbery published *A Pretty Little Pocket-Book*, which contained a rhymed description of "base-ball" along with a small picture illustrating the game. The book was extremely popular in England, and it was reprinted in American cities several times between 1762 and 1787.[3]

It is evident from occasional literary references that girls played rounders or baseball, at least in England. The protagonist of Jane Austen's novel *Northanger Abbey*, completed in 1803, was a girl named Catherine, presumed to be an autobiographical reference to Austen. Catherine plays baseball and cricket and is a girl who prefers physical freedom outdoors to the restrictions society intended for her life. Austen chides the respectability of her day in this sympathetic description: "And it was not very wonderful that Catherine, who had by nature nothing heroic about her, should prefer cricket, base ball, riding on horseback, and running about the country at the age of fourteen, to books." Virginia Woolf was also familiar enough with baseball to be able to publish a 1915 essay about the early-nineteenth-century baseball writings of Ring Lardner.[4] Whether the English game was called rounders or baseball, it was rough. One unathletic Englishwoman recalls her less-than-happy brush with the game: "I played rounders at school, but not with much enthusiasm. I got a hard wooden rounders ball in the solar plexus one day, and that rather put me off!"[5]

Women's Collegiate Baseball

Baseball was played at women's colleges in New York and New England, and at public coeducational institutions in the Midwest in the middle of the nineteenth century. Only after baseball was distinguished from softball in the 1890s, and the two sports were categorized "male" and "female" did women play anything other than regulation baseball, to the extent that regulation baseball existed. American women had been playing organized baseball for three decades before softball and basketball were created in the 1890s. At the same time that Albert Spalding was working to mythologize baseball as a manly American game, both softball and basketball were invented, designed to be easy enough for girls to play without being overly competitive or physical. Both sports were originally intended to be played indoors, away from inappropriate gazes of passersby and men. But girls and women failed miserably at their commission to stay only moderately involved in the sports they played. Like their brothers, father, and boyfriends, they became passionate, competitive, and physical when they liked what they were playing. They were proud of victory and coveted the awards, such as college letters and team trophies, bestowed upon victorious athletes.

College women loved baseball and petitioned to play it rather than do the calisthenics that had recently been found beneficial to the health of young ladies. This implies some familiarity with the sport from girlhood. In the early twentieth century, there were all-women's teams at coeducational universities, as well as at women's colleges. However, the earliest college women's baseball emerged at the same time as men's college baseball: in the mid-nineteenth century. For almost as long as young women have been attending college in this country, they have been playing baseball. Students demanded to play baseball at Vassar College in 1866, just five years after the college was founded. It was first played at the collegiate level by men at Williams and Amherst only a few years earlier, in 1859. A photograph of the Vassar Resolutes shows the nine ballplayers with belts displaying the team name, baseball caps, and the full-length dresses of the day. The team poses with a hardball, bat, and looks of resolve: the girls are wearing their game faces for the photograph. Vassar alumna Sophia Richardson, who was a freshman during those early years, recalled,

> About twenty years ago, when I was a freshman, seven or eight baseball clubs suddenly came into being, spontaneously as it seemed, but I think they owed their existence to a few quiet suggestions from a resident physician, wise beyond her generation. The public so far as it knew of our playing was shocked, but in our retired grounds . . . we continued to play in spite of a censorious public. One day a student, while running between bases, fell with an injured leg. We attended her to the infirmary, with the foreboding that this accident would end our play of baseball. Not so. Dr. Webster said that the public doubtless would condemn the game as too violent, but that if the student had hurt herself while dancing the public would not condemn dancing to extinction.[6]

Smith, Mount Holyoke, and Wellesley soon followed with their own intramural teams. Barnard and Radcliffe added teams several decades later. While the women's game in the nineteenth century may have gotten its start as a desirable substitute for calisthenics, it is clear that the girls took the game seriously. In the later decades of the nineteenth century, baseball disappeared from Seven Sisters' athletics, but it reemerged in the first decades of the twentieth century. The reason for the temporary eclipse of collegiate women's baseball is unclear although the first two decades of the twentieth century are years when the first wave of the women's movement began picking up its second wind as it reorganized and mobilized in the push for suffrage during the first two decades of the twentieth century.[7]

Sports for women in both the nineteenth and early twentieth centuries were intramural, not intercollegiate. Too much competition was regarded as unhealthy for girls although it is obvious that the girls who participated in sports completely ignored the warning. Travel was also believed to be too strenuous and unsuitable for the health and morality of the young women, which is why intercollegiate athletics were forbidden. Women engaged in sports were not to be seen in public, with mussed hair, sweat, and the inelegant, uncomposed facial expressions that accompany athletic effort and involvement. The college athletic experience remained confined to campus events. However, photographs and letters from the girls involved in sports indicate commitment and passion in spite of the efforts of their guardians to suppress it.

Smith undergraduate Margaret Townsend, class of 1911, wrote her parents in 1908 to ask them to send her a baseball glove; one of her brother's mitts would do, if he was willing to part with it: "Please ask Morgan if he has a baseball mitt he can send. We are practicing all the time now and trying curves, and playing with a real baseball. Sometimes I can throw an in-curve. Marjorie Browning spent the afternoon over yesterday and we played baseball . . . until we were weary, and then we went in the tank."[8]

Baseball was popular at Smith on many levels in the early decades of the twentieth century. A 1916 photo shows Smith College president Marion LeRoy Burton dressed in a baseball uniform. Since all of the students at his college were women, it is unlikely that he donned the uniform to participate in a man's game. Students also attended baseball games played by Amherst's men and had their own baseball organization on campus, which was prominent enough in 1917 to warrant a regular student representative.

Baseball was also played at Vassar in the early twentieth century, with baseball skills being part of the annual spring Field Day. In May 1911, eighteen-year-old freshman Dorothy Smith broke two long-standing collegiate women's records, in the standing long-jump and the baseball throw for distance. She threw the ball 204 feet, 5 inches and received the coveted letter sweater with a V on it. The *New York Herald* sent a reporter to the campus to cover the athletic feats and found the students had gone "wild with joy" because Smith's records had raised Vassar's already high standing in college sports. The reporter was particularly "amazed" by Smith's baseball throw, since, he wrote, "Girls do not throw a baseball further than the average boy without some sort of training. . . . Girls are popularly believed not to know how even to hold a baseball. And as for throwing it straight and true, it isn't expected of them."[9] The reporter was further astounded by Smith's report that she had no special training in baseball at all and no brothers although, she did allow, "I have always played ball with boys ever since I can remember." The newsman was won over by the young athlete, writing that she was "tall and slim and lithe," and "the modern type of girl athlete . . . not marred by overdeveloped muscles, but so well trained that every bit of her strength counts . . . the modern variety [of girl athlete] has all the charm of the sweet young girl, to which are added a strength and a knowledge of sports [of] which her alma mater has reason to be proud."

If the reporter had done his research, he would have found that while Smith's throw was indeed record-breaking, she was not the first Vassar student to throw a baseball a significant distance on the annual Field Day. A. Belding, class of 1907, threw a baseball 195 feet, 6 inches in 1903 and 193 feet, 3 inches in 1906.[10] It is evident that the "baseball throw" was more than just an annual Field Day event and that the girls played frequently on their own. A 1909 photograph shows two Vassar students, one standing at bat, the other crouched behind her wearing catchers' gear. Somebody must have known how to pitch in order to have thrown to a catcher who needed protective equipment and obviously knew what she was doing. The Vassar student newspaper, *Miscellany News*, of May 4, 1917, reported a game between the students and faculty. The article was titled "Slaughter of the Faculty." A photograph shows the victorious team posing with their faculty coaches. A photograph shows left-handed pitcher Esther Daly, class of 1920, following through on an overhand baseball pitch. Her eyes are focused and intense, her hair is unkempt with the athletic effort, and she appears to be competitively engaged. Not quite the traditional stereotype of a "Vassar Girl" in the Roaring Twenties, but Vassar was proud of its history of athletic excellence and had been from its earliest days. The 1924 team photograph shows a group of smiling girls in short sleeves and bloomers (no longer the serious, fully clothed Resolutes), some leaning playfully on their teammates in an uninhibited fashion. A mural in the restaurant of the Vassar Alumnae House depicts a variety of activities at the college in the early days, including a game of baseball.

In the nineteenth and early twentieth centuries, women's intramural baseball teams received favorable coverage in the local press. An article in a 1914 Boston

Vassar Resolutes, 1866 (courtesy Vassar College Archives)

Class of 1924 Vassar baseball team (courtesy Vassar College Archives)

Esther Daly, Vassar College, class of 1920, pitching overhand (courtesy Vassar College Archives)

paper was headlined, "Girl Players in a Pitching Duel: Wellesley College Juniors Beat Seniors in Indoor Baseball Game." The article went on to note that "Miss Hoyt proved to be a star, for in addition to pitching what was, for girls, 'airtight ball,' she knocked out a three-base hit and fielded her position like a major league veteran."[11] A 1910 article in the *Cincinnati Enquirer* announced a game in which "The Barnard girls will play on a diamond of regulation size with bags, mitts, bats and other accouterments from a regulation sporting goods house. They will play genuine baseball with all its complications."[12]

But women's baseball was not only a collegiate sport. Women of all classes and races wanted to be a part of the game, and in the late nineteenth century, women's professional and semiprofessional leagues sprang up across the country. Women's baseball historian Gai Ingham Berlage notes, "The popularity of baseball crossed sex, class, and color lines. Socially prominent upper-class women formed private baseball clubs and women from middle- and lower-class backgrounds played on their own semi-professional teams."[13] In the early days, the women played in long dresses, which did not facilitate acquiring skills to match the men, although it did result in some interesting rules. For a while it was legal for a player to stop a grounder or a low line drive by trapping it in her skirt. There was a rule on a Pensacola, Florida, team in 1867 proclaiming that if a player got entangled in her hoop skirt and fell, she was immediately expelled from the club.[14]

In spite of the handicaps of respectable feminine clothing, a ban on unlady-like intercollegiate competition, and the secluded playing fields demanded of respectable women in the nineteenth century, the players developed skills.[15] Male and female college students played together in pick-up games on their campuses, which, predictably, caused "adult" concern about the propriety of men and women playing together. The result was usually that the women were thrown off the diamond. Women were encouraged, and in some cases required, to observe and support the men's sports programs, but there were questions about whether it was proper for men to observe the women's games. In the early twentieth century, college administrators were so obsessed with separating the sexes at athletic events that at the University of California at Berkeley—an elite institution with a self-proclaimed reputation for progressive thinking—women who wanted to watch men's football and basketball were required to sit in a separate section from the men and were prohibited from using the same yells as the men to cheer on the teams.

American students had little compunction about playing baseball with each other in coed games, but the adults who supervised their lives could not bear to see the morality of their charges so compromised. In 1904, for example, a group of University of Pennsylvania men organized a game of baseball on the college lawn. Some women joined in, and one of them lined a two-base hit, which "produced pandemonium"; faculty members were drawn out of their offices to see what the commotion was about. When they learned that a woman had gotten the best hit of the game, they banned women from playing baseball at Penn.[16] The rationale, presumably, was the overstimulating response, which involved both male and female students losing their composure in the company of each other.

There was undoubtedly also a class-based response reflected in the concern over such passion exhibited in a mixed-sex environment; there may not have been such outrage over a display of boisterousness among the working-class young.

In the first decades of the twentieth century, baseball became a major sport for women at coeducational universities in the Midwest. The teams formed in the first decades of the twentieth century may have begun as "indoor baseball," or softball teams, but the women's rapidly increasing skills and the allure of the open Midwestern plains in springtime soon drove them outdoors, using regulation baseball diamonds and equipment. The University of Missouri's yearbook, *The Savitar*, of 1915, in the section on women's sports, includes a page with the heading "Baseball as a Game for Girls." There were four squads (one team for each student class), and the game was described enthusiastically. The newness of the sport for girls meant that it was somewhat risky, but all were relieved to find that "no dreadful thing resulted" when girls played baseball for a season.

> Until recently baseball has been considered strictly a boy's game. Within the last few years, however, it has become a fairly widespread sport for girls. In many places the general sentiment of the community was against young ladies participating in such a man's game. But, owing to the interest the girls showed and to the fact that no dreadful thing resulted from their playing baseball, the game is fast becoming a popular girl's game. . . .
>
> A few years ago Missouri started regular baseball as the spring sport for girls. The interest manifested has increased each year. The outfit used is the same as that used by any boy's team.

In the spring of 1914, there was much enthusiasm for the interclass games. The championship was finally won by the class of 1916. The freshmen were captained by Rachel Stutsman, the sophomores by Bess Arbuthnot, the juniors by Lorruli Rethwilm, the seniors by Lila Dalton.[17]

In spring of 1917, girls' baseball was also introduced at Indiana University, as reported in several articles in the *Indiana Student Daily* and the year book, *The Arbutus*, which said, "Baseball has been introduced as a new sport this spring and about fifty girls were out for the first practice. Class teams will be selected and the championship will be played off."[18] The *Daily Student* of May 18, 1917, ran an article headed "Girls' Baseball Games to Be Played Saturday. If War Takes All Men, Girls Will Defend Class Honors of University." The article proclaimed,

> Hurrah! The teams for girls' baseball have been picked and the first game of the season will come Saturday morning at nine o'clock between the junior-senior team and the freshmen in the girls' gymnasium, with no admission.

Interclass baseball among the boys is no more, too many stars having left for service either in training camps or on farms. The girls trained and ready, are filling their places even in athletics. If conscription takes all the athletes, it will be up to the girls next year to keep up Indiana's athletic reputation.[19]

The next day's newspaper lauded the turnout in "great numbers" of freshmen girls and reported that the competition for the freshman team was stiff and the girls were ready to face the "mighty junior-senior team." The article reported, "Baseball has become one of the most popular sports of the season." The other sport that enjoyed extreme popularity among the women students was tennis.[20]

When the war ended and the men came home, Hoosier women kept playing baseball. An article in the 1921 *Arbutus* shows a picture of the girls' baseball squad and some action photographs of a pitcher winding up, a batter at the plate, and a long view of the entire game. The article begins "'Slide, Lizzie, slide.' 'All right, Mid, right over the plate.' 'Catch it! Catch it!' 'Watch out for the bat,' are a very few of the shrieks that disturbed the Sigma Chi's siestas last fall while Indiana's feminine Ty Cobbs and Babe Ruths were cavorting on the Dunn Meadow diamond." For the first time in the university's history, women's baseball was played outdoors because the gymnasium had become "too small for line drives and because outdoor exercise was more conducive to red corpuscles. . . . Coach Helen Coblentz led some sixty devotees of the national game to the newly-laid-out diamond across the Jordan." The rest of the article describes the season, the players, and the differences between the men's and women's game: distances between the bases are somewhat shortened (no dimensions were given), a padded baseball and smaller bat are used, and only the catcher is allowed a mitt. However, these alterations for the women resulted in larger scores, some of which, the writer proclaimed, "need to be counted on an adding machine."[21] That fact would lead one to believe that the Hoosier ladies would have done just fine with a regulation diamond and equipment.

Women's Semipro Baseball

Working-class women of all races and religions also played on organized baseball teams in the 1920s. There were insufficient funds or institutional organization to support regular leagues, but there were enough players and interest to enable a lively barnstorming circuit to develop. One such team was Madame J. H. Caldwell's Chicago Bloomer Girls. In 1920, she placed an ad in the *Chicago Defender*, a well-known African American newspaper, that read, "Wanted—Ladies to Play Ball." She promised that her team would meet all challengers, white or black, male or female, and boldly stated, "Our women are voting now, so why not be able to play a real game of baseball?"[22] Caldwell's ballplayers were African American women—although she had a white pitcher and catcher she would occasionally substitute for her usual battery, which created a stir among both the fans and opposing players—and brought in enough gate receipts (at twenty-five cents each) to enable the team to travel to Michigan and other nearby states. On the road, the Bloomer Girls faced male and female opponents of different races and ages. At home in Chicago, Caldwell's Bloomer Girls played boys' high school teams, a Sunday school team from Grace Presbyterian of Chicago, and a team that called themselves the Hebrew Maidens from Chicago's Hebrew Institute. The vision of a team of young black women playing ball with a team of Jewish girls is particularly heartwarming and truly renders baseball worthy of the title "the American game" when we recall that such ethnic and gender diversity was considered an athletic as well as a cultural impossibility in the men's well-paid version of the game during the same era. In the same city, at the same time that Madame Caldwell's Bloomer Girls played the Hebrew Maidens, the Chicago White Sox were immersed in major league baseball's worst scandal.

Several men who were destined to achieve baseball greatness actually drew their first paychecks as professionals playing baseball with women on Bloomer Girls barnstorming teams. Smoky Joe Wood and Rogers Hornsby are two of the more illustrious Bloomer Girls. Hall-of-Famer Wood remarks in his memoir, "A funny thing happened in September of 1906 that I'm not too keen about talking about, but I guess it wouldn't be exactly right to act like it never happened. In a nutshell, that's when I started my professional career, and I might as well just take a deep breath and come right out and put the matter bluntly: the team I started with was the Bloomer Girls. Yeah, you heard right, the Bloomer Girls."[23] Wood had been pitching for his local team when a team of barnstorming Bloomer Girls came through town. They were a good team, accustomed to winning, and when Wood's team defeated them, the Bloomer Girls' manager asked if he would be willing to join them to finish out the season and receive $20 for his effort. Wood was tempted, but he refused to wear a wig in order to "pass" as a woman, which was sometimes the custom on the "coed" teams. The manager assured him it would be unnecessary: "With your baby face you won't need one anyway." That convinced Smoky Joe, and he turned pro playing infield with the Bloomer Girls.

Rogers Hornsby, another Hall of Famer who still holds second place for lifetime batting average (.358, behind Ty Cobb, .367, with only Shoeless Joe Jackson and Ted Williams close) had a similar experience at the start of his career. Ironically, Hornsby, who began his professional baseball career playing

Girls' baseball game, Hebrew Institute of Chicago, 1909 (courtesy Chicago Historical Society)

with women, insisted when the Dodgers were about to bring Jackie Robinson up in the mid-1940s as major league baseball's first black ballplayer that racial integration "will never work." Perhaps Hornsby would have approved if the Dodgers had attempted to bring up Babe Didrickson instead.

Some of the women's individual achievements were noteworthy, and comparable to the performances of the most accomplished men. In 1912, Amanda Clement threw a ball 275 feet, believed at the time to be a record for a woman.[24] Babe Didrickson, the great multisport athlete of the first half of the twentieth century, made a measured throw of 296 feet, and in one game hit three home runs and threw a ball 313 feet, from center field to home plate.[25] The distance from the outfield fences to home plate in most major league ball parks is less than 400 feet. Few men can throw that far. Didrickson's diminutive stature of 5 feet, 4 inches and 125 pounds makes the feat even more remarkable.

No matter how accomplished the women became, however, they were never permitted to play major league baseball. As with all social segregation, separate is never equal. In this case, the men were free to play on women's teams, but the reverse was not possible, just as men are now allowed to play baseball *or* softball, but women only softball. Detractors have tried to dismiss women's baseball as vaudeville, or a freak show, or anything except serious athletes playing baseball well. But it's unlikely that perception was shared by the women who played the game. There were simply too many serious and impressive performances. In Huntsboro, Alabama, a team called the Mrs. Jane Duffy Club beat a local men's club by a score of 20–11. On December 24, 1884, a Philadelphia girls' team defeated a men's club, the Mutual Baseball Club of Jackson, Mississippi, by a score of 13–11. In 1883, a twelve-year-old girl in Pottsville, Pennsylvania, was credited with being able to pitch "as well as the average male amateur pitcher." If all of these were events staged simply to draw a paying audience to witness the spectacle of men being humiliated by women, there must be a masochistic streak in the American male psyche that warrants study by social psychologists.

It is clear that there was plenty of women's baseball in the United States during the years when baseball was growing in popularity, becoming organized, institutionalized on multiple levels, and professionalized. Baseball's rise to popularity as a national sport paralleled the United States' rise as a world power. Those decades of American history involved social and economic upheaval and demands from women, immigrants, and people of color for full citizenship rights. The more associated the game became with American identity, the more stridently it fought to maintain its white male exclusivity. There were specific ways in which women were erased from baseball history and denied a baseball future. The first was the effort to mythologize baseball's history as male only, the initiative for which can be attributed disproportionately to Albert Goodwill Spalding. Secondly, women's future with baseball was seriously challenged with the invention of softball. Although "indoor baseball" or softball was created by and for men who wanted to play baseball in confined spaces and bad weather, it was soon found acceptable for women to play instead of baseball. The next two chapters consider the rise of the "male only" baseball ideology, and the adaptation of softball as women's baseball.

THREE

A. G. Spalding and America's Needs

Baseball did not begin as an exclusively boys' or mens' game, nor as America's "national pastime." The appropriation of baseball for American manhood was the result of developments that explicitly removed the game from the hands of girls and women and delivered it to white middle-class American men. While so enormous a theft could only have occurred if it served preexisting needs for American culture, it happened at a specific moment in American baseball history. The dissociation of baseball from anything female was accomplished in two parts: by the rewriting of baseball history and by the invention and use of softball as a substitute for baseball. One man, Albert Goodwill Spalding, was the first to publicly state that baseball was not for women and make it stick.

Mothers

A. G. Spalding was born in 1850, the first child of Harriet and James Spalding, in the farming village of Byron, Illinois, not far from Chicago. Two other children followed Albert: a sister, Mary, born in 1854, and a younger brother, James Walter, born two years afterward. Harriet had been widowed before she married James, and brought a considerable inheritance to her second marriage, which enabled the couple to provide their children with a spacious country home surrounded by the amenities of respectable, middle-class life. James Spalding did not farm: he rented his land out for farming, acquired several houses in town as investment property, and raised horses. He was a real estate investor and landlord, rather than a farmer, and his wife had brought sufficient wealth to the marriage to enable him to spend his time managing his properties and overseeing his horses. The family seems to have been playing the part of gentry in its rural Illinois hometown, and they were ridiculed for their "gentility."

In 1858, however, James succumbed to a year-long illness and died. Albert was eight, his sister four, and his brother two. According to Spalding's biographer, Peter Levine, Spalding's family reported that the young son "never realized the extent of this loss, for the widowed mother, with constant devotion, wonderful strength of character, and inspiring heroism, filled the place of both father and mother to the little children left to her care."[1] As Spalding's story is told by family members, he was sheltered from the full blow of this misfortune because his mother determined to be both parents to her children, to put their welfare before her own. Harriet was responding to her late husband's dying request that she "bring her boys to industrious habits." She vowed "to live entirely for [her] children . . . with all [her] heart and all [her] thought centered on them."[2] She was determined to immerse her children in respectable middle-class values, and found the citizens of Byron too rough-hewn. The citizens of Byron were not enamored with the Spalding family. Albert and his siblings were teased for wearing "fine shoes and silk clothing." The men of the town were inclined to idle away their time on rainy days in the town's general store, "with their trousers tucked into their boots, sitting on kegs, cracking jokes and talking."[3] This was not the model of industriousness and morality that her husband intended in his final message to her. Harriet moved her eldest son, Albert, to the town of Rockford, Illinois, which advertised itself as a model community in which a young man could make his fortune by dint of hard work and respectable surroundings. It was an early suburb of Chicago, at the crossroads of urban and rural life. Albert was only twelve years old when his mother arranged for him to live in a boarding house while she closed her family's affairs in Byron and moved with her two younger children to join Albert a year later.

The agony of firstborn sons separated from their mothers and siblings in order to receive social and educational advantages has set much history in motion. For young Albert Spalding, that year of painful loneliness may have changed the access women have had to baseball, for it was through a ball game that he started making connections in his new community. Fifty years later in his memoirs, Spalding claimed he had been so lonesome and homesick that it still haunted him "like a nightmare." He was, in his own words, "an overgrown, unbaked country boy, as green as the verdant prairies," and so shy and withdrawn that he was "almost afraid to go out of doors, lest I should meet and be spoken to by someone not a member of my family."[4]

The only relief he found from this loneliness and anxiety was watching other boys in his new town play baseball on the commons. He would sit beyond the outfield boundaries and watch, but he could not muster the courage to join the games. As he relays the story, "No mother, parted from her young, ever had a stronger yearning to see her beloved offspring than I had to break into those crude games of ball." He could not bring himself to take the initiative of asking to play, claiming that he would "rather have died than suggest such a thing." But fate was destined to bring Spalding and baseball together. In what he later referred to as an act of "special providence," one day a ball was hit straight at him as he sat in his usual place beyond center field. It was a powerfully hit line drive, and he responded like a ballplayer: "That ball came for me straight as an arrow. Impulsively I sprang to my feet, reached out for it with my right hand, held it a moment and then threw it home on an air line to the catcher." After the game, the ballplayers came over to congratulate him, inviting him to play ball with them the next day. Spalding blushed and stammered but managed to accept the invitation. From that day on, he was a regular member of the team, and "when sides were chosen I was usually among the first to have a place. And this was my first real introduction to the game."[5]

Spalding's ego was as big as his ambitions, and his autobiography exemplifies his ability to mythologize his life. Regarding his romanticized, self-aggrandizing autobiography too seriously is foolish and will not reveal the secret truth of baseball history. However, a few suppositions are plausible. Losing his father at eight years of age had to have been traumatic. In Byron, Albert must have been self-conscious, at ease with nobody but his mother, sister, and much younger brother.

He must have felt both superior to the local boys and insulated from them by his material circumstances and socially ambitious parents. But he also must have felt isolated: shy, lonely, and wanting the company of the boys and their games.

Not long after the death of his father, his emotional shelter was disrupted when his mother decided he would be better off as a boarder in Rockford rather than either remaining in the safety of his family or hanging out with the rough country boys of Byron. In Rockford, Spalding found himself alone in a new town, on the cusp of adolescence, missing his mother and siblings, and probably also harboring resentment at his abandonment and feeling envy of his younger siblings. He spent an entire year in this painful emotional state until joined once again by his family. In the meantime, however, the shy boy, whose only model of strength and survival thus far had been his mother who was unavailable for the year, found a substitute family in a group of baseball-playing boys. His baseball arm was his ticket to inclusion in this new family. He won his place on the team by returning an errant fly ball that came to him as he watched from the sidelines, wanting to participate, as he put it, with all the longing of a "mother parted from her young."

That is, he must have hoped his mother yearned for him as desperately as he yearned to join the boys in their baseball games. Insecurity and fear of abandonment might also have haunted young Albert. It is remarkable that the image that came to mind while watching the boys play, or at least the image he later associated with that incident, was that of a mother separated from her child. It is evident that he missed and identified with his mother. His longing for her and what he hoped was her longing for him are merged in his mind. Imagine the power of baseball to fulfill Spalding's wishes of being reunited with his mother yet also separated from her in a world for boys and men only. Baseball allowed him to be independent of his mother and at the same time to internalize her, to keep her close by experiencing what it might be like to be a mother yearning for her child. On the diamond, he was masculine in a way that was out of reach for him when he lived in Byron with his mother and sister, teased by the boys for his genteel pretensions and dress. That masculinity had also been out of his reach in Rockford before baseball, when he had felt bereft and emotionally dependent on the woman he had lost. Baseball provided a magical cure for his feelings of childishness and dependence. It enabled him to control his vulnerability and sense of inadequacy, embodied by the most important woman in his life. Baseball made a man of Albert Spalding, and he would not leave the game for a moment during all of his adult life. Indeed he credited baseball specifically with "making men," and the opening pages of his five-hundred-page tome,

America's National Game, asserted that no girls or women may play baseball for it is too strenuous for them.

Spalding's charged emotional dependence on baseball for his sense of adult masculinity is clarified by this story, whether it truly happened or was apocryphal, constructed for its compatibility with his self-made legend. His separation from his mother was actually initiated by Harriet Spalding herself. She was hardly clingy and overprotective toward Spalding. But he felt unequal to the challenge of being his own man at twelve years of age, even though he probably believed he should be up to the task. He must have been told that he was "the man of the family" after his father died. But by the time he was twelve, he had been without a masculine role model for over one third of his childhood. Shy and ashamed of his weakness and emotional neediness, he found in baseball both consolation and a sense of adequacy. And so he built a wall to keep the infantilizing women away from that experience, and perhaps also to exact revenge on his mother for excluding him from the family circle. No longer would he be embarrassed by country boys making fun of his sissified clothes or by his neediness of the women in his family. Baseball was the male family he sought, the band of brothers. Keeping women away was the means of controlling emotional dependence on his mother.

Spalding was a gifted athlete. He became a star pitcher for the Boston Red Stockings and later a pitcher and player-manager for the Chicago White Stockings, which brought him back to his Illinois home. He helped businessman and reformer William Hulbert form the National League in an effort to ensure that gambling interests did not entirely take over baseball, became president of the Chicago White Stockings, remained involved in the administration of the National League, and was instrumental in defeating an effort by baseball players to form their own league, dictate their labor conditions, and compete with the National League. He and his brother founded the legendary sporting goods company A. G. Spalding and Brothers (it included his brother-in-law, too), which held a monopoly on the manufacture of sporting goods in America for a long time. He used his stature in baseball to publish *Spalding's Official Baseball Guide*, an annual advertising catalogue for Spalding and Brothers that also contained baseball news. He retired to San Diego with his second wife and their young sons, where he wrote *America's National Game*.[6] The energetic Spalding was not one for a quiet retirement, and he obviously had a genius for anticipating cultural trends and financial opportunities. He soon became involved in real estate development in Southern California, ultimately waging an unsuccessful campaign for senator. Through his wife, he became involved in a mystical religious sect in Southern California called the Theosophic Society, which baseball historian David Block describes as "perhaps the first major organization in America to study and disseminate Eastern esoteric teachings."[7] Spalding, in the forefront of whatever was happening in his time, participated enthusiastically in an early version of California New Age culture. None other than Abner Doubleday was an officer of the Theosophical Society, which, Block hypothesizes, made him all the more attractive to Spalding when Doubleday was mentioned as the founder of baseball. Spalding died in 1915 of two successive strokes, in the bosom of his second family, in Southern California.

No question about it, Spalding epitomized the nineteenth-century American "self-made man." Although born to the comfortable middle class, he suffered some painful difficulties in childhood and overcame them in spectacular entrepreneurial fashion. He interpreted his life as a rags-to-riches story in spite of his materially comfortable childhood, and he exploited, developed, and profited from the game that brought him early self-esteem. He converted baseball into a well-organized business, offering it for consumption to as much of the world as he could, diversifying into the business of manufacturing the necessary tools of the trade, and then expanding that business to one that still fulfills the insatiable American need for leisure and professional-quality sporting goods. Meanwhile, he convinced himself and the world that his genius for profit was actually a moral mission to infuse America with respectable, middle-class values by means of baseball and leisure sports. He even retired to San Diego and became involved in West Coast spirituality. Spalding was an unmitigated American success story whose need for self-aggrandizement reflects an anxiety and self-doubt that are emblematic of the successful American entrepreneur.

Albert Goodwill Spalding, the exemplary nineteenth-century man, tapped a ready and enthusiastic market for what he valued. But he did not foist baseball on America. America volunteered, forked over its money willingly, and enthusiastically participated in making baseball a national obsession. Baseball was about to become the first of what now exists as the mega-industry of American professional athletics. Spalding's obsessions dovetailed with America's needs for self-righteousness and masculinity.

Fathers

Spalding's life suggests that it was personally important for him to separate baseball and women. The text of *America's National Game* helps us to understand why his needs resonated with those of the nation. The exclusion of anything feminine is a theme that emerges in the very first pages of Spalding's history of baseball. *America's National Game* is suffused with nationalist and gender chauvinism. Baseball, the game that was loved by all who played it in colonial and early-nineteenth-century America, is presented one-dimensionally as male and Anglo-Saxon. This creates inconsistencies as Spalding attempts to distinguish it from cricket, which he condescendingly associates with repressed English character. Spalding's volume is a long, meandering history of the game from the origins Spalding himself fabricated. He extrapolates development of baseball rules from unsubstantiated hypotheses about spontaneous boys' games; describes its evolution to a professional sport that Spalding himself enabled; its corruption through gambling and drink and the "threat" of a ballplayers union; and applauds its salvation, again by A. G. Spalding himself, with a little help from his friends William Hulbert (founder of the National League) and Henry Chadwick (founder of baseball statistics). Spalding celebrates baseball's role in bringing democracy and civilization to every part of the world that it touches. In *America's National Game*, Spalding's life is presented as inseparable from the history of baseball, which is presented as inseparable from America. The book's dedication reads, "To the memory of Henry Chadwick, 'The Father of Baseball,' To the memory of William A. Hulbert, The Savior of a Nation's Pastime, And to the National League of Professional Base Ball Clubs That has borne the brunt of battle During thirty-five years of development of America's National Game."[8]

Chadwick and Hulbert served as father figures to Spalding. Both men were reformers of baseball, and by extension American life. Spalding presents them in saintly terms throughout the volume. Indeed, his paean to baseball is suffused with references to Christianity, beginning with the dedication to Chadwick the "Father" and Hulbert the "Savior." Spalding apparently viewed himself as one of the apostles writing the Gospels. Baseball was associated with Anglo-American Christianity well into the twentieth century.

Although Spalding himself epitomized the nineteenth century "self-made man," his need for a fatherly presence is not surprising given the early death of his biological father. He also remained close to his mother for the rest of her life, and she accompanied him on the first leg of his world tour of baseball in 1888, as he and the two teams traveled from Chicago to San Francisco to board a steamship to Hawaii and Australia.

In spite of the fact that Spalding seemed to play the part of an exemplary son to his mother and his surrogate fathers, in the first few pages of his five-hundred-page book, he puts women in their place, which is *not* on a baseball diamond. Chapter 1 begins by asserting Spalding's obsession: baseball is profoundly, originally, inherently American *and* masculine. Page 1 begins with a rhetorical question: "Have we, of America, a National Game?"[9] Proof that baseball is the American *national* game, says Spalding, is the fact that people will pay money to attend, unlike any other public event of the day. "It must also be admitted that it is the only game known for which the general public is willing day after day to pay the price of admission. In exciting political campaigns, Presidential candidates and brilliant orators will attract thousands; but let there be a charge of half a dollar imposed, and only Base Ball can stand the test." Lest the reader think that the willingness to shell out half a buck is the only definition of American character, he elaborates:

> I claim that Base Ball owes its prestige as our National Game to the fact that as no other form of sport it is the exponent of American Courage, Confidence, Combativeness; American Dash, Discipline, Determination; American Energy, Enthusiasm; American Pluck, Persistency, Performance; American Spirit, Sagacity, Success; American Vim, Vigor, Virility. Base ball is the American game *par excellence*, because its playing demands Brain and Brawn, and American manhood supplies these ingredients in quantity sufficient to spread over the entire continent. No man or boy can win distinction on the ball field who is not, as man or boy, an athlete, possessing all the qualifications which an intelligent, effective, playing of the game demands.[10]

This begins to narrow down the American character: male and willing to pay for spectator sports. What else? "Not English," is the next thing Spalding tackles. "Cricket is a splendid game, for Britons. It is a genteel game, a conventional game, and our cousins across the Atlantic are nothing if not conventional. They play Cricket because it accords with their country so to do; because it is easy and does not overtax their energy or their thought."[11] Having dismissed British character as lazy and conventional, Spalding declares that baseball is also more suited to America because it is more democratic and more warlike. "The genius of our institutions is democratic; Base Ball is a democratic game. The spirit of our national life is combative; Base Ball is a combative game."[12] "He may be the Swellest Swell of the Smart Set in Swelldom; but when he dons his Base Ball suit, he says good-bye to society, doffs his gentility, and becomes, just a Ball Player!"[13] Baseball is an equalizer of men much like the military is. Indeed, the exclusion of "coloreds" and women also resembles nineteenth-century American military life. African Americans played their own baseball, and had their own military regiments. Or they were the servants of American officers. While no men of color played on his teams, an African American man named Clarence Duval accompanied the tour as the White Stockings mascot. The ballplayers were fond of rubbing his "wooly" head to bring them luck during games.

Baseball's racial segregation and Spalding's impulse to establish baseball for profit around the globe is more in keeping with colonialism and militarism than the democratic values Spalding claims to have promoted with the spread of the sport. Baseball itself may seem less militaristic than other more obviously territorial field sports, such as football of both the American and English varieties. But Spalding was adamant and explicit about what he believed was America's warlike national character. "Cricket is a gentle pastime. Base Ball is War! . . . The founder of our National Game became a Major General in the United States Army! The sport had its baptism when our country was in the preliminary agonies of a fratricidal conflict. . . . Base Ball, I repeat, is War!"[14]

Finally, because of its warlike, energetic, virile, and masculine essence, which is to say its nationalism, women must take their seats on the sidelines. "Neither our wives, our sisters, our daughters, nor our sweethearts, may play Base Ball on the field . . . but Base Ball is too strenuous for womankind, except as she may take part in the grandstand."[15]

Part of Spalding's nationalistic baseball crusade involved making it profitable and professional. This development was consistent with a trend in American culture in the late nineteenth century. Routinization, specialization, and professionalization were intended to create order in the increasingly complex social and economic system of industrial turn-of-the-century United States. Professionalization also meant money, which raised the value of the game and fueled desire to keep rewards controlled by the fewest men possible. Spalding associated baseball with the identity of the nation, with the spending and earning of capital, with the waging of war, and the desire for worldwide domination. No sooner does he proclaim the impossibility of women playing baseball than he asserts that baseball deserves the honor of being the American national game because it "follows the flag":

> It followed the flag to the front in the sixties, and received then an impetus which has carried it to half a century of wondrous growth and prosperity. It has followed the flag to Alaska, where, under the midnight sun, it is played on Arctic ice. It has followed the flag to the Hawaiian Islands, and at once supplanted every other form of athletics in popularity. It has followed the flag to the Philippines, to Porto Rico and to Cuba, and wherever a ship floating the Stars and Stripes finds anchorage to-day, somewhere on a nearby shore the American National Game is in progress.[16]

Immaculate Conceptions

Spalding's insistence on the *American* origins of baseball may have served to disguise what he more urgently needed to believe, which was that baseball was a masculine game. If baseball evolved from rounders, played by girls as well as boys, then it was of questionable manliness. If Spalding's primal encounter with baseball had helped him to control his emotional dependency on his mother, it was most important to him that baseball retain its masculine purity. The origins of baseball and its male exclusivity preoccupied Spalding enough to muster a group of "experts" to confirm his need; there had to be an alternative to the thought that baseball was related to an English game—whether rounders, cricket, or both—that had been played by English girls and women. When Henry Chadwick publicly declared at Delmonico's restaurant in 1889 that baseball was derived from rounders, it must have been mortifying to Spalding, as though his father had publicly teased him about his manhood. Spalding's "Special Commission on Baseball" redeemed it from "Father Chadwick's" implicit accusation that the game that made Spalding a man was also played by girls.

In the event that his commission's fabricated report wasn't sufficient to establish baseball's American origins, Spalding gives us another version. After all, the Bible has two back-to-back, contradictory stories about the beginning of humankind (did God create a man and a woman in God's own image, or did God create man first and, when he complained about loneliness, put him to sleep, remove a rib, and present him with a female companion?). Certainly there can be two parallel stories about the creation of baseball. Not to be outdone by God, Spalding offered a "natural" origins myth in addition to the "historical" origins myth of Doubleday drawing a diamond in the dirt. The natural origin of baseball involves a generic American boy and a ball. "Placing the Ball in the hand of the first lad who happens along, we may be assured that he will do the rest. And he does. In less time than it takes in the telling, he is bounding the sphere upon the ground. Down it goes; up it flies. Leaving the boy's hand it strikes the ground, and, returning, is caught. In this completed act we have the first crude and elementary step in our National Game, with just a boy and a ball."[17]

This act doesn't seem particularly American, and chances are that any girl given a ball would do the same thing with it. But let's follow Spalding's logic. Spalding claims the boy will naturally go looking for a friend to show off his new ball to, and, finding a playmate, the boys will play "Throw and Catch": The second stage in the evolution of the game has been achieved with "Two Boys and a Ball." Soon the two boys get bored playing catch with each other. They find a barn, one throws the ball against the barn, and the other tries to hit it with an axe handle. Or as Spalding's hypothetical boy, Tom, says to his hypothetical friend, Dick, "I'll throw the ball against the barn. You get that old axe-handle over there and strike at it as it comes back. If you miss the ball and

I catch it, you're out; or, if you hit the ball and can run and touch the barn and return before I can get the ball and hit you with it, you count one. If I hit you with the ball before you get back to your place, you're out. See?"[18] They try it, it works, and soon another boy joins the game, and another, and before you know it, there are so many boys that they have to add a base to the barn, and another, and another, until baseball is born. Masculine and close to the soil, this is something that could only have happened in America. The English milkmaids who created the same sort of game several centuries earlier have disappeared from the natural origins myth, written out of the birth of baseball entirely. As Spalding proclaimed in his book, "Baseball is a man maker."[19]

But the history of major league baseball is what really interests Spalding, and this to him is as much a history of business as it is of sport. His suppression of the players' union and his battle with various corruptions that genuinely threatened the game's existence is presented as a moral quest to insure that baseball represented only the best middle-class values. His success in driving out all rivals, all gamblers, as many alcoholic players as he could, and his defeat of the players' union amounted to the creation of a baseball cartel. Spalding's perspective on what is and what is not important to baseball history is the story that has prevailed. The history of the major leagues is the definitive history of baseball, and success and recognition as a ballplayer ultimately requires playing in "the show."

Did Albert Spalding run women out of baseball all by himself? Should he be held responsible for creating the American hierarchy that favors professionals, excluding men of the "wrong" race and religion and excluding women from the inner sanctum of the game he called "national"? Or did Spalding merely give voice to existing nineteenth- and early-twentieth-century values, perhaps articulating them publicly and putting them into print for the first time. His sporting goods company and catalogue and his talent for successful entrepreneurship positioned him to circulate his ideas widely, enabling him to act as an historical catalyst. Spalding was clearly an important figure in the history of baseball and in the development of sports as big business in America. He was that exceptional individual with more energy, and a more urgent drive to be recognized, who fit a niche that was waiting to be filled. If Spalding hadn't appeared on the scene when he did, most likely somebody else would have soon afterward, and done the equivalent work of turning baseball into a professional sport that could be marketed to the world. His particular obsession with keeping women out is likewise characteristic of his own life yet reflecting a general cultural context.

Historians agree that nineteenth- and early-twentieth-century American men had a need to convince themselves of their manliness; that sport was one avenue of accomplishing that goal; and that women were the best audience to confirm their success.[20] Less well-noted is the fact that women fought back: many women struggled to extricate themselves from their confining lives as appreciative spectators of men's accomplishments. Women would have fought for their right to strength and health, as well as to fun and games, and met with severe resistance with or without the specific presence of Albert Spalding. But the iconization of baseball specifically as a "national pastime" where no girls are allowed is attributable to Spalding in greater part than is usually recognized.

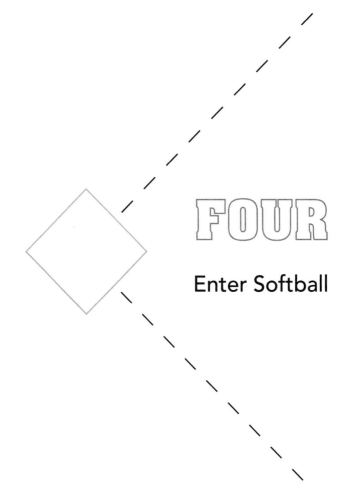

FOUR

Enter Softball

The History of Softball

Baseball had to be commandeered as a boys' only sport. Softball was not invented as a girls' game, but it quickly gained that moniker. The unwillingness to allow girls to play baseball at all, forcing them, if they want to play baseball, to buck enormous social and cultural pressure at a young and vulnerable age and to play primarily with boys, is glaringly unfair. How did women lose their right to choose which stick and ball game they would play?

Unlike baseball, the history of softball is well documented and free of mythology. Its moment of origin is accurate almost to the hour: Thanksgiving Day 1887, immediately after the Harvard-Yale football game. It was spontaneously invented by a group of twenty or so young men in the gymnasium of the Farragut Boat Club on the edge of Lake Michigan, in the 3000 block of Lake Park Avenue in Chicago. The guys had gathered to follow the progress of the football game by telegram as it was played in New England. When the final results came in (Yale beat Harvard 17–8), the young men were in high spirits. Engaging in light-hearted horsing around, one fellow lobbed a stray boxing glove at another who fended it off with a pole that happened to be close at hand, batting it across the room. All were delighted with the results, and one, a young reporter for the Chicago Board of Trade named George Hancock, used the glove's laces to tie it into a ball and declared, "Let's play ball!" They chose sides, played a spirited game, improvised rules as they went along, and softball was born. Hancock enjoyed the game so much he offered to compile rules, have a ball made that duplicated the weight and size of the boxing glove, and provide a rubber-tipped bat smaller than a regulation baseball bat, so that the indoor playing area would be safe from damage. He believed "indoor baseball" would catch on as a way to play the summer game during cold Chicago winters.[1]

Chicago's indoor baseball had a younger sibling, born several years later in Minneapolis. In 1895, a Minneapolis fire department officer named Lewis Rober reinvented baseball in the confines of an empty lot next door to the firehouse, to keep his men in shape with something more interesting than medicine-ball conditioning exercises. The next year, Rober was assigned to a unit of firefighters on the campus of the University of Minnesota, and he formed an "indoor-outdoor" baseball team that called itself the Kittens. The nickname "Kitten Ball" was given to this early Minnesota version of softball, and it stuck, to the point of generating a rule book for "Kitten League Ball." Within the next few years, the game spread throughout the nation, with "interesting and totally confusing variations in everything from ball size (from ten to twenty inches) to what the game was called."[2] However quickly the popularity of "indoor-outdoor" baseball spread, and however boisterous a game it may have been, it was always regarded as baseball's stepchild and belittled with nicknames such as "mush ball," "melon ball," and "panty waist."

With such unthreatening associations, it was quickly approved for girls. It served the purpose, so much on the minds of turn-of-the-century health and education experts, of providing women with a safe, nonviolent way to get exercise, and it removed the threat to baseball of contamination by female participation. The men who gave indoor baseball prissy nicknames such as kitten ball and sissy ball were broadcasting their attitude: it was only surrogate baseball. They enjoyed indoor-outdoor baseball as a way to keep swinging a bat during the off-season, in response to the constraints of bad weather or limited space. But they self-consciously mocked themselves for playing it as though they were embarrassed to be engaging in a pastime so lacking in violence and danger. Meanwhile, the softer version of baseball seemed perfect for girls and women: it solved the problem of how to get exercise to the average, nonathletic girl, without running the risk of supporting "games of strife" that might make America's girls too competitive, brave, strong, and passionate about something not in the service of men and family. And it was played indoors, discretely out of the view of spectators.

Although the new game was obviously regarded as "soft," it was not actually given the name "softball" until 1926, when a meeting was held in Colorado to standardize the way the game was played in that state. Denver YMCA director Walter C. Hackanson suggested the name, which gained standard usage although the game remained amenable to variations, depending upon the age group and the inclination of the players. It was an accessible, less formal, less demanding version of baseball, and it quickly became popular.

Softball might have remained as it began—makeshift, informal indoor winter baseball—if not for another American athletic development that had taken place a few years earlier. When basketball was invented in 1891 by James Naismith, women physical educators quickly picked it up and taught it to girls, who took to it enthusiastically. Basketball and indoor baseball became immensely popular among the young and restless of both sexes, and by the turn of the century, basketball and indoor baseball were competing for gym space. Basketball won claim to the indoor courts, as we know, and bounced indoor baseball outdoors, although a women's-rules variant of basketball was also developed. Indoor baseball, which had begun as a temporary winter stopgap for men waiting for the real baseball season, was pressed upon girls, who were urged to play indoor baseball outdoors and to forego hardball altogether.

When indoor baseball was invented, it appeared to solve the cultural problem of women's enthusiasm for playing the national pastime. While the inventors of the milder, safer form of baseball had been manly as could be, firefighters staying fit, or young professionals letting off steam after following a Thanksgiving Day football classic, and while the Chicago version that caught on so quickly was a rough-and-tumble, though informal game, the reputation indoor baseball developed across the nation was not completely masculine. Dickson observes, "Indoor baseball . . . was initially little more than a pale imitation of baseball, lacking even the hint of violence, or at least that was the common perception."[3] The first balls were "dumpling soft" and hit with a bat much smaller than a baseball bat. In terms of sexual imagery, not much more needs to be said: baseball had hard balls and big bats, while softball had big soft balls and little bats.

In 1895, the first women's team was organized at Chicago's West Division

High School. A. G. Spalding, ever ready with an opinion about which sports were manly and which not, claimed that the first women's softball games were disappointing because of the "lack of natural ball playing ability of the girl" but went on to note that 90 percent of the girls who were exposed to the game played it with enthusiasm and increasing skill.[4] He apparently mistook "natural playing ability" for knowledge and practice. Girls took to softball as quickly as they had to baseball. The game's inventor, George Hancock, was surprised and deeply pleased with the degree to which the game had become a women's game. He wrote just after the turn of the century, "It is surprising to note the expertness with which girls can play the game after short practice."[5]

Stolen Bases

Baseball has thus been twice stolen from American girls and women: once when softball was invented as "substitute baseball for girls" and once through the obliteration of girls' and women's ball playing history in the United States and England. It is not a coincidence that the moments are closely intertwined. The uproar at Delmonico's over Chadwick's remark about rounders occurred in 1889, two years after softball was invented. Softball was officially endorsed as a less strenuous form of baseball, more appropriate for girls, by the Sub-Committee on Baseball of the National Committee on Women's Athletics of the American Physical Education Association at their first meeting in April 1927. In 1933, the Amateur Softball Association made the term *softball* official, and the name was adopted for the modified baseball games that girls had been playing. A few years later, in 1939, Little League baseball was organized by Carl Stotz in Williamsport, Pennsylvania, for boys ages eight to twelve, for the purpose of "developing the qualities of sportsmanship, citizenship, and manliness." Girls were officially banned from youth baseball just as baseball on all levels was associated exclusively with manliness. Baseball was given the task of building male citizens at the same time that softball was allocated to girls. Defying gender stereotypes, however, softball developed into a serious sport with many skilled players and avid fans, and women never completely gave up playing baseball.

The raw facts about women's participation in baseball have been well documented and are available in a wide range of recent scholarly books about women and sports.[6] What is missing from the canon of baseball scholarship is ongoing dialogue about and analysis of the nation's tenacity in *keeping* women from playing the national sport, which has involved burying the history of their interest and participation, legally barring them from playing, culturally insisting that baseball is a boys' and men's game (indeed, definitive of American manhood in some ways), and when all else failed, foisting a substitute game upon girls and telling them it was the only form of baseball they could play.

Without unduly disparaging softball itself, the game has been imposed upon girls and women, and they have been given no choice about whether they prefer their balls harder or softer, smaller or larger, or their pitches coming from above or below. It is a fair bet that given a choice between softball and baseball, boys certainly will choose the latter, and many more girls would choose hardball than currently play the game. Why? First, there is the matter of aesthetic preferences. The games are not identical. Softball tends to be dominated by pitching, so any ballplayer with a preference for the hitting and running game, and for the speed of both infield ballhandling and the intricacies of base stealing, will probably favor baseball over softball. Second, there isn't a comparable history and infrastructure creating cultural support for softball. You cannot read about your favorite softball player, for six months of the year, in every newspaper in America. The nation does not direct its attention during the month of October to division and league playoffs and finally the World Series of softball.

Just as there is nothing inherently masculine about baseball, there is nothing inherently feminine about softball. A modern softball is the approximate size and color of a grapefruit. It is bigger but not noticeably softer than a baseball. In the hand, it feels more like a lightweight shot put. "Soft" is not a descriptive name for the little cannonball that girls are encouraged to throw at each other because it is supposedly safer than a "hard" ball. Nonetheless, the ideology of "softness" and femininity is conveyed by insistence on the term. The softball diamond and outfield are smaller than in baseball. In fact, they are approximately the size of a Little League baseball field, giving the clear impression that grown women are only as big, fast, and powerful as six- to twelve-year-old boys. Perhaps the rationale is that women are smaller than men and so require a smaller field. Why, then, is the ball so large?[7]

But the size of both baseball and softball diamonds and the average size of American people have changed since the nineteenth century, underscoring the fact that there is no anatomical basis for the sizes adopted for either baseball or softball. The official size of a baseball diamond evolved in the nineteenth century and only became standardized when baseball was becoming professional and claiming its "inherent" manliness. It has not changed in more than a century, although the size of professional ballplayers certainly has. Meanwhile, the size and strength of women has also evolved. So when 90 feet was agreed upon for regulation baselines, the men who ran those base paths were no bigger than the women who would be running them today. There is nothing essentially masculine about the distance of 90 feet. What matters is that women's size is always perceived as debilitating: smaller and weaker than men, no matter what size field the men play on. That men are bigger and stronger than women is advertised in every cultural artifact of our society, from school crossing signs with big boys and little girls to steroids to make men bigger and eating disorders and diet drugs to make women smaller. A stroll through any mall in America will reveal "size 0" clothes in chic boutiques for teenage girls and size XXXL athletic jerseys in stores that sell professional and college teams' logo wear for boys.

The difference in size between softball and baseball diamonds has an impact on the games. The rules and action of softball are affected by its field dimensions. Because the distances between the bases are relatively short and the pitcher is so much closer to the batter than in baseball, base stealing is allowed only after the pitcher has released the ball, just as in Little League baseball. The purpose for the rule in Little League is to protect the players, who are children in need of limits for their own safety. Allowing base stealing whenever the ball is in play causes the pitchers to change the pace of the windup when a runner is on base in order to be able to throw quickly to the open base *or* to the catcher. The likelihood that the young pitchers' and catchers' skills are sufficiently developed to keep the ball under control under those circumstances is slim, posing the risk of players getting hit by wild throws as well as colliding on the base paths with defending infielders. For the youngsters' protection, that sophisticated aspect of the game is postponed until they are teenagers. Because the dimensions of an adult softball diamond are the same as a child's baseball field, advanced softball players are also deprived of a thrilling and suspenseful aspect of the game, which requires the development of highly skilled base running and infield defense.

Proportionate to the dimensions of the softball diamond, outfield fences are placed at between one-half to two-thirds of the distance of a regulation-sized baseball outfield. This speeds up the pace of the game but allows less fielding and base-running drama. Many of baseball's moments of suspense and tension are missing in the quick, short action of softball. Softball fans would probably respond that what baseball fans regard as suspenseful is simply boring. One unimpressed football fan remarked while watching the World Series on television, "There sure is a lot of staring in this game." Baseball is painfully slow, with long periods when nothing appears to be happening. It is, critics might say, out of touch with the fast pace of contemporary life. To others, that slowness, "the mental game," defines baseball's allure. The slow pace allows spectators to strategize along with coaches and players. It allows time to think, watch an outfielder waiting for the pitcher's next move, or the batter in the on-deck circle adjusting his batting glove, or the pitcher rubbing up a new ball. It allows time to get a beer and a hot dog and return to your seat (although every baseball fan who has done this will testify that as soon as you leave your seat or let your mind wander, some thrilling play will take place, and you will miss it and kick yourself for the rest of your life).

For baseball fans, the leisurely pace of baseball compared to softball allows for the most subtle, most intriguing aspects of the game. Softball's short outfield fences do not allow for a long, high fly ball that draws outfielders back, back, and back far enough so that even after the ball is caught, the runner can tag up and make a dash for the next base while the fielders quickly relay the ball to try to make the out. The baseball fan could find softball crimped without baseball's pasture-sized outfields. The collective suspense of that pause, while players and spectators alike await the outcome of the ball's flight, is missing in softball. So is the renowned "mental" aspect of baseball. The long stares between pitcher and batter, the challenge posed by a fast runner on first trying to steal second while the pitcher splits his attention between the batter and the runner, do not exist in softball. Baseball's long at-bats that require, with a runner on base, almost subliminal communication between the infielders and continual changes in strategy by the batter as the pitch count changes, are not part of softball. It's a different game.

What is important to note is that the dimensions and the pace do not stem from a woman's physical "limitations." A contemporary woman athlete is entirely capable of running the distances in a baseball outfield to chase down a fly ball. But the choice of which sport she will play has been made in advance for her, and it is not the one Americans pay to see. Even if she accepts the fact that very few women can become wealthy playing any team sport, once she becomes good at softball, it is difficult to switch to baseball. The reverse is not the case. If the pace of the game is determined by the size of the field, the mechanics of play are affected by the equipment used. The larger size of the softball requires entirely different throwing and batting techniques. A baseball can be gripped with the thumb and two fingers and hurled with arm fully extended as a rock from a sling. The softball must be grasped with all five fingers to be held securely and tossed with a shorter motion. This is then disparaged as "throwing like a girl." Once a girl has been trained to throw like this, it is difficult to make the transition to throwing a baseball, difficult to learn to swing the bat to hit baseball's smaller, faster-moving ball with its longer trajectory and extended time for unpredictable movement (change-ups, sliders, knuckle balls, and curves that have time to drop "off the table" before most batters can even see them). The wrist action, hip balance, and follow-through of a baseball swing are significantly different than the quicker, shorter movement required to hit a softball effectively. The skills required are not regarded as merely different, however: girls are told they are "not good enough" to play baseball, while boys are regarded, rightly or not, as having less difficulty down-sizing to softball if they so desire.

These differences do not imply that either baseball or softball is inherently "better." The point is that sexes are segregated and given no real choice about which game to play. Boys who play softball are assumed to be not good enough to play baseball. All understand that baseball is the real national pastime and softball is a modified version. Given the pace at which young athletes develop today, starting late forecloses much of a career in sport.

Although socially and institutionally deprived of the right to choose baseball, individual girls continued to play baseball with boys throughout the first decades of the twentieth century. Often, when one girl became a standout in a given venue, all girls were prohibited from playing in that locale. In 1928, a fourteen-year-old girl named Margaret Gisolo played American Legion baseball with exceptional talent. Gisolo was the star of her (otherwise all-male) team, playing second base and batting .429 in the championship tournament in Chicago. She became a national celebrity, featured in newspaper articles and Movietone News. One sportswriter was so electrified by her playing he wrote, "Perhaps it won't be long before some young lady will break into the lineup of a professional baseball team." Her young teammates welcomed her contribution to their team. The adults, however, gatekeepers for the enforcement of gender roles, made sure no girl would ever again lead their sons at the national game. Her league changed its rules the following year to explicitly exclude girls from play.

In 1935, before rulings were passed prohibiting it, a fifteen-year-old high school sophomore, Nellie Twardzik, gained national publicity when she tried out for and beat twenty-five boys to make the Bartlett High School baseball team in Webster, Massachusetts. She too was at first celebrated and then ejected from the sport. Newspapers referred to her as the "Babe Ruth" or "Babe Didrickson" of Webster, and one AP sportswriter wrote, "Babe Ruth may be the greatest drawing card in the major leagues but as far as comparisons go, he is just another ball player when one considers the crowd appeal of fifteen-year old Nellie Twardzik."[8] It was estimated that as many as 1,500 spectators showed up for the high school games that used to draw only 200 or 300 supporters.

Local bans against girls playing baseball held up until they were challenged in 1973 by parents who filed civil rights complaints on behalf of their daughters who wanted to play Little League ball. When it was clear that Little League baseball could no longer legally forbid girls to play, other tactics were attempted to discourage the children, the most successful of which was a diversionary tactic with which we still live: Little League baseball spawned Bobby Sox softball as "Little League for girls." This siphoned girls away from baseball for life, as the softball leagues became feeders for high school and college softball teams. The existence of parallel universes where girls play softball and boys play baseball is suspect egalitarianism, considering girls had to be manipulated into relinquishing hardballs. The fact that girls and women have played organized baseball since it was introduced to American soil is not denied, merely ignored. It is regarded as a nonevent, and inevitable that American girls who tenaciously continue to play baseball are just as continually thrown off the field.

The dynamic of exclusion is evident in Harold Seymour's classic three-volume history *Baseball*, written between 1960 and 1990. In the volume treating the years 1900 to 1930, *The Golden Age*, Seymour opens with an observation about baseball's early hold on American culture: "In short, baseball was ingrained in the American psyche. Its importance in the first decades of the twentieth century was astonishing . . . Why did the game have such a strong grip on the public? Perhaps Zane Grey's explanation is as good as any: 'It fulfilled the American need for expression because it was open and manly, and full of risks, surprises, and glorious climaxes.'"[9] The American psyche is manly, Seymour and Grey suggest. But in Seymour's third volume, *The People's Game*, women's participation is discussed in detail over several chapters. Seymour notes, "It is ironic that the game of baseball, so closely associated with men as to become a male preserve, should have a partly feminine origin."[10]

His alertness to this fact doesn't get women in the front door. At the very beginning of volume 3 he presents a diagram, a house with a flag flying from the roof proclaiming the house of baseball "The People's Game." In the attic, or penthouse, is the Hall of Fame. The story just below is "Organized Baseball." The levels of the house move down through college players, town teams, industrial teams, semipros, armed forces players, and finally, softball players, far beneath the Hall of Fame and organized baseball. In the basement are Indians and prisoners, and then, below them, forming the foundation of the house of baseball, are boys. A separate building called "the outbuilding" houses black baseball. Connected to the main house, in a separate wing called "the annex," are women. They are marginalized in spite of the fact that Harold Seymour himself acknowledges that they were among the first players of the game. Softball players are "in the house," although on a low level. Perhaps they are included because men, too, play softball. Only women and blacks are represented in segregated wings from the big house of baseball.

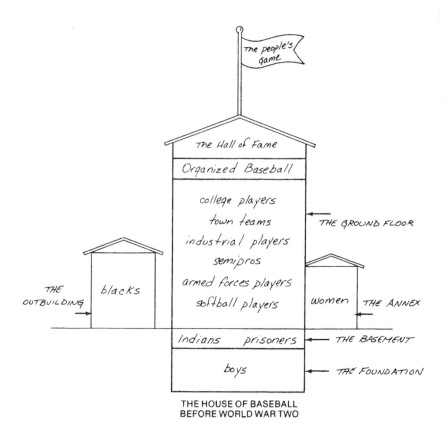

THE HOUSE OF BASEBALL
BEFORE WORLD WAR TWO

House of Baseball diagram with women's baseball in the annex (Harold Seymour, *Baseball: The People's Game*, Oxford: Oxford University Press, 1990, viii. By permission of Oxford University Press)

The Danger of Competitive Girls

In the 1920s, a debate emerged that would dominate discourse on women's athletics for the next half century: was athletic competition healthy for girls? Education experts were beginning to advocate more physical exercise for girls, although most were leery of encouraging competition. The young women of the new century were showing themselves capable of becoming very involved in the competitive outcome of their games. In basketball, special rules were required to restrain female players from becoming too physically aggressive. Softball's appearance on the national scene in the early twentieth century served the purpose of the educators who wanted to discourage demanding, "violent" competitive sports for girls. In its earliest incarnation, softball was designed to be such an easygoing game that it was hard to get too intensely engaged in the competitive outcome.

Only a minority of physical education experts of the early twentieth century argued that *team* sports as compared to individual exercise were beneficial for girls. Gertrude Dudley, director of the women's department of physical education at the University of Chicago, and sociologist Frances A. Kellor were two who believed in the benefits of team sports for girls and women. Dudley and Kellor sought to bring girls out of the sheltered environs of their households and make them useful members of society. The qualities that the middle class sought for its men and believed athletics would instill, were also desirable in women. "The point is that women can no longer live in such a way that they influence only their own homes, family and immediate circle," the educators asserted.[11] Athletics for women would engender "good personal habits and improved appearance," as well as "a group consciousness, with its many varying expressions of graciousness and power." Athletics enhance the lives of individual women and improve society as a whole. "The organized game is the active expression of one's natural self, the life in many essential details which is lived later away from school and college and a miniature of the democracy which envelops one in later years." Athletics taught the mental skills of "observation, attention, concentration, memory, imagination, initiation, judgment and will-power." When these qualities are achieved, they lead to "the attainment of a presence of mind and self-control in which accuracy, coolness, quickness and good judgment are called into use. Every one knows how essential these are in any field of activity and how indispensable they are to efficiency."[12]

Physical robustness and self-control are conventional middle-class values. However, Dudley and Kellor's belief that the same values were equally desirable in American girls and women as boys and men was very progressive. The scholars argued the type of athletics that most readily engender these qualities are "the various games of ball, from the simpler ones, such as long-ball, captainball, push-ball, volley-ball and drive-ball, up to those requiring fine team work, such as indoor baseball, basketball, and hockey."[13] Dudley and Kellor advocated *team* sports as directly beneficial to the education of girls. In 1909, this qualified as a revolutionary educational theory. Team ball games would also improve girls' ability to reason, to control their instincts and exercise common sense and judgment; to develop self-control, unselfishness, honor, self-sacrifice, fairness, modesty, decision, courage and responsibility, loyalty, and discipline; and would train them for citizenship. These values would not only help middle-class girls to take their places as citizens but would socialize the working class, the poor, and the children of immigrants by teaching cooperation and self-control.

> Take a struggling mass of little East Side children. They want to be "on the go" every instant and to show off, and have hitherto done this by chasing each other, shoving, pinching and kicking, complaining, sulking, tattling or even going home with a "mad on." Obedience to orders is the first step out of this maze of energy—obedience when every sense and perception is alert. They must listen to rules, must play the position given, and fouls are called unceasingly when they do not obey. In a little while they are actually controlling themselves and are preventing fouls and delays.[14]

Dudley and Kellor regarded fair play and group loyalty as indispensable to a strong and orderly society. The character building usually associated with boys was equally important for girls.

> If a sense of honor and loyalty are made to mean anything, after a little training most girls will be found standing bravely with their team in defeat, congratulating the other team or modestly accepting their share of the team's victory. It is a great thing to learn to be a good loser. It is also a great thing to share victory and feel that some one else has done as much as one's self to win it. There are many girls who have never had this sense of sharing victory or defeat in the guise of group loyalty.[15]

Dudley and Kellor expected American girls to become active citizens rather than homebound objects of sentimentality and emotionalism. If girls were allowed to focus on something larger than themselves, to learn to cooperate as a part of a group and to respect rules, they could step out of their sheltered existence and the self-preoccupation of their confined household worlds and become useful participants in civic life. Team sports would help them achieve this larger life.[16]

But the two educators drew the line at too much emphasis on winning. Team sports were healthy, but only if competition was limited. Traveling teams were unhealthy because they placed too much "nervous strain" on the girls, who, given the chance, would become overly preoccupied with their team and with winning. "They get interested in their game and spend so much time at it that they neglect their studies . . . they try every means to meet in the library, halls, and lavatory and talk game, of course. They very often go insane on their particular game, and do not care for any all-around work. . . . This training to professionalism is to be condemned; too much time is lost, carting around the country."[17]

In other words, given a chance, the girls would behave like any other school athletes. The rhetoric about natural athletic *differences* between the sexes reveals underlying fears about *similarities*. If girls were "naturally" less competitive, less combative, less aggressive, made of gentler stuff than boys, the behavior described above would not arise. But given the opportunity to play sports seriously and competitively, many girls succumb to the same temptations as boys. And in fact, when involved with athletic teams that practice and compete to win against other athletic teams, girls have demonstrated their ability to become as "insane" or unbalanced as any sports-crazy boy. Boys are indulged when they behave that way, but girls are not. It is not regarded as strange for grown men, married and with children, to be obsessed with a particular sport or boyhood team. A man can rush from the dinner table or stop at a sports bar on his way home from work to watch his team play Monday Night Football or the World Series or basketball playoffs. But let Mom stop off on her way home, or neglect the household, or fail to have dinner ready because she was watching the same game on television, and she is likely to be viewed as selfish and irresponsible, an unfit wife and mother, and a candidate for individual or family counseling.

The real problem is that we don't *want* our girls and women to become sports fanatics, or overly involved in athletics, and we know that given the opportunity, they can fall victim to the temptations of sports. Somebody in the family has to be an adult, available to drive the kids, do the shopping, and prepare dinner. Therefore, do *not* take the risk that girls and women will fall in love with a sport for life, taking precedence over family at certain times of the year. Do *not* allow them to play competitively and take themselves seriously as athletes. Even the progressive educational theory of Gertrude Dudley and Frances Kellor withers at the thought of girls overly involved in sports. While our two educators encourage a mild exposure to the social benefits of organized games, too much of a good thing is dangerous. Enter indoor baseball.

The Benefits of Softer Balls

Dudley and Kellor wanted to include baseball among the games played by girls precisely because its complexity and orderliness promised to instill the values they believed would benefit American girls. They saw the same benefits for girls that male social reformers saw for boys. "Baseball . . . possesses the greatest educational possibilities, for it is the most highly organized of all games." But they believed girls were not interested in playing baseball for four reasons: "There have been four causes of the lack of interest: the hard ball, the heavy bat, the long-distance throws, and the complexity of the rules."[18] Indoor baseball, or softball, provided a remedy for all four obstacles.

The ball used is soft; the bats are short and light; curves are not much used; the pitching is the straight arm, which is especially easy for girls, as it is the way they ordinarily throw; gloves and masks are not required, as the element of injury is greatly minimized; sliding bases is but little practiced, owing to the rule that the base-runner cannot leave the base until after the ball has passed the batsman or while the pitcher holds it; bunting is much used, so strength does not count for a great deal; and the distances are short, so the throws need cause no strain. A high degree of exertion is required only at intervals and then is not prolonged. Above all it is a pretty game with much fun in it. The only remaining difficulty is the complexity of the rules.[19]

Dudley and Kellor believed that the newly invented game of softball would give girls access to the benefits of baseball while avoiding the risks. "[Indoor] Baseball can be played by girls not strong enough to endure the constant strain of basketball [and indoor] baseball like basketball requires a good body and good lungs, but there is so little strain that almost any girl can play."[20] They embraced softball, both indoor and outdoor, as a toned-down version of baseball, which, they concurred with Spalding, was too strenuous for womankind. Sadly, even these most forward-thinking of educators were stopped in their tracks when it came to advocating baseball for girls.

In April 1923 a delegation approached Mrs. Herbert Hoover and obtained her assistance in calling a conference in Washington. The Women's Division of the National Amateur Athletic Federation was the result. Three years later under the sponsorship of the Women's Division, Gladys Palmer of Ohio State University created a special set of baseball rules for women. The reason was that regular baseball was too "strenuous and dangerous" for "the weaker sex." In April 1927, the Subcommittee on Baseball of the National Committee on Women's Athletics of the American Physical Education Association adopted Palmer's rules as the version of baseball that girls would play.

FIVE

How Baseball Became Manly and White

Baseball and Women's Rights

Softball was thus adopted as the form of the national sport appropriate for the "gentler sex." The need to separate women from men and to make everything women do smaller and more contained than what men do reflects a need to control and confine women. The glorious expanse of pasture in a full-sized baseball outfield invites freedom of movement: hitting a ball as far as it can be hit, running forever after a long fly ball to try to snag it, dwelling in—and perhaps trying to control for a moment—the limitless freedom of open land. The assertion that a baseball diamond is too big for women, but a softball field is just right, has the effect of confining women's space. The playing field may be level, but it is smaller. Confined spaces and limited choices are designated women's domains not because they are "naturally" feminine, but because they segregate boys and girls and create gender hierarchies.

The domination of space by physical possession, verbal assertiveness, or psychological control is one of the most important means of establishing masculinity. Masculinity as physical and psychological occupancy explains why the spaces set aside for girls and women were so dramatically confined. To be feminine meant to be dominated and confined. Traditionally bounded by the household, modern women's worlds were also severely constricted, if not limited entirely, to the home. In sports, girls got half a basketball court, three bounces, use of fields and gyms only when boys' and men's teams didn't need them. Instead of being allowed to roam the outfields of baseball, girls got the fenced-in dimensions of the softball field, a game that was designed with spatial constraints in mind.

This is neither a new phenomenon nor an original observation. Women have long been defined as private rather than public beings, confined within households rather than free to participate in the larger world. But women's lack of access to baseball is more than a simple continuation of archaic history. Organized sport in general and American baseball in particular gained preeminence and became a site for gender, race, and class contestation during an era of rapid social and economic change. Baseball's rise to national popularity paralleled nineteenth-century urbanization and industrialization, the end of American slavery, an influx of working-class immigrants, and, most importantly for the purpose of this book, the nineteenth- and early-twentieth-century women's movements in Europe and the United States. The pursuit of a separate version of the national game for girls to play reveals the contested nature of gender in the United States, always defined in terms of both class and race. In this chapter, the role baseball played in consolidating and enforcing emerging American race, class, and gender roles is explored.

The American women's movement of the nineteenth century germinated in the antislavery movement and reflected national racial and class tensions even while it demanded political, economic, and social rights for women. The earliest public utterances of nineteenth-century American women were demands by both black and white women in the 1830s for an end to slavery with particular reference to its sexual abuse of women. The 1840s were an important decade for launching women into the uncharted realm of political protest, culminating in 1848 in the first American women's rights convention in Seneca Falls, New York—not too far from Cooperstown. The first public expression of the American women's rights movement thus took place during baseball's first decade of life, if Spalding's public relations myth about Abner Doubleday in Cooperstown in 1839 is taken to mark the game's origin.

This vision is only slightly ironic. The idea of baseball and American women's rights born as twins is not a social scientific observation, nor does it imply a causal connection between the two nineteenth-century American phenomena. For an American woman baseball lover, however, the parallels between the rise of baseball and women's rights are both amusing and uncanny, and they continue into the twentieth century. The last decade of the nineteenth century and first years of the twentieth century marked the reunification and revitalization of the pre-Civil War women's movement, which had shattered over racial issues in the 1870s. At the end of the nineteenth century, women reorganized and renewed their campaign for the right to vote. In 1920, they achieved their goal after having overcome unimaginable resistance. Baseball's history during the same decades was marked by the advent of professional baseball, the formation of the National League, and the first attempt at international expansion. American baseball, proclaimed Spalding, should "follow the flag." Uncertainty about the possible impact of newly won women's rights on traditional American gender roles caused anxiety for many. Indeed, Madame J. H. Caldwell called, in 1920 in the *Chicago Defender*, for women to play baseball now that they could vote: "Wanted—Ladies to Play Ball." Her willingness to take on all challengers whether black, white, male, or female must have provoked concern for those worried about where women's suffrage might lead. The text of the ad explicitly associates the right to vote with the right to play baseball: "Our women are voting now, so why not be able to play a real game of baseball?"[1] The idea that African American women were ready to challenge both gender and racial boundaries in politics and sports underlines the radical threat to American social order. It might be too late to repeal women's suffrage, but they could still be kept off the nation's baseball diamonds!

Baseball, whose arrival in North America in the early nineteenth century was embraced spontaneously and nearly universally, was appropriated by its first generation of professional owners and managers as a means of promoting and reflecting American values. Baseball became not only a profitable business with international aspirations, but a means of ensuring that American manhood was associated with white middle-class mores. Those regarded as insufficiently manly, insufficiently white, and insufficiently civilized were excluded from the national game, an object lesson in what constituted a bona fide American. "Democracy's game" thus reflected and enforced the segregation of race, class, and gender. It helped to construct American masculinity in the nineteenth century and acted as a gatekeeper for integrating the various "masculinities" represented by different races and classes into a single white, Christian, middle-class norm. It both forged and reflected the victory of middle-class "rationalism" and consumerism, the dominance of European American Christianity through the exclusion of nonwhites and non-Europeans from the game, and a reassertion of dominance over newly mobile women, both by exclusion from play and by asserting that the masculine qualities required for athletic excellence were the same as those required for American citizenship. As Michael Kimmel notes, "The masculinity reconstituted on the ball field or in the bleachers was a masculinity that reinforced the unequal distribution of power based on class, race, and gender. In that sense, also, baseball was truly an American game."[2]

Race, class, and gender do not exist in nature. Not only must they be erected and maintained with cultural glue, but they cannot stand alone: each assumes and requires the existence of the other two. The sections that follow explore the interrelations of race, class, and gender during American baseball's adolescent years.

Sport Builds Modern Men

Rapidly changing economic roles brought about by nineteenth-century industrialism contributed to American and European consternation about the definitions of masculinity and femininity. The new industrial order promoted increasing rationalization and compartmentalization of society accompanied by pseudo-scientific theories about the differences between men and women. For the first time in history, the concept of gender, defined as the social roles of men and women, was linked directly to biology. As Todd Crosset writes in "Masculinity, Sexuality, and the Development of Early Modern Sport," "Women first gained and then lost economic and political power to men in the early stages of urban industrial growth. The loss of power was, in part, the result of a cohesive heterosexual male bourgeois ideology that defined men and women in terms of biology and sex. This ideology was promoted by a myriad of new scientific theories and social institutions that concerned themselves with sexuality and that justified the privileged position attained by the male bourgeoisie."[3]

Organized, professionalized sport originated during the late nineteenth century and played a critical role in socializing men to define themselves as biologically superior to women. Crosset suggests that organized athletics emerged in the late-nineteenth-century United States explicitly in order to reassert male dominance over the changes in women's social role. "The nineteenth century was marked by drastic social transformations in the roles of men and women. Whereas an increase in power and roles for women occurred during the first half of the century, the second half of the century was characterized by a reactionary male bourgeois movement that emphasized male superiority and distinct sex spheres. Social institutions of the post–Civil War era, including sport, helped to promote these gender distinctions and separate gender roles."[4] The institutionalization of sports was used to "produce" men by making participation virtually mandatory for all "normal" boys and men, which in turn taught and promoted a set of values and behaviors that appeared natural. Defining athletics as unfeminine assured that the girls and women of the middle class, discouraged from all but the mildest exercise, did in fact remain physically weak.

The more strident the proclamation of men's "natural" athleticism, the more doubtful is the concept. You don't need to work so hard at something that comes naturally. David Whitson in "Sport in the Construction of Masculinity" observes,

> It is important to register just how much time, effort, and institutional support is given over to *masculinizing practices*. It is also important to understand just how much urgency is usually attached to the success or failure of such projects, by parents and indeed by the boys themselves. What such effort and concern immediately belie is any notion of biological destiny. If boys simply grew into men and that was that, the efforts described to teach boys how to be men would be redundant. We can suggest, then, that "becoming a man" is something that boys (and especially adolescent boys) work at.[5]

Medical science itself was mobilized to prove the natural superiority of men. Biologist Anne Fausto-Sterling describes medical and scientific studies at the turn of the twentieth century that claimed to establish chemical and biological differences between men and women "justifying" rigid sex segregation in activities with little obvious link to sex. She describes the era as "a period when the populace of the United States and many European nations had begun to reevaluate traditional constructions of gender and sexuality. . . . New debates opened up over the rights of homosexuals and women—while what historians have called a 'crisis in masculinity' developed in both Europe and the United States."[6]

Moral superiority associated with physical prowess and muscular strength was an ethic also articulated at the time in the "muscular Christianity" movement that emerged in England during the mid-nineteenth century. Olympics organizer Pierre de Coubertin and Thomas Hughes (*The Manliness of Christ*, 1880) contributed to the definition of masculinity as separate and superior to femininity by virtue of muscular prowess. The muscular Christianity movement reconceptualized the image of Jesus from "a beatific, delicate, soft-spoken champion of the poor into a muscle-bound he-man whose message encouraged the strong to dominate the weak."[7] The masculine norm fashioned by sports was white, Christian, and middle class. The muscular Christianity movement in England, France, and the United States placed athletic fields at the center of boys' education. Acquiring manliness meant learning to dominate that space while developing their bodies to be bigger, faster, and stronger.

On an emotional level, the white American men of the nineteenth-century middle class needed to reassure themselves that they were still the warriors, protectors, and providers that nature intended them to be, even though their work was no longer physical. Athletic life offered one method of reinforcement. The image of virile athletic manhood proved reassuring, especially for professionals, merchants, and white-collar workers. Fortified by rigorous exercise and competition, well-to-do men could cultivate their physical superiority, restore their confidence, and regain the hard edge required for effective leadership. On a political level, athletics helped to establish the fitness of the middle class for moral and political leadership while attempting to channel the "unruly passions" of the working classes. The discipline of organized sports held the promise of encouraging the social integration required to be citizens and consumers in the newly emerging economy.

The working poor used sports in their own way, which was not always compatible with middle-class intentions. The "unruly mob" was interested in athletics as a distraction from the physical hardship of their lives. Working-class men created a male sporting culture that included baseball clubs, prizefights, boat races, footraces, and gambling halls. They engaged in a more rough-and-tumble style of competition that included gambling and drinking mixed with athletics: a rejection of the dominant ethos of self-discipline and delayed gratification that presented a rebellious underside to proper Victorian culture.

For contradictory reasons, then, middle- and working-class men cultivated competitive athletic cultures in order to define and assert the changing mores of masculinity in an era of rapid social change. The middle classes sought a masculinity defined by rationality, discipline, and Christian morality, while the lower classes asserted their independence from that enforced order and asserted their masculinity by roughness and passionate physical toughness. Women represented a threat to both versions of athletic culture, even though all classes of women were also becoming more interested in sports. But the more sports became organized and popular in the nineteenth century, the more athleticism became associated with masculinity. Susan Cahn observes, "American men confronting the changes wrought by industrialization, urbanization, and mass immigration looked to sport as a crucial avenue for defining and expressing their manhood. It is not surprising, then, that women who tried to carve out a place in the athletic world met with some resistance."[8]

Racialized Gender and Class

In the United States, concepts of masculinity and femininity are racialized as well as associated with economic class. Stereotypes dictate how "white" and "nonwhite" women and men will behave. The refined, rational "manliness" expected of a wealthy white man differs from the rougher, more passionate masculinity of a man who works with his body. Race and class thinking intersect in the sense that few men of color are expected to be wealthy. Working-class men of different races are set at odds with each other as society teaches them to focus on racial rather than economic hierarchies. American culture has tried to teach that racial hierarchies are "natural" and immutable while economic hierarchy, or class structure, is the just reward for hard work. Instead of directing anger about exploitation at their bosses, the working poor are encouraged to see the source of their problems as working people of other races, immigrants, and women. Their attention is diverted to racial and gender hierarchies instead of class divisions. When unemployment rates are high and wages are low, workers are taught to blame minorities' willingness to work for less money, or feminists who encourage women to take men's jobs. This directs attention away from the fact that the economy itself requires low-wage workers. White workers are encouraged to feel superior to and threatened by men of color and all working women instead of becoming angry at a system of exploitation.

Though most of the economic power in the United States is controlled by men, European and African American women have also been pitted against each other in a template of gender stereotypes that contaminates every racial and cultural group. Racial and sexual mistrust that initially began with the European conquest of Native Americans can be seen in dramatic relief in slavery. The polarized caricature is that white women are too delicate and "good" to be physically strong and sexual, while "other" women—Native American, African American, Latin American, and so forth—are too strong and sexual to be feminine. It may be true that white men and "other" men also suffer from polarization, with white men regarded as rational and controlled but always in need of proving their strength and sexuality, and "others" regarded as strong and sexual but having to prove their rationality. European American men, however, have cornered the power to define, as well as most of the economic and political power in our society. All are robbed of their full humanity by these destructive dualities.[9]

Working-class white women fell into a netherworld similar to that of working-class men as race eclipsed class as the most significant social signifier in America besides gender. They weren't fragile enough to be regarded as feminine and "protected" sexually, but they were encouraged to distance themselves from black women. Working-class men were tough but not rational like middle-class men; yet they were encouraged to believe they were intellectually superior to men of color. As European workers immigrated to the United States, each group went through a process of distancing themselves from the race of the freed slaves. Thus American racism was actually encouraged, in part as a way to keep working people from developing any sense of class solidarity.[10]

European Americans worried about who they were and whether they were manly enough, feminine enough, or white enough. Since these qualities are not self-evident, people clung defensively to what they thought they *should* be, reassuring themselves by distinguishing themselves from blacks, "non-Americans," non-Christians, and in the case of women, "unfeminine" women. Men were determined to distinguish themselves from anything female.[11] In the United States, where no classes were believed to carry a life sentence, the line between the working class and the middle class was blurred. There had never really been a peasantry in this nation, although there were slaves and, after slavery's abolition, former slaves and "white trash," both landless farmers who were forced into sharecropping arrangements with little to distinguish them from the European peasantry. Since the American aristocracy was not officially hereditary, the middle class was at pains to distinguish itself from the working class, which was at pains to distinguish itself from the poorest of the poor, both white and black. All the uncertainty about social boundaries in the nineteenth-century United States manifested itself as defensiveness: prejudice and exclusionism capable of mushrooming into a virulent racism and sexism.

Early Baseball's Struggles with Gender, Race, and Class

Baseball reflected all of the anxiety about gender, race, and class, including the ability to turn fear into exclusion in the name of morality and democratic values. Early baseball developed an ideology that was male, white, and middle class, and worked hard to make it true. Historian Warren Goldstein refers to the discord between working- and middle-class masculinity when he notes, "No single word carried more virtue or praise in sporting language than 'manly,' and few words carried so much disdain as 'boyish' . . . the realm of 'manliness' was defined by what lay outside it: anything that was not 'manly' was roundly condemned. Here too, however, their language betrayed them. So much vehemence infused this effort as to suggest that the ideal of manliness was as fragile as it was vague."[12] Goldstein observes, "Baseball was straddling a cultural boundary during those years, a position it has never managed entirely to escape. The game appealed simultaneously to the culture of the urban streets—a culture that was losing some of its principal institutions by the late 1850s, and to the respectable and newly vigorous culture of middle-class Victorian men. Participants in the baseball fraternity would find these two cultures difficult to reconcile."[13]

In baseball as well as other American industries, class conflicts between labor and management manifested themselves as racial exclusionism and concern with styles of masculinity. The first generation of professional baseball promoters, led by A. G. Spalding and William Hulbert, organized the National League in 1876, using the language of morality, discipline, and manliness to justify controlling the independence of professional baseball players. While early professional baseball had been plagued by gambling, corruption, and general rowdiness that infected players and spectators alike, the desire to rescue baseball from "its slough of corruption and disgrace," in the view of Spalding and Hulbert, required disempowering the ballplayers themselves. The National League would oversee baseball *teams* with clearly delineated roles distinguishing management from players, who had previously thought of themselves as members of baseball *clubs*, with their own responsibility for running everything from securing grounds to setting schedules and managing the actual play. Now managers were hired by owners to oversee the administrative aspects of staging competitions in order to "free" ballplayers from any distractions apart from actual play. This professional specialization was actually disempowering, as ballplayers had less responsibility and less opportunity to determine their own playing conditions. Historian Adrian Burgos notes, "The National League founders created an exclusive organization and enacted a multipronged approach to maximize profits through domination of labor and cultivation of new markets. The league now dealt with players as 'club subordinates' and adopted a new contract that 'provided a penalty of expulsion of any player violating his contract, and anyone thus expelled was to be forever ineligible to reinstatement in any League club.'"[14]

This was the beginning of the "reserve clause" that bound players to a particular team and gave the team management the right to exclusive use of the players under contract. The system remained in place until the mid-twentieth century, when players successfully organized to demand free agency. In the nineteenth century, the National League players actually supported the reserve system because they believed it would create more job security. In the early years, it also enabled players to influence who else would play on their team, as they collaborated with management about the respectable manliness of professional baseball. That is, they shared a white middle-class masculine consciousness, rather than identifying themselves as workers in conflict with management. They had a stake in perceiving themselves as professionals and distinguishing their careers as ballplayers from the labor of both the working class and non-whites. But it was a fine line between being professional specialists and children without any responsibility except playing ball. This tension heightened the need for professional ballplayers to distinguish themselves from both boys and girls. Racism made men of color "boys" while sexism devalued anything associated with girls. Burgos notes,

> Labor also collaborated with management in shaping popular perceptions by engaging in class- and gender-based discourses that presented the professional game as respectable work performed by gentlemen. Discourses about masculinity and respectability also contributed to justifying the exclusion of colored players. By collaborating with management in the formation of a color line, players wielded influence in determining who could participate in organized baseball. The color line boosted the status of white players as professionals while also creating an artificial scarcity of available talent.[15]

The reserve system did not really create job security but instead undermined the independence of the players and contributed to the psychological pressure to distinguish themselves from children or slaves. Once a ballplayer signed a contract with a professional baseball team, he was bound to that team for the duration of his professional career. Since management's primary concern was with profit, they were tempted to find excellent players who might be cheaper to hire: African Americans, Latin Americans, Native Americans, and so forth. But this threatened the white ballplayers not only because of their lack of freedom to negotiate their own careers but because it blurred the racial line that distinguished them from slaves. Burgos writes, "Outspoken players complained of being treated like chattel, mere property to be bought and sold by team owners. Treatment as property at a time not far removed from the era of slavery imposed on ballplayers a condition associated with blackness. Concerned players sought to avoid the subordinated status of 'colored' Americans, who had been excluded from organized baseball."[16] To assert that they were free, white, middle-class professionals, the players formed a labor organization, "The National Brotherhood of Base-Ball Players," and resisted any effort on the part of management to hire any man of color. The ballplayers' insistence that baseball was a profession for whites only held out to all European American men, even the most newly arrived, that whiteness could be earned and was more important than material rewards for labor. Race eclipsed class as the most important signifier of American manhood.[17]

Even more intense than the fear of being thought of as black was the fear of being considered unmanly. Terror of being feminine transcends race *and* class lines. It is the final insult for men who have been robbed of their "manhood" by racism. It was an insult for a man of color to be called a "boy," but it was even more traumatic for any boy to be called a "girl." Femininity is also a threat to middle-class men whose masculinity has been defined as no longer physical but rational, controlled and controlling, and dispassionate. Sexuality for these men is paradoxically a reflection of their ability *not* to lose control, even to their sexual desires for a woman. The emerging and still shaky redefinition of modern American masculinity required distinguishing it from anything feminine as well as anything nonwhite. Being an American man is a precarious business. It requires effort and a difficult emotional and physical journey. The rewards for those who accomplish it are first access to the best of everything the nation has to offer.

Still Crazy after All These Years

The struggle to be masculine has not been resolved. Nobody grew up and men are still worried about not being men. William Pollack, professor of psychiatry at Harvard, has spent his career studying the paradox of modern manhood. He offers the "Boy Code": injunctions boys must follow if they are to become "real boys" rather than "sissy boys" or effeminate boys. The issues Pollack addresses are primarily those of white middle-class men who have struggled with gender identity since the advent of industrial capitalism in the mid-nineteenth century: (1) Men should be stoic, stable, and independent, never showing weakness, pain, or grief. They are to be "sturdy oaks." (2) Men should "give 'em hell," be daring and risk-taking: "the misconception that somehow boys are biologically wired to act like macho, high-energy, even violent supermen." (3) Boys and men should achieve status, dominance, and power. "Or, understood another way, . . . avoid shame at all costs, . . . wear the mask of coolness, . . . act as though everything is going all right, as though everything is under control, even if it isn't." (4) "Perhaps the most traumatizing and dangerous injunction thrust on boys and men is the literal gender straitjacket that prohibits boys from expressing feelings or urges seen (mistakenly) as 'feminine'—dependence, warmth, empathy."[18]

These boyhood imperatives hinder the ability of boys and men to make emotional connections. They foster an unrealistic sense of personal independence and shame in any boy displaying vulnerability or "femininity." By the time boys are of school age, says Pollack, they feel isolated, ashamed of emotional neediness, depressed by their essential solitude, and capable of expressing only one "acceptable" masculine emotion: anger. Girls and women represent a dangerous threat to this unrealistic emotional state. Anything feminine is experienced as a primal threat because it disrupts the emotional toughening process of boyhood, which involves premature separation of boys from their mothers. By age four or five, little boys are made to feel shame if they cling to their mothers. If masculinity is defined by emotional independence from women, girls and women forever remind men of their forbidden, but very human, emotional neediness. Pollack cites psychologist Jean Baker Miller, who has observed that boys are "made to fear *not* being aggressive, lest they be found wanting, be beaten out by another, or (worst of all) be like a girl. All of these constitute terrible threats to a core part of what is made to be men's sense of identity, which has been called masculinity."[19]

While Pollack's sophisticated critique of "gender straitjacketing" is promising for the emotional futures of men and women, it does not acknowledge what it is like to be *outside* the straightjacket. To be born female is to be used as an implement with which the spirits of boys are controlled and crushed. The most shameful insult for a boy is to be called a girl. This is not a whispered insult: it is shouted in every schoolyard and playing field in America. What are the girls within earshot, or indeed playing *with* the boy, to believe about themselves? The crippling segregation between male and female is destructive to both boys and girls because it creates a hierarchy in which half the population is given to believe it is inferior and embarrassing while the other half lives in fear of being like the inferior, embarrassing half. The whole business is emotionally disabling and carries potential physical consequences as boys are forced to be strong and aggressive and girls are encouraged to be weak and passive. It is an invitation to sexual violence and self-destructiveness. It is an utter disgrace for a boy to be "girly," or feminine in any way, and that diminishes the value of being a girl at all. Boys are regarded as *better* than girls, not just the "opposite," although that identification is always in danger of collapsing and in need of bolstering. It is not nearly as damaging to a girl's self-conception to be referred to as "tomboyish" or "studly" as it is for a boy to be called a "sissy" or "girly." At stake for boys who fail to act in a demonstrably masculine matter is their position of power and privilege on the gender hierarchy.

Statistics and the Civilizing of Baseball

The culture of early baseball, its audiences, and the evolving rules of play reflected an explicit effort to distinguish the newly proclaimed national game from anything boyish, as well as anything feminine. Even the gentlemen's clubs of the earliest era of American baseball were concerned that they not be seen as engaging in "boys' play," and made a point of inviting women as spectators, hosting elaborate dances for their club "reunions" in the off-season. Warren Goldstein describes the genesis of the term "baseball club" in contrast to the emerging "professional baseball team." He emphasizes the importance of upper-class social masculinity.

> Members of baseball clubs were proud of their ability to attract women both to observe their baseball skill and to participate in their social events. . . . The *Clipper* observed that the Eckfords had "long been noted for the number of ladies who assemble upon their grounds, as spectators of their playing." . . . Similarly, the winter social calendar of the Bowdoin Baseball Club of Boston was a tribute to the club's members, who "gave evidence," according to the *Clipper*, "that they were as much at 'home base' in the ball room, with the ladies, as on the ball ground with their friendly opponents."[20]

But even more important than the need for middle- and upper-class amateurs to establish their graciousness with the ladies was the work of rendering the sport itself compatible with modern standards of disciplined, rational masculinity. Credit for this accomplishment goes largely to Henry Chadwick.

There is nothing inherently masculine about baseball. Its claim to that title was self-consciously constructed with rule changes and statistical science. These are hardly traditional paths to masculinity, but they were compatible with the emerging definitions of the modern man. Henry Chadwick, who has been referred to as "Father Baseball," was born in Exeter, England, in 1824 and immigrated to the United States as a boy. He came from an illustrious line of intelligent and socially active men. His grandfather, Andrew, a disciple of John Wesley, had devoted his life to the promotion of "measures for the improvement of the condition of the population."[21] Henry's father, James, was prominent in regional intellectual and cultural circles, a follower of Thomas Paine, supporter of the French Revolution, and a journalist who advocated radical causes. Henry's half-brother Edwin, twenty-four years his senior, was already out of the house and following in his father's and grandfather's footsteps when Henry was born. He became one of the most famous men in Great Britain, knighted for his work as the architect of Britain's public health laws. His nickname in England was "The Sanitary Philosopher." The half brothers greatly admired each other, and it is likely that Henry's concern with making baseball a rational and moral sport for Americans was influenced by the same passion for order that motivated the rest of his family.

Edwin was Henry's role model in reform. In 1842, while sanitary commissioner in Britain, Edwin published a landmark work of social research, the *Report on the Sanitary Condition of the Labouring Population of Great Britain.* His research made use of voluminous quantities of accurate statistics on the working poor of England, interviews with doctors, and public health statistics. His highly respected document was the basis of the Public Health Act of 1848, of which he was the primary author. While Edwin devoted his life to cleaning up English working-class sewage, Henry devoted himself to sanitizing baseball in the name of respectable manliness. Henry's mission was to use baseball as "a moral recreation" and "a remedy for the many evils resulting from the immoral associations [that] boys and young men of our cities are apt to become connected with."[22] He vowed to accomplish this by making baseball both "scientific" and "manly." His brother once joked, "While I have been trying to clean up London, my brother has been keeping up the family reputation by trying to clean up your sports."[23]

Henry Chadwick never drew a diamond with a stick on a dirt field, but he was responsible for creating much of what modern baseball is. He invented the box score and was the first to keep the statistics that are the core of professional baseball history. He was a sports reporter for major New York newspapers and edited *Beadle's Dime Base Ball Player* and the *Spalding Baseball Guides*. In inventing statistical analysis of the game, he invented a system that enabled baseball to keep track of its history as well as to measure and judge various aspects of the game. Chadwick had played rounders as a boy in England, cricket as a young man in Hoboken, New Jersey, and finally became so smitten with baseball that he was "struck with the idea that base ball was just the game for a national sport for Americans."[24] From the moment of his epiphany, he devoted himself to promoting and improving the game in a way that would ensure its middle-class respectability and moral cleanliness.

Chadwick was not universally beloved for his efforts. He was strident in his beliefs and somewhat priggish. He favored a game that emphasized "displays of skill, control, and intellect over those reliant on unbridled power."[25] His system of scorekeeping enabled each game to be interpreted moralistically as well as athletically. His efforts to make baseball a more "scientific" game were in tune with nineteenth-century reformist zeal. Historian Jules Tygiel observes, "To Chadwick, for whom the promotion of baseball served a moral purpose, statistics were a means to this higher end. . . . box scores were not just game reports, but a series of mini-morality plays. Players should receive credit for their achievements, and through the category of errors, acknowledgement of their flaws. . . . Just as reformers made distinctions between the 'deserving and undeserving poor,' Chadwick attempted to distinguish between positive achievements and those that befell a team or athlete as a result of opponents' misplays."[26] In addition to the box score and the score card, Chadwick was the first to keep track of and to systematically define a relationship between hits, earned runs, and the errors. The only hits that counted should be the result of pure hitting, and not the result of "skillful base running and the fielding errors such running involves."[27] He reduced the number of balls required for a walk from five to four, for safety's sake, because "it would moderate the dangerous speed in delivering the ball to the bat." (If a pitcher knew he might put a runner on base with four rather than five pitches, he would have to be more careful with each pitch.)[28] He was more impressed with good fielding than with strikeouts, which were, he believed, the result of poor hitting rather than good pitching. Home runs were the result of poor pitching rather than good hitting. He clearly advocated an early version of "small ball," but his strident moralism smacked of puritanical religion as much as scientific interpretation of an intriguingly complex game.

Two things are certain about Henry Chadwick's lifetime efforts to make baseball masculine and scientific: they were enormously influential, at least to the ideology of modern baseball, and they were profoundly middle class. The manliness with which he was concerned reflected that class bias as did the efforts of reformers on both sides of the Atlantic to make the working classes conform to middle-class standards of morality and comportment. When Henry Chadwick referred to baseball as an "invigorating exercise and manly pastime,"[29] he was referring not so much to the specific physical demands of the game as to the middle-class virtues of controlled competition and rational play that can be understood statistically. Commentaries from baseball's early years employed almost exclusively the language of discipline, training, skill, and specialization. Regular team practices and specialization of positions were the products of this era. A team would rather describe itself as disciplined workers than as exceptional talents who were loath to practice hard. The rational, disciplined manliness of middle-class baseball paralleled the dominant definition of manhood in nineteenth-century America.

Gloves, Balls, and Masculinity

While the culture of baseball in the nineteenth and early twentieth centuries was forging its masculine identity, the rules and equipment were also evolving. Each stage in the game's development was measured and evaluated on a scale called manliness. What qualified a change in the game as manly seems capricious from a modern perspective. Early baseball closely resembled what we now call softball. It was played on a smaller diamond than modern baseball with a larger ball, which might be harder and livelier or softer and "dead," depending upon the choice of the competitors in any given game. Nineteenth-century teams often used livelier balls for practices and then would agree on a deader ball for games. The livelier ball made hitting easier and fielding more difficult, especially in the absence of any sort of protective gloves. Even using a catcher's glove was considered cowardly, so the catcher would stand a good distance behind the batter unless there were runners on base. Pitchers usually pitched underhand, and batters called for the pitches they wanted. Strikes were based upon the pitchers' ability to get the ball where the batter called for it.

The evolution of the sport along with technological developments in the manufacturing processes of equipment resulted in further changes to the modern game. The modern baseball itself is more tightly wound than any used in the early years. It is much livelier, enabling batters to hit it farther without being any stronger than earlier players. Changes in bat size and style of swing corresponded to the changes in the ball. Since the game's early years, there have been dramatic changes in the pitchers' delivery, in the sizes and shapes of infielders' and outfielders' gloves, in rules about designated hitters and substitutions for pitchers, and specialization of middle- and late-inning relievers. The livelier ball allowed for more power hitting, but it made life more difficult for pitchers, who developed new pitches to foil batters and paid a price in wear and tear on their arms. Nobody expects modern pitchers to pitch a full nine innings except in exceptionally brilliant outings. There are specialist pitchers who come in to work the middle innings when their team gets in trouble and "closers" who specialize in ninth inning pitching. Designated hitters have saved American League pitchers from having to bat at all.

Larger, more highly padded gloves evolved and have changed the nature of fielding. The size of modern outfielders' gloves would have been regarded a century ago as sissified, if not outright cheating. Darryl Brock, in his historical novel *If I Never Get Back*, describes the reaction to his time-traveling twentieth-century protagonist's request for what passed as a catcher's mitt when he stepped in as a substitute catcher during an 1869 game against a rough team called the Haymakers: "The Haymakers pointed and guffawed, a reaction that spread through the crowd. Flynn minced in dainty circles, fitting his hand into an imaginary glove. Craver roared, 'First the milksop, what'd he call it, *bunts* the ball? Now he's turned out like some Nancy boy with his little pinkies in a . . . *glove!*' It was too much for them; several actually rolled on the ground."[30]

Batting helmets are an even more recent development than gloves and protective catchers' gear. By nineteenth-century standards, it is more masculine to risk being killed at the plate by a fastball than to protect the head. What about slugger Barry Bonds' use of wrist and elbow protectors to prevent injury from inside pitches? He wore them at bat and discarded them when he reached base. Young boys emulate him by also wearing protective pieces on their elbows because they were deemed "cool" and made them feel like Bonds. One can imagine the taunts a boy who put them on would have drawn before Bonds made them a baseball fashion statement. But the game continues to be defined as quintessentially masculine, in spite of all these "sissy" developments.

One early significant change in the rules was the subject of a major dispute in the nineteenth century. Before 1865, a ball hit and caught on one bounce was considered an out. Since the players of the day used no fielding gloves at all, it was not as easy to catch a batted ball "on the bound" as it may seem to us today. However, in keeping with the general concern that baseball be "manly" rather than "boyish," there was a reform movement afoot to change the rule so that an out was counted only if the fielder caught the ball "on the fly," before it hit the ground. As Warren Goldstein notes, "Simply put, the reformers considered the bound catch a 'boy's rule.' By eliminating the bound catch in favor of the fly catch, they hoped to make baseball a more manly sport."[31] Proponents of changing the rule argued that catching the ball on the fly was more like cricket, which for once nobody denied was a "manly" game. It made the game more difficult, it looked "prettier" and, said Chadwick, catching a ball on the bound was "a feat a boy ten years of age would hardly be proud of." He urged players to try to catch balls on the fly even before the rule was implemented, because "Nothing disappoints the spectator, or dissatisfies the batsman so much, as to see a fine hit to the long field caught on the bound in this simple, childish manner." The rule, as we know, was changed to accommodate the reformers, nineteenth-century upper-class amateurism coming to be replaced by a middle-class work ethic, with its emphasis on professional skill, hard work, and discipline.

The game continues to evolve, as does its association with masculinity. One way the "New Man" of the late nineteenth and early twentieth century demonstrated his professionalism and manliness was by getting to a fly ball and catching it before it fell. Contemporary defenders of the essential masculinity of baseball would probably point to the home run as the definitively masculine characteristic of the game. "Women can't hit the ball 500 feet!" one can almost hear them say in response to the suggestion that women can play baseball. But the home run and its importance to the modern game is no more essentially manly than the fly ball rule. It is a cultural development, and it was not regarded as manly or admirable by Henry Chadwick. Two decades after the Babe added power to twentieth-century baseball, another sort of excellence entered, or perhaps more accurately *reentered*, the game. In 1947, when Jackie Robinson was finally allowed to play in the white major league, he brought a negro league style of ball with him that once again changed the game and its conception of masculinity. Robinson's daring and aggressive base running was unfamiliar to white ballplayers, who believed hitting the ball long was as manly as things got. Black ballplayers of the era regarded white men's play as conservative to the point of being timid and unimaginative. As one African American ballplayer remarked, "The white men just hit the ball and then stood there at first base and waited for somebody else to hit it!"[32] Robinson brought the ability to steal bases apparently at will. A white minor league manager whose team played against young Robinson remarked, "He stole everything except my infielder's gloves!" He could generate runs without waiting for anybody else to hit, driving pitchers to such a state of distraction with his shenanigans on the base paths that they would balk him home from third base.

This dimension was not immediately identified as "manly," at least not in the same sense as the home run, which is still taken to be the quintessential expression of masculine power both in the game and metaphorically in American life. Robinson and the black ballplayers who followed him added speed and cunning to the brute power of the home run. Baseball's "essential" manliness has proven very adaptable, with an uncanny ability to claim as its own whatever great thing is happening in the game. Perhaps the most consistently manly thing about baseball is its preoccupation with keeping women out.

American Womanhood and Athletics

As masculinity was being redefined on a white middle-class model in the nineteenth and twentieth centuries, modern femininity was also struggling to emerge from the confines in which it had been held. Athletics was one important testing ground for establishing manhood, organized by both class and race. But athletics was also one of the arenas that young women attempted to claim as they emerged from the shadows of severely limited traditional lives. The battle for access to their own strong and healthy bodies was in some ways even more daunting than their access to political power, or at least to the vote. The sports that girls and women were able to access were sorted by race and class, as were men's sports. Their experiences struggling to participate in athletics in general establish a context for understanding their exclusion from baseball. Access to women's track and basketball have involved some of the same areas of contestation as baseball: control of physical space and competition involving speed and power. But baseball remains a final frontier for women, while other sports, including track and basketball, have been opened to women, albeit with restraints based on race and class. What have been the issues in American culture that have made women's access to sports so difficult?

Sports Are for Boys

Gender is neither a fixed concept nor an essence but an evolving process. Some feminist theorists claim that all gender is "performance," the ability or compulsion to act the way society expects us to act. Biological sex does not naturally or inevitably translate into "masculine" and "feminine" behavior. Feminist theorist Judith Butler suggests that we are trained to act in conformity with the behavior that is stereotypically associated with our assigned gender.[1] Gender is imposed upon us by everything in the social environment, from mass media to toy manufacture to parental interest in helping children to "fit in." We attempt to freeze masculinity and femininity into concepts that transcend class or race, yielding debilitating contradictions.

If masculinity as defined by American society is intrinsically impossible because men are asked to be superhuman, needing nothing from other people, pure femininity is equally impossible because women are asked to be less than fully human. They have been defined biologically only as nurturers and mothers and psychologically only as dependents. They have been required to constrain and repress other human qualities, such as ambition, competitiveness, intellectuality, and physical courage. The refined, delicate, middle- and upper-class woman is presented as the only authentically feminine woman. Women who are strong, independent, and actively sexual are slammed as "unnatural," unfeminine, aggressive, and worse. They are disparaged as "virtual men" because of their behavior and ignite fear that they must be stealing masculinity from men. The "masculinization" of women will result in the "feminization" of men, a threat that must be stopped. If athletics are used to build men, then athletic women present a challenge to their assigned gender.

From the moment a baby is wrapped in its first diaper, *everything* is encoded with gender. Is the baby dressed in pink or blue? Are its toys baby dolls or Bob the Builder, Barbie cars or Tonka trucks? Will it be offered cheerleading and softball, or Pop Warner football and Little League baseball? We receive intensive gender instruction from the moment we are born, and it is an education so thorough that masculine or feminine behavior is indistinguishable from "natural" behavior. Although William Pollack is hardly the radical feminist that Judith Butler is, both scholars arrive at remarkably similar conclusions about our unnatural presumptions about gender behavior. Neither suggests that men and women are identical creatures, but simply that our inflexible definitions of male and female are socially constructed rather than a product of biology. Genes and hormones may create differences between biological maleness and femaleness, but they do not translate into specific behaviors.[2] "Masculine" and "feminine" are more accurately understood as a continuum defined by human beings than a dichotomy created by nature.

The Athletic Middle-Class Girl Next Door

In the late nineteenth century, medical experts focused on a way to find sufficient exercise for middle-class girls and women to keep them healthy enough to be attractive and fertile partners for their husbands. White Christian America feared the influx of immigrants from "undesirable" parts of the world and believed that middle-class women needed to bear sufficient offspring to keep pace with the immigrant birth rate. White middle-class babies would defeat the threat of "race suicide" as people of the "wrong" color or religion appeared to be outreproducing Anglo-Saxon Protestants. But the right balance had to be struck. Overly strenuous exercise programs risked masculinizing the young women, undermining their fertility and threatening the masculinity of their male counterparts. The scientific community expressed fears that if women were too physically developed, they would be unable to bear *male* children. Arabella Kenealy, a British doctor with a substantial American following in the early twentieth century, gave voice to fears that athletic women would steal masculinity from men. In her judgment, a female athlete was drawing her virility from the store available to her future sons: "A woman who wins golf and hockey matches may be said . . . to energize her muscles with the potential manhood of possible sons . . . since over-strenuous pursuits [could] sterilize women as regards male offspring."[3]

Medical authorities recommended a moderate dose of calisthenics, just enough to get young women's blood circulating and oxygen into their lungs. Serious competition would jeopardize their femininity and their fertility. Besides, overexertion was just plain ugly in a female. Who would date a girl with her hair mussed up, breathing and perspiring heavily, with clothing in disarray? (Remember that this was the turn of the twentieth century, and disorder was not yet regarded as sexy.) College girls were bored to tears as they were forced to take classes that required them to perform tedious, repetitive exercises, never break a sweat, weigh themselves repeatedly, and have their posture and spinal alignment checked regularly, with success measured solely by weight gain or loss. One Radcliffe freshman recalled being "thrust into Miss Arrowsmith's class for the over-fat and over-thin and those of the crooked spines," while another "learned of my insignificance by orders of the Gym department to write my insufficient weight weekly on a horrid tablet that all could view."[4] Still, no exercise at all would reduce them to flabby, pasty-faced matrons, as unattractive to men as the unfeminine athletes were sure to be. What was an educated middle-class girl to do? American women got conflicted messages about femininity distorted by race and class. Women athletes had a problem that no man ever faced: sports themselves were claimed for manhood, and so, to the extent that any woman, from any race or class, was an effective and passionate athlete, she had also to "prove" that she was a woman.

Americans struggled to reconcile femininity and athleticism; race and class has profoundly affected the acceptance of female athletes. There has always been an element in every society that is hostile to women with developed muscles and competitive spirits. However, there is also a deep-seated spirit of fair play among the American people, who have attempted to embrace, however awkwardly, the anomaly of athletic girls. One of the more attractive stereotypes is "the girl next door," that fresh-faced, usually white, all-American girl with hair in pigtails, a broad friendly smile, and freckles. Picabo Street, Mary Lou Retton, Dorothy Hamill, and Chris Evert are examples: conventionally pretty women and accomplished elite competitors, willing to broadcast their heterosexuality in subtle and not-so-subtle ways. A variation on the athletic girl next door was the athletic beauty queen. In Grantland Rice's article "Leading Ladies" in the April 6, 1929, *Collier's*, Rice begins his discussion of swimmers, golfers, and tennis players with "James Montgomery Flagg had just been introduced to Martha Norelius as this famous young swimmer emerged from the ocean at Palm Beach. 'Have you, by any chance,' he said, 'just fallen off a frieze on the Parthenon?'"[5] More contemporary examples are women athletes who advertise products in sexually suggestive poses.

The girl next door and the beauty queen represent efforts to reconcile the "contradiction" between femininity and athleticism. The stereotypes may have been well intentioned, but they reveal the fear lurking beneath the surface of the American consciousness that female athletes are not feminine. A report may reveal appreciation of an athlete's prowess, as in this description of Helen Wills: "This is Helen Wills, who has developed the knack of hitting a tennis ball harder than any other woman that ever played." But the same journalist will then undermine the impact of his respect by sharing some information about the athlete's conventional femininity: her physical beauty, the presence of a boyfriend or husband, her culinary skills, or her joy at housekeeping. *The Literary Digest* of 1932 contains a laudatory article about Babe Didrickson, entitled "The World-Beating Girl Viking of Texas." Didrickson's appeal is clearly that of the "girl next door" variety, as the subtitle reveals: "Only a Slim, Sunburned Girl, But, Oh, What Dynamite!" In one moment, the article is fabulously admiring: "Babe Didrickson, heroine of the Olympic Games, breaker of records, and winner of championships in an amazing variety of strenuous athletic sports, threatens to outdistance the home-run king as a figure of captivating interest to all the nations of the world." But in the next moment, the threat of such prowess pops to the surface: "Perhaps she supplies the proof that the comparatively recent turn of women to strenuous field sports is developing a new super-physique in womanhood, an unexpected outcome of suffragism which goes in for sports as well as politics, and threatens the old male supremacy even in the mere routine of making a living."[6] The vote has given women the idea that they may appropriate the world's finite store of masculinity. Athletic success will bring designs on money and political power, all intrusions on male turf.

The article concludes with expressed admiration for Babe's domestic talent. "It's a mistake to think, however, that Mildred's [now it's not Babe's, but "Mildred's" . . .] talents are purely muscular . . . The Babe can sew and cook a mean meal. In the wardrobe that she brought with her from Dallas is a blue crepe party dress which she made herself.'"[7] The befuddlement of the American mass media and public about what to do with a "girl athlete" would be almost touching were it not for its destructiveness. In attempting to wrestle women athletes into palatable images, they were reduced to two-dimensional stereotypes.

The athletic woman of the early twentieth century walked a delicate line. Was she in vibrant good health, ready to become an attractive wife and bountiful mother, or so strong that her femininity and fertility were compromised? Serious women athletes were expected to possess both personal charisma and physical beauty in addition to their athletic talent. They fell from grace if they allowed their feminine image to be overshadowed by athletic achievement. The "good woman athlete" was an active and sexually attractive "new woman," of either the girl-next-door or healthy beauty queen variety. The "bad" woman athlete was so successful at her sport that she ceased to be feminine and became instead one of those unattractive muscular women doing a bad imitation of a man.[8]

Race, Class, and Women's Athletic Competition

Changing gender roles in the early twentieth century provoked a battle over the direction of girls' and women's athletics. Two national organizations struggled to define the role of women's sports in America. Women's physical educators and specialists on women's health issues formed two interlocking organizations: The Committee on Women's Athletics of the American Physical Education Association (CWA), and the Women's Division of the National Amateur Athletic Federation. Both found themselves at loggerheads with the Amateur Athletic Union (AAU), whose members included men who were involved in women's competitive athletics. The ideological lines of the rivalry have persisted, dogging women's sports throughout the twentieth century until the absorption of the Association for InterCollegiate Athletics for Women (AIAW) into the men's NCAA in 1984. The difference in philosophies between the female- and male-led organizations is interesting. The two early women's organizations (the CWA, later referred to as the Women's Section, and the National Amateur Athletic Federation's Women's Division) were comprised of women who believed exercise was good for young women but the strain of competition was not. These educators were firmly ensconced in white middle-class mores of traditional femininity and womanhood. They were horrified by the "excess of zeal" competition bred and believed that too much investment in the outcome of athletic contests would destroy American womanhood. Women of color and working-class women, less fearful of competition and athleticism and not as delicate as their sisters in the leisure class, were regarded as cautionary examples by protectors of middle-class morality.

The male-led AAU, on the other hand, saw benefits of women's competition and participation in "games of strife." The AAU worked closely with the International Olympic Committee in promoting women's involvement in elite sports. The battle for the soul of women's athletics on the collegiate circuit since the passage of Title IX has shaped up as a battle between advocacy of truly amateur student athletics and the preprofessional, "winning is everything" mentality of men's collegiate sports. The Women's Division accused the AAU of exploiting innocent young women, urging them into unnatural competitions for the amusement of audiences and the profit of promoters, or transforming them into masculine freaks. Innocent American girls, it was feared, were being turned into either prostitutes or lesbians by their male handlers.

If the male-led promotion of women's sports was undermined by these inconsistencies, at least it wasn't characterized by class-based ideas about femininity.

The AAU encouraged serious athletic competition among women, signifying more broad-mindedness about American femininity if only to the extent that women athletes were worthy of investment capital. That willingness to exploit women for athletic competition opened a door for working-class women, who in turn used organized athletics as a way to travel, see the world, or at least the country, and to make a reasonable income doing something they loved. AAU's more progressive attitude toward women's athletic competition also opened American eyes to the possibility of women's team sports. In the more traditional view of women's physical education experts, swimmers, tennis players, golfers, and archers were the only acceptably feminine athletes. Less expensive team sports such as baseball and basketball, which did not require access to country clubs or swimming pools, were regarded as too masculine. Working-class women were drawn to the team sports. African American women in the 1920s and 1930s drew the attention of the world to U.S. track and field.

Black female educators and the black community in general encouraged girls' and women's athletic competition at the highest possible levels. Strong, educated women were seen as good for the community and potential leaders. Many African American girls in the mid-twentieth century faced the same sort of criticism from their communities as did white girls if they were "too" athletic and tomboyish. Olympic track athlete Willye White described herself as a " tomboy and outcast" who was discouraged by her parents from going to the playground where she played ball and raced with boys. It was, she said, "not acceptable in American society."[9] But to a far greater extent than in the white middle-class community, for African Americans strength was not incompatible with femininity. In contrast to white educators, African American educators promoted a sane and self-confident sense of femininity in their girls, even while white America was denigrating black women as "strong" and "masculine," stereotypes that were remnants of slavery. Tuskegee physical education director Amelia Roberts wrote a letter to the African American newspaper the *Chicago Defender* arguing for the importance of women's physical education. Another black woman leader, Ruth Arnett, YWCA secretary of girls' work, dismissed undue worry about tomboyish athletes with the conviction that competition nurtured strong, vital women that "real men" would not be threatened by: "Let's encourage our girls to be 'tomboys.' Let them enter any game of sport and recreation that the boy enters. Let's teach them to be real girls."[10]

One result was international dominance of track and field by African American women in the mid-twentieth century, although black women had to rise above white America's notions of what constituted femininity. Martha Hudson, a Tennessee State University track athlete of the 1930s, noted, "We were just so prepared for a lot of things—criticism—our coach would talk to us. Things that a lot of people worried about, we didn't. We would discuss it, we would talk about it, but it didn't bother us." Teammate Lula Hymes noted, "They gonna think and talk and say what they want to say anyway, regardless of how you feel about it. I never pay any attention to what people say."[11] Olympic champion Alice Coachman was not bothered either, proclaiming joyously about her track career, "When I look back at it now, I just say, 'Lord, I sure was a running thing!'"[12] Coachman was the first black woman to win an Olympic gold medal. Her event was the high jump, but so unacknowledged is she that Americans barely recognize her name much less claim her as a hero. It is clear that she rejoiced in her gift of speed and saw her success as being true to who she was.

Another Gentle Women's Sport

Basketball, like baseball, has a history of migration between class, race, and gender in the United States. Although college and professional basketball are now dominated by African American men, the game, like baseball, had feminine origins. It was invented in 1891 by James Naismith, a YMCA worker who intended it to be an inexpensive indoor winter game for boys and girls. The game quickly caught on at women's schools and settlement houses where women played on small indoor courts, out of public view. Men also played in the early days, but basketball was originally regarded as a sport appropriate for women, not only because they took to it so eagerly but because as an indoor game with limited physical contact and a relatively small playing surface, basketball had all the earmarks of a girls' sport. Still, the women who first played the game occasionally alarmed observers with just how rough they could make it. In 1892, a Massachusetts newspaper described a Smith College match as "a mad game" marred by "wild play and riotous cheering." They took particular pleasure in batting the ball out of opponents' hands and aggressively shoving opponents out of the way. It was feared that the girls were becoming "rough, loud voiced, and bold."[13] A photograph of Vassar women playing basketball outdoors on a grass field also shows what is clearly a full-contact sport. A referee caught between two players battling for possession of the ball appears to be in immanent danger of injury.[14]

West Coast girls also played rough when on April 4, 1896, Berkeley and Stanford coeds engaged in the nation's first women's intercollegiate athletic contest. The basketball game was reported in depth by the *San Francisco Examiner*, the *Daily Palo Alto*, and the *Berkeleyan*. It was a celebrated event with a

Early women's basketball looking rough. The referee appears in immanent danger. Vassar College, 1911 (courtesy Vassar College Archives)

sellout crowd of women only at the San Francisco Armory Hall. The *Examiner* described the fans in attendance: "There were old women, and young women, and short-haired women, and long-haired women, and pretty women, and plain women, and new women and—well, there may have been middle-aged women. But the really remarkable thing about them was the immense volume of noise they managed to create."[15]

The *Examiner* article described the dramatic entrance of the teams onto the court. The California players appeared first, wearing blue bloomers with white sweaters that had a blue U and a gold C interlaced and a knot of blue and gold ribbon on the left shoulder. They wore black stockings and athletic shoes, and they raised the roof as they "ran into the big hall. They came in single file. They skipped and danced, these dainty co-eds, keeping time with the meter of the college yell." The Stanford team was more sedate, wearing black bloomers, red sweaters, and soft red silk caps. According to the *Examiner,* the Stanford team was not "frisky, like the Berkeley girls. They came in slowly, walking one behind another. They were all dark-haired, and looked more like a group of gypsy maidens than college athletes." The game described sounds more like indoor rugby than basketball, similar to the game played by the Vassar students. Whatever the rules of the day, it was not a gentle sport. The *Examiner* reports:

> The fighting was hard and the playing good. Anything to keep the ball out of the opponent's basket—anything to intercept a clever throw. The girls jumped, scrambled and fell over one another on the floor, but they didn't mind it. They were up as quick as a flash, chasing after the ball again. Captain McCray of the Stanford team was a terror to the Berkeley girls. She was agile, quick and a good catcher. Many were the times she kept the Berkeley coeds from making their score. [Berkeley] Captain Griswold was equally clever in her way. She understood how to change the whole aspect of a play by tossing the ball backward over her head.[16]

Stanford won (as anticipated by the title of the *Daily Palo Alto* article, "Stanford Never Loses"), but it was not for want of effort by the Berkeley girls. Ella Wing, captain of the Castilleja basketball team, analyzed the game for a local newspaper. She reported that in the second half, "Stanford opened aggressively. . . . Berkeley shows good interference, but her men [*sic*] are inclined to foul by running and tackling. Stanford shows quicker playing, better catching and stronger centers."[17]

Women's basketball spread rapidly. Industrial leagues were formed for working-class girls and for African American schoolgirls. Then an odd thing happened. In the 1920s, basketball's popularity spread to boys and men, and soon the game was considered "too masculine" for girls. By the 1920s, although women had loved basketball first, they were viewed as interlopers. Rules for men and women were differentiated, resulting in the infamous "girls' rules" that developed such a negative reputation with so many young women throughout the first three-quarters of the twentieth century and probably drove many potential players away from the game. Dribbling was limited to three bounces only, and there were six players on a side, three guards and three forwards, who could stay on their side of the court only, until a rule change designated one "rover" on each team who could travel from defense to offense, allowing four-on-four action at each end of the court. Nonetheless, the revised girls' game lacked the athletic demands that had made basketball appealing to the girls who first played it. Title IX lawsuits were required before rules were restored that allowed girls to play the full-court version of the game that exists today at the high school, collegiate, and professional levels.[18] What was enforced by women's three-bounce, half-court basketball was the definition of femininity characterized by bounded space, restricted movement, and a lack of physical contact. The feminine ethos was reinforced throughout American culture, with confining dress styles, domestic duties that confined women to the space within their homes, and a lack of leisure time or access to sport. Women's basketball succeeded in breaking out of those boundaries. However, women's baseball does not enjoy the same level of acceptability. The lawsuits of the early 1970s that were brought in an effort to enable girls to play Little League baseball succeeded legally but resulted in the establishment of organized softball rather than girls' baseball. Girls succeeded in using Title IX to reclaim the full-court press but not in gaining access to a full-sized baseball diamond.

SEVEN

Cricket

Before turning to the modern history of girls and baseball, a comparative moment will permit us to see women's absence from baseball in light of another venerable and manly national sport in another democratic nation. The history of women's cricket in England strikes a sharp contrast with American women's baseball history: women actually play the game. Cricket is as sacred to English men as baseball is to American men. It has been referred to as England's national game, a "manly" game, and "something akin to a religion."[1] Both cricket and baseball have been reluctant to include women. Women cricket players in England today do not regard the word "equality" as an appropriate description of the state of the men's and women's games. Women cricketers don't make sufficient salary at their sport to cover even travel expenses, and most must take time off from their "day jobs" to participate in tournament play. In contrast, men have long been able to enjoy the material rewards of athletic stardom at their chosen sport. Women have taken second place to men in access to facilities for play and until recently were not allowed to play at Lord's, London's vener-able hallowed ground of cricket and the home of the Marylebone Cricket Club, synonymous with England's national team. Sociologist Jennifer Hargreaves notes succinctly, "The men's game is financially and ideologically powerful and exclusionary; women have traditionally been refused membership of major clubs and organizations which wield power and control resources."[2] Women's cricket has undeniably been relegated to second-class status in the country of the sport's origins. However, English women cricketers have been more successful than their American counterparts in gaining access to their sport. This is not to minimize their battle to play and be recognized but rather to gain perspective on how excessive America's exclusion of women from baseball has been.

Lasses and Ladies

Women have played cricket in England since at least the fourteenth century. The earliest known image of women playing cricket is in Oxford University's revered Bodleian Library. Nancy Joy, in her 1950 classic *Maiden Over*, describes a 1344 illustration by Johann de Grise that illuminates the *Romance of Alexander*. The scene shows "the ancestress of women's cricket to be a nun holding a ball; she is faced by a monk who brandishes a club, and a group to the right stands with upraised hands in an attitude of rapt attention denoting either prayer or concentrated in-fielding."[3] Joy goes on to chronicle the long history of women's involvement in the game in both the rural lower class and in the aristocracy. The first recorded public match was played in 1744, and the first published account of a women's cricket match appeared on July 26, 1745.[4] *The Reading Mercury* reported, with lavish praise, a competition between the young women of two villages, describing how eleven maids of Bramley and eleven maids of Hamble-ton played "the greatest cricket-match that was ever played in the South part of England." The Hambleton girls beat the Bramley girls 127 notches to 119, and the newspaper exulted, "There was of both sexes the greatest number that ever was seen on such an occasion. The girls bowled, batted, ran and catched as well as most men could do in that game."[5]

The next publicly reported village engagement took place on July 13, 1747, referred to in the press as "the match of cricket, so long expected, between the women of Charlton, in Sussex, against the women of Westdean, and Chilgrove, in the same county." The match was interrupted by a brawl, which made it neces-sary to suspend play and finish the game the next morning. The 1747 news story reported that the match had been interrupted when a fight in the stands spilled onto the playing field, requested that the spectators "be so kind as to indulge [the players] in not walking within the ring," and assured that "all gentlemen and ladies who have paid to see this match on Monday, shall have the liberty of the ground, to see it finished, without any other charge." A second match was scheduled for the afternoon with "several large sums" depending on the outcome of the match. "The women of the Hills of Sussex will be in orange, and those of the Dales in blue: wickets to be pitched at one o'clock, and begin at two. Tickets to be had at Mr. Smith's."[6]

The casual attitude with which the women absorbed their brush with violence is an example of vintage British stoicism, the proverbial stiff upper lip. Compare that eighteenth-century English news account with a painful moment a century later in Poughkeepsie, New York, when a Vassar College undergrad hurt her leg while playing baseball and it was feared that the college president would ban the game as too dangerous. Violence at a women's cricket match was not perceived to be sufficient reason to ban the sport entirely. Perhaps American women have been the victims of overprotection.

Village matches were held frequently throughout the eighteenth century in England, most often between married and single women in a given village, or between villages. In 1765, "A cricket match was played by Upham, Hants, by eleven married against eleven maiden women, for a large plum cake, a barrel of ale and a regale of tea, which was won by the latter. After the diversion the company met and drank tea: they spent the evening together and concluded it with a ball."[7] In 1768, there were three matches recorded between the young women of Harting and Rogate, attended by several thousand spectators. The second match was reported to have been "exceedingly contested on both sides," being decided by only two notches. The news account noted "the great cheerfulness and agility with which these female gamesters performed their several parts afforded the most agreeable diversion for near 2,000 spectators. We hear they have agreed to play two other matches: the first is expected on Wednesday next, on Rogate Common."[8]

The games attracted spectators and wagers, and were followed by social occasions on both the upper- and lower-class levels. The competitions between maids and matrons, unmarried and married women may also have had a sexual subtext: a sort of spring ritual that attracted eligible bachelors as well as husbands. At any event, participating in the sport was hardly regarded as unfeminine. Newspapers recorded the local matches, often between maids and matrons, in a matter-of-fact manner. In 1775, six single women beat six married at Moulsey Hurst by seventeen runs, a game attended by "many London Gentlemen" who made "great bets" on the outcome. The maidens were victorious in a three-game match at Felley Green, Surrey, in 1778. Matrimony triumphed hands down on Bury Common in 1793, where the matrons beat the maids by eighty notches. The Bury women seem to have been a cocky bunch, as the news account reported, "So famous are the Bury women at a cricket match that they offer to play against any eleven in any village in their own country [county] for any sum."[9] The prize for swagger, however, must go to eleven women from Hampshire, who in 1772 challenged twice the number of Hampton gentlemen to play them for £500. Apparently the local fans believed they could prevail, as the early odds were in favor of "the female professors of that noble exercise."[10]

These were village matches, played by rural women. Upper-class women had a circuit as well, though. Predictably, the rural village matches were rowdier than the aristocratic events. Lower-class women and men gambled and drank heavily at cricket and other sporting matches. In the late eighteenth century, there were many women's cricket matches in the south of England, with teams usually bearing the names of the villages they represented. Relatively large sums of money, frequently over £1,000, rode on the outcome of the matches.[11] The scenes at these women's matches were robust, colorful, boisterous, rowdy, and often inelegant. Men and women in the stands drank, swore, shouted, and gambled. Only once, in 1833, were women players reported to have conducted themselves in an excessively undignified manner, as "by their deportment as well as frequent applications to the tankard, they rendered themselves objects such as no husband, brother, parent, or lover could contemplate with any degree of satisfaction."[12]

Not to be outdone by their rustic counterparts, the fashionable set in England also picked up bats and balls. The late-eighteenth-century aristocratic women cricketers quickly made a name for themselves, even attracting suitors with their prowess. We know this because the upper-class women had names that were recorded. In 1777, a match was "played in private between the Countess of Derby and some other Ladies of quality and fashion, at the Oaks in Surrey, the rural and enchanting retreat of her ladyship." Miss Elizabeth Ann Burrell, sister of Peter, first baron Gwydyr, and one of the best batswomen at the White Conduit Cricket Club, achieved lasting fame by scoring more notches in the first and second innings than anybody else in the entire game. The *Morning Post* reported that "Diana-like, [she] created an irresistible impression" with the result that the eighth duke of Hamilton is reported to have fallen in love with her on the spot and married her before the next cricket season.[13] Whether or not the story is apocryphal, it is clear that the noblemen appreciated athletic women.

Another eligible bachelor among the onlookers at the match, John Frederick Sackville, third duke of Dorset, made a drawing of the game for his absent lady friends. He remarked, "What is human life, but a game of cricket? And if so, why should not the ladies play it as well as we?" The duke sent his drawing to his circle of ladies along with a letter mocking unenlightened men who were intolerant of women's cricket:

> Methinks I hear some little macaroni youth, some trifling apology for the figure of a man, exclaiming with the greatest vehemence. How can the ladies hurt their delicate hands, and even bring them to blisters with holding a nasty filthy bat? How can their sweet delicate fingers bear the jarrings attending the catching of a dirty ball? . . . Mind not, my dear ladies, the impertinent interrogatories of silly cox-combs, or the dreadful apprehensions of demi-men. Let your sex go on and assert their right to every pursuit that does not debase the mind. Go on, and attach yourselves to the athletic, and by that convince your neighbours the French that you despise their washes, their paint and their pomatoms, and that you are now determined to convince all Europe how worthy you are of being considered the wives of plain, generous, and native Englishmen![14]

The ballplaying ladies of Surrey clearly made an impression on these gentlemen friends, who either proposed on the spot or sought to recruit absent lady friends to the sport. The duke of Dorset was such a cricket enthusiast that he also attempted to introduce the game to cricket-deprived Frenchmen. But before he could muster a team to join him in Paris to demonstrate the English sport, he was forced to flee from the French Revolution and return to Dover. Discretion being the better part of valor, it appeared safer to teach the game to English women than French men.

The fashionable set in England continued to play in the nineteenth century. A match took place on October 2, 1811, between "the Hampshire and the Surrey Heroines (twenty-two females)." The ages of the players ranged from fourteen to sixty, with sixty-year-old Ann Baker celebrated as "the best runner and bowler" on the Surrey side. Reporters accurately listed the names of all the players but had some difficulty describing their attire. *Monthly Magazine* reported "loose trowsers with short fringed petticoats descending to the knees, and light flannel waistcoats with sashes round the waist." This sounds like the undergarments of the day, and Nancy Joy surmises that the "undress uniform" was the result of "the peculiar exertions of a three-day fixture," musing, "Have they, perhaps, taken something off?" Imagine the scandal in the United States in 1811 had there been a news account of well-to-do women stripping down to their knickers to be more comfortably dressed for a three-day baseball tournament. Nearly two centuries later, national headlines were made when American World Cup soccer's Brandi Chastain exuberantly tore off her jersey and raced around the field in celebration of her game-winning goal, revealing the modest sports bra she wore to the ninety thousand spectators in the stadium and the millions in the television audience. The "oohs" and "ahs" subsided only when American sportswear manufacturers realized they could capitalize on the newly respectable state of women's athletic undress.

Suitable sporting attire appears to have been a constant challenge for early-nineteenth-century women cricketers. In 1821, Christina Willes, while pitching to her brother John, came upon a solution to the encumbrance of voluminous skirts. She invented overhand pitching, known to the English as "round-arm bowling." However, her brother took credit for the revolutionary development. Big brother John Willes regarded the overhand bowl with such pride that his tombstone bears the inscription, "He was the first to introduce round-armed bowling in cricket." Squire Willes attempted to introduce the move to his team-mates in an 1822 match at Lord's cricket grounds in London, but resistance to the unorthodox bowl was strident. An umpire ruled Willes's overhanded pitch a foul, and Willes, in response, "threw down the ball, jumped on his horse and rode away, out of Lord's, declaring he would never play again." Nor, reports Joy, did he, although his sister's invention was incorporated into the rules six years later and remains required form for bowling to this day.

Both noble and village women played regularly during the early part of the nineteenth century. By this time even the village women's names were noted in news articles covering the games. Once, in Hampshire in 1823, two teams of lady haymakers in the employ of rival farmers challenged each other. On August 28, 1822, the *Annals of Sporting* reported that an "extraordinary match" took place between maidens and matrons, which caused a traffic jam of "carriages, and even wagons" carrying people to the event. "The pink maidens gave the blue matrons a fine trouncing, skittling them out in the first innings for 15 runs. The matrons cried revenge, and the return match again excited such intense interest that the roads were literally crammed and covered with crowds hastening to the expected scene of enjoyment." Youth prevailed in the rematch, too, and two of the maidens, Miss Budd and Miss Ruth Stonen, scored forty-one and seventeen runs, respectively, and were congratulated in the report of the game for their "scientific play" and "manly exertions."[15]

During the middle decades of the nineteenth century, there was a short decline in the popularity, or at least visibility, of girls' and women's cricket, and data on women's play is difficult to find. This temporary eclipse may not imply that women's play disappeared entirely but that it either declined or was veiled, perhaps along with the necks and ankles of Victorian women and the legs of their furniture. In the 1880s and 1890s, it was once again respectable for women to take the field, and women's cricket came roaring out of hiding. "Cricket weeks" had long been a summer fixture for wealthy young men at their country estates. The matches would go on all summer long, week after week at various estates, with the men playing cricket and their lady friends scoring and applauding, and dancing with them until late in the evening. Now, at the end of the nineteenth century, women's cricket made its appearance at the exclusive festivities. "It was natural, what more so, that the ladies should demand their little game. So the gentlemen umpired, and the ladies did their playing, quite charming and delightful, and that was that—away they tripped in boater and bustle, to the next week."[16] Cricket continued to emerge from Victorian shadows on all levels of play, writes Joy: "Cricket in the great country houses, professional women cricketers on tour, cricket in the schools, the colleges, the villages, the colonies. Cricket in *Punch* and in the pages of J. M. Barrie."[17] Cricket was now included in the sports curriculum of several of the most prestigious private schools, and for the first time, the middle class got in on the act. "Middle class girls all over England were also picking up the game, often having to find their own ground which they rolled and marked. They often played before school started, with bats far too big borrowed from fathers and brothers, and of course always used the men's full-sized ball."[18]

A League of Their Own

With increasingly widespread involvement in cricket, it was inevitable that women should seek permanent status for teams and leagues. Upper-class women first provided the formal organization and continuity required to stabilize women's cricket. The White Heather Club, which still exists, was founded by eight women of means whose names are inscribed in its first leather score book. White Heather flourished, growing to fifty members in the first three years. As other women's clubs were founded, play was organized among them with occasional challenges to men's clubs as well. In 1887, a Miss Grace made 217 runs at Burton Joyce, Nottinghamshire, "against the really good bowling of four men." Another woman, listed as "Miss D.," played on the men's team of the village of Bingham and was described as "able to hold her own with the best of them."[19]

In 1890, a second professional cricket club was organized called the "Original English Lady Cricketers," or the OELC. A prospectus was published in the leading periodicals of the day, proclaiming, "With the object of providing the suitability of the National Game as a pastime for the fair sex in preference to Lawn Tennis and other less scientific games, the English Cricket and Athletic

Association Ltd. have organized two complete elevens of female players under the title of *The Original English Lady Cricketers*."[20] The OELC was not as serious about its game as White Heather, as it was essentially two touring teams that played each other in exhibition matches with the goal of spreading the game both in England and abroad. One young man who watched a match in Wales was unimpressed with the quality of play, saying they might be original and English, but they were neither ladies nor cricketers.[21] A uniform worn by one of the original members of the OELC, circa 1888, is on permanent loan and prominently on display along with other memorabilia from the era in the museum at Lord's Cricket Ground in London.

English women's cricket was always played on the same size pitch, or field, as the men's. An Englishman named Alfred Reader designed a cricket ball for women one half ounce lighter than the men's regulation five and a half ounce ball. He even took matters the proverbial extra mile, believing it would please the ladies if their cricket balls were colored light blue instead of the traditional red. The women found the blue ball difficult to see in the grass and went back to using the men's equipment. Soon the lighter-weight ball was manufactured in traditional red.[22] To this day, the women's regulation cricket ball is lighter by one half ounce than the men's ball, and heavier by one half ounce than the children's regulation ball. Male and female cricketers still use a red ball when playing in white uniforms but have switched to a white ball when wearing colors, which is a very modern development. Traditionalists refer disparagingly to the colored uniforms as "pajamas."

The minor alterations in equipment allowed the women cricketers to excel on the same size pitch as the men. The result was that women's cricket play progressed consistently, since no special fields had to be constructed. Women's clubs challenged each other and men's clubs, and arranged matches involving men and women on the same team. In 1926, several women organized two teams to play a tournament in the south of England. Local men refereed the games and entertained the women in the evenings. The tour was regarded as an enormous success, and on October 4, 1926, the women met and established the Women's Cricket Association (WCA), modeled after the men's flagship Marylebone Cricket Club. It remained the governing body of women's cricket until 1998, when it was merged into the England and Wales Cricket Board (ECB), which administers both men's and women's cricket in Great Britain.

The declared purpose of the WCA was "simply to enable any woman or girl wishing to play cricket to do so; and to play the game with strict order and decorum."[23] It was hoped that the WCA would encourage the formation of more clubs from which county teams might be built. In the WCA's first year, forty-nine matches and a festival cricket week were arranged under the auspices of the organization. Within that first year, the WCA grew to 347 individuals, ten clubs, twenty-eight schools, six colleges, and two business houses. The organization continued to grow at such a rate that by year three, 1929, it was time to arrange a public, or "test" match. Heyhoe Flint and Rheinberg remark, "In the early 1930s, with its enthusiasm, its dedication and its leadership, came the start of what might be called to-day the Golden Age of women's cricket."[24] A match was scheduled at Beckenham on July 17, 1929, between teams from "London and District" and "The Rest of England." By all accounts, the quality of play established that women's cricket had come of age. "A day of lively cricket brought a close finish (Rest beat London, 215–176 for 9) and the most talented women cricket players in England were on parade for all to see."[25] Several of the players had honed their skills and developed their reputations while playing on men's clubs.

The "representative match" had arrived on the scene to stay. Women's cricket thrived, and by 1934, the WCA oversaw eighty teams, which increased to 123 local and college teams during the following four years. Women's cricket was now ready for international play. A team of the best players in the country was selected to travel to Australia in 1934 and 1937, and women's international cricket was launched. Similar to the moments in American women's sports history when men's organizations absorbed previously segregated women's athletic organizations, the women's organizations grew quickly after the mergers although they lost autonomy. The most recent parallel in American women's sports was when the NCAA took over the AIAW in 1984. The culture of women's intercollegiate athletics changed, but its prominence and, some would argue, level of competition increased exponentially.[26] When ECB took over the running of women's cricket in 1998, the number of women's clubs increased even more rapidly. The year 2003 saw a 33 percent increase in the number of new clubs, with many more girls playing the game at primary and secondary schools. In 2003, the ECB announced that, for the first time, there were more than 2 million girls playing cricket in England.

Playing Hard Ball with the Old Boys

However, women's cricket did not grow without opposition. As the game became more public, antagonists became more vociferous. "Even tolerant comment was often synonymous with condescension and patronizing humour," says Jennifer Hargreaves.[27] The battle for Lord's Cricket Ground is representative of the tenacity of male resistance. Men of the Marylebone Cricket Club (MCC) fought women's membership to the wire, giving in only when the economic incentives to admit women became irresistible. The MCC is the oldest, most prestigious cricket club in England. It is a distinct social privilege to be selected, its 18,000 members are admitted for life, and there is a waiting list many decades long. Members enjoy unlimited access to the spectators' pavilion and to the grounds for play. Its American equivalent would be having lifetime season tickets to Yankee Stadium that include the privilege of playing baseball whenever the Yankees weren't using the field.

Marylebone Cricket Club was founded in 1787 as an exclusive club for the aristocracy. The wealthy elite always regarded cricket as their own, but the popularity of cricket grew rapidly throughout Britain, and upper-class women had begun staking their claim to the beloved sport. The select crowd of men in the London area were accustomed to playing at White Conduit Fields at Islington, but as general interest in cricket blossomed, so did the crowds that gathered to watch them play. The aristocracy grew impatient at having their matches spoiled by noisy spectators. Thomas Lord, a bowler (pitcher) for White Conduit, leased a private ground in Marylebone and the MCC was born. They played at the Marylebone field for a few years, establishing a code of cricket rules to which MCC still holds the copyright. In 1814, MCC moved its fields to what was at that time a more rural location near St. John's Wood, north of central London, the current site of Lord's. They built a pavilion for spectators, which burned down and had to be rebuilt. The second structure, completed in 1889, is still standing and is one of the most famous landmarks in international sport.

So long as the MCC was a private club, it could not receive public funds. In 1968, there was a major reorganization of cricket throughout England. The MCC set up the Cricket Council as the governing body of cricket, and the Test and County Cricket Board to administer the professional game. The MCC Cricket Association was converted into the National Cricket Association and given the task of overseeing the recreational game throughout the land. Its efforts to reach out to the general populace earned the MCC the right to receive government funding, akin to an American corporation using charity donations as tax write-offs. The MCC gained financial advantage with government support, but it remained a private and exclusive institution, completely under the sway of its wealthy upper-class members. The Marylebone Cricket Club insists that it "never tried to control the Women's Cricket Association," but it did wage a major battle to keep women out of the club, as both players and spectators. A battle royal was set to occur as English women of all classes were playing cricket by the middle of the nineteenth century, while the most exclusive men's cricket club would not countenance any women except the queen in their club. When the oldest old boys' club in the world said "No Women Allowed," it meant no women on the field *or* in the stands. Until 1998, the only woman who had ever set foot on Lord's grounds was the queen of England. With women playing cricket at all levels in Britain, the entrenched resistance at Lord's was shaping up as a mighty provocation.

In the 1990s, "modernizers" both within the ranks of the MCC and without put sufficient pressure on the membership to call for a vote about admitting women. Among those leading the assault on the male stronghold was Rachael Heyhoe Flint, retired captain of the English women's cricket team, author of *Fair Play*, the classic history of women's cricket, and a woman described affectionately by one admirer as "that old soldier."[28] The question of whether to admit women was so important that a two-thirds majority was required to pass the measure allowing women to join. At a special meeting at Lord's on February 24, 1998, the vote was held, and while a simple majority of the members present voted in favor, the modernizers could not muster the two-thirds required.[29]

In light of the MCC's recently acquired eligibility for government funds, the failure to admit women was perceived as hypocrisy. There was an outcry for another vote, including pressure from Prime Minister Tony Blair. Conservatives were appalled, some threatening to quit the club rather than allow women to join. David Heald, an MCC member for seventeen years, resigned ahead of the scheduled second vote and proclaimed, in a letter to London's *Daily Telegraph*, that the members of the MCC committee who agreed to the second vote were "posing as gallant Lancelots" while in reality "abjectly bowing to the diktat of political correctness."[30] Heald seems to have missed the point. The contest was financial expediency versus traditional privilege.

The "modernizers" prevailed in the second vote with 69.8 percent voting to admit women and 30.2 percent voting against. The men supporting women's admittance won the day neither because they were gallants nor because they were caving in to pressure from feminists. Most were simply pragmatic, voicing recognition of the changing social climate in the belief that it was for the good of the club's image in Britain. Members had never deigned to acknowledge that the general English public had referred to them as a gang of "flannelled fools" for most of the club's existence. By the late 1990s, however, they were sufficiently aware of public opinion to admit that the time had come to recommend that women be admitted. "The principal reason for reaching this decision was the positive effect it would have on MCC's public role which is now being redefined as the International Cricket Council seeks to develop the game worldwide."[31]

The English press was blunt: "Mercenary motives have entered the membership debate, and they appear to favor the ladies. Last year the MCC was offered £4.5 million ($7.2 million) in national lottery money for building a new grandstand at Lord's, but was told that to qualify it must drop its all-male rule. The MCC is now reminding members that if they vote for the status quo they will be saying goodbye to the lottery money."[32] Darcus Howe, spokesman for racial justice, a native of Trinidad who had immigrated to England, called out the members of the MCC in a critical commentary in the *New Statesman*.[33] He stated that admitting women was an empty gesture. True equal access for women would take a more widespread and concerted effort.

> From the general female public, the reactionaries need fear nothing. The waiting-list is so long that it will take a woman who applies now some twenty years to get to the top of it. Further, a woman will have to be proposed and seconded by an existing member. Then she will have to satisfy the committee that she has a reasonable knowledge of the game. This requirement reminds me of one of the reasons for the civil rights uprising in the southern states of America. In order to win the right to vote, blacks had to convince the electoral authority that they had a reasonable knowledge of the constitution of the United States. . . . No doubt applicants for membership of the MCC will be asked to define a googly or a chinaman.[34]

Howe said women's cricket is in a deplorable state: "This miserable exclusion of women is reproduced in almost every county cricket club in the land and abroad, too. Stephen J. Bull of the University of Brighton, who has served as team psychologist for the England women's team states, 'Although women's cricket is well established . . . it is not accorded high status and has received little public interest.'"[35] These observations, coming from men who are sympathetic to women's cricket, are undoubtedly true. Although women have played cricket for centuries, they are not professional athletes. They are required to make a living apart from their sport, which creates distractions and problems in the quality of play that full-time professional athletes never face. The women cricketers do not receive the fame and glory enjoyed by successful male athletes, much less the salary. And while English law rewards cricket clubs that have women members, if the women play on separate teams, they must still compete with the men's teams for resources and access to practice and match facilities.

Still, the women play. Children, both boys and girls, flock to the English national women's team players, offering the adulation that all athletes need, seeking autographs, standing near the edge of the outfield during play, cheering and offering encouragement. Sociologist Hargreaves, who is pessimistic about the state of women's sports in general in England, admits, "There have been some recent advances for women's cricket in England. Although in comparison with Australian players, who receive federal government grants, support from the Australian Sports Commission and corporate sponsorship, English players are woefully short of substantial financial support. . . . if women's cricket in England draws large crowds, as it does in Australia, India, New Zealand and the West Indies, it will create a stimulus for regular media coverage and increased sponsorship."[36] English law requires county teams to either field women along with men or on separate teams. It also provided the context that forced the MCC to admit women. While it is futile to measure degrees of oppression, it does seem that English women are not as deprived of cricket as their American sisters are of baseball. There are laws and institutional structures in place that provide access to established male teams or to establishing their own teams and using county grounds. It is not legal to deprive English women access to their preferred sport nor are they forced to play a different game, such as rounders, in its stead.

Rounders and Softball

Cricket has been referred to by contemporary enthusiasts as "chess on legs" and "an educated person's game."[37] These aspects are what originally made it "manly," but not so manly that both upper and lower-class women didn't want a piece of the action, too. When the middle classes began playing cricket in England, there was no more precedent for excluding women from cricket than from any other sport. Cricket had never been used to define English masculinity in the same way that Americans have been prepared to say that any American boy who doesn't like baseball isn't a "real" boy. David Block observes, "At home in England, base-ball had been a popular activity for both sexes. Once arrived in the American colonies, however, its play was apparently denied to girls due to more rigid standards for unladylike behavior. Unsurprisingly, this deprivation paralleled the stirrings of interest in the game among American adults."[38] I have surmised that the "rigid standards" of American femininity to which Block refers actually mask American middle-class anxiety about gender.

If there is an indigenous English equivalent to American softball, it might be rounders. Softball was contrived to fit specific needs when baseball was not available. It was designed to be a smaller, less formal version of baseball. Rounders, and a variety of other English bat and ball games, evolved more organically than softball, evolving and developing independent of cricket. But cricket and rounders fill needs in the United Kingdom that parallel the roles played by baseball and softball in contemporary American culture.

Rounders is an old and still-popular game for both children and adults in Britain, and it takes less space and organization than cricket. It is a shorter game that can be more easily offered as part of a physical education program in schools. It uses four bases, a smaller bat, and a smaller, softer ball than cricket. It has fewer possibilities for detailed strategizing and lacks the mental element found in the adult versions of both cricket and baseball. It takes its name from the fact that the batter can only score by hitting what Americans would call a home run: a "rounder." A player who hits the ball must advance around the bases and beat the fielded ball home or be called out. In cricket the batter can always choose not to run, but in rounders the hitter must always run to all the bases. The fact that it is a less formal sport than cricket means that a school can work it in to whatever space and time it has available. The outfield can be limitless or small, and the rules can be varied to accommodate the needs of a particular group of players. Rounders is cricket's "poor relation" not because it is a girls' game but because it is a less expensive game, more adaptable to a variety of venues.

There are parallels, then, between cricket and rounders in Britain, and baseball and softball in the United States. Cricket and baseball are the "official" games of national identity. They are the more highly respected, the more complex, the ones with a wealthier class history, and the ones that are lucrative professional sports for men. Rounders and softball are less well-respected as sports but much beloved informal games in both nations. They are regarded as "easier," more appropriate for informal children's games and for school sports. They don't have the prestige of professional leagues associated with them. Rounders and its variations, stool ball and base ball, were never exclusively masculine: English girls have always played them. Softball was handed to American girls as a substitute when American middle-class men stole baseball.

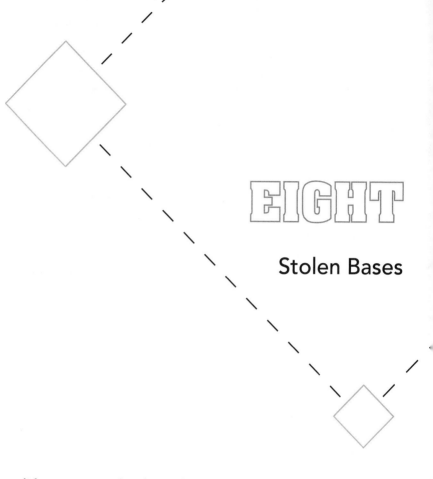

EIGHT

Stolen Bases

English women insisted on their right and ability to play the national game, and English men made way for them, sometimes begrudgingly, sometimes good-naturedly. While the men kept the money for themselves, women at least liberated the sport from an inextricable association with English boyhood and manhood. In the twenty-first century, American men are still insisting on baseball's manliness while American women battle to participate in the joys of the game.

Civil Rights Background

It is legal for girls and women to play baseball in the United States. From the standpoint of federal law, it has been legal since at least 1868 with the passage of the Fourteenth Amendment. Not until 1972, when Title IX of the Education Amendments was passed, did some girls and their parents attempt to claim that right. Neither the Fourteenth Amendment nor Title IX makes specific reference to baseball. The Fourteenth Amendment was passed by Congress in 1866 and ratified into law in 1868 to protect the rights to due process and equal protection of recently freed slaves. It was an emergency measure, necessary after the Civil War to protect the lives of the new citizens from the wrath of their recently defeated former owners. It defines former slaves as citizens and guarantees full rights to legal equality: "All persons born or naturalized in the United States and subject to the jurisdiction thereof, are citizens of the United States and of the State wherein they reside. No State shall make or enforce any law which shall abridge the privileges or immunities of citizens of the United States; nor shall any State deprive any person of life, liberty, or property, without due process of law; nor deny to any person within its jurisdiction the equal protection of the laws."[1]

But there was a catch. Section 2 of the amendment appeared to exclude women from American citizenship by referring to "male inhabitants of such State, being twenty-one years of age, and citizens of the United States." This was the first time the word "male" had been used in the constitution, and to women's rights activists of the day it begged the question of whether women were actually citizens. These leaders feared that this interpretation of the Fourteenth Amendment might be used to prevent them from gaining legal rights such as the vote. Their fear was amplified by the passage of the Fifteenth Amendment, which granted black men the right to vote but ignored suffrage for any women. Only after the 1920 passage of the Nineteenth Amendment were early feminists satisfied that the Fourteenth Amendment could be used to achieve protection for women as well as men.

The Fourteenth Amendment became important again more than a century after it passed in securing girls equal access to sports, although Title IX is the higher-profile legislation that prompted the lawsuits. In the context of the progressive sociopolitical culture of the 1970s, Title IX motivated girls and women to seek access to rights and privileges previously reserved for boys and men. The civil rights legislation passed in 1964 included Title VII, guaranteeing equal pay for equal work, protection from wage discrimination, and protection from sexual harassment in the workplace. Originally, that legislation was intended to provide protection only from racial discrimination, but Representative Martha Griffiths (D-Mich.) fought to include sexual discrimination. Title IX of the Education Amendments of 1972 was passed and signed into law by President Richard Nixon. It provided equality of access for all people to all aspects of any educational program that received any form of federal funding: schools, colleges, universities, and recreational and extracurricular programs run by educational institutions.

Few Americans of the late twentieth and early twenty-first century would openly deny girls equal access to educational opportunity. However, the idea that educational opportunities include the right to participate in athletics on an equal footing with boys and men is a different matter. It stirred and continues to stir intense controversy. According to Title IX, all schools, universities, and youth programs that serve the public and receive federal funds must achieve gender parity or lose their federal subsidies. In 1975, two years after passage of Title IX, the Department of Health, Education, and Welfare (predecessor of today's Department of Education) issued regulations to implement and enforce Title IX. In 1979, a three-pronged standard of evaluation was added. An institution must regularly report on the progress it is making toward proportionality of opportunity for both sexes.

The three primary areas used to determine whether an educational institution is in compliance with Title IX are whether (1) the funds available to male and female athletes are proportionate to their enrollment in the institution, (2) the athletic interests and abilities of male and female athletes are equally accommodated, and (3) other program areas—equipment and supplies, facilities, travel accommodations, scheduling, and so forth—are proportionate. The first and third criteria are straightforward and easily measured. The "interests and abilities" criterion is more difficult to evaluate, and so there are three questions to determine interest and abilities in a given institution: (1) Are the levels of participation opportunities for male and female students who wish to participate in sports proportionate to their enrollment? (2) Where the members of one sex have been and are underrepresented among intercollegiate athletes, can the institution show a history and continuing practice of program expansion that is demonstratively responsible to the developing interests and abilities of that sex? (3) If the members of one sex are underrepresented among the intercollegiate athletes and the institution cannot show a continuing practice of program expansion, can it be demonstrated that the interests and abilities of the members of that sex have been fully and effectively accommodated by the present program? These measures require subjective evaluation, and so establishing the existence of interests and abilities continues to be problematic, in spite of efforts to enforce proportionality.[2]

President George W. Bush attempted to weaken Title IX by claiming that interests and abilities can be measured by a one-time e-mail survey of current college women to ask them what their interests and abilities are. Supporters of Title IX respond that such a survey would foreclose the possibility of extending collegiate athletic offerings to future generations, who may just be beginning to develop their skills and interests. The absence of a variety of sports on university and college campuses can hinder development of interests and abilities in students. Northwestern University's championship women's lacrosse team of 2004 was recruited in part from athletic women already on the Northwestern campus who had never played lacrosse before. For the most part, however, interests and abilities of high school and college athletes are developed during childhood: interest in college students demonstrates the presence or absence of opportunity in childhood. If there is no youth baseball for girls, there will be insufficient interest and ability to warrant a high school girls' baseball team. And if there is no high school girls' baseball, there will be no collegiate women's baseball.

Title IX does *not* require a women's football team for every men's football team, a women's soccer team for every men's soccer team, and a women's wrestling team for every men's wrestling team. But if sufficient interest and ability exists for one gender to warrant a team, the school must create that team or allow those interested athletes to try out for an existing team, even if the existing team is of the opposite sex. The one exception made by Title IX is for "contact sports." An educational institution is not required to allow a mixed-sex team for a contact sport if a woman wants to participate and there is no women's team. Contact sports have been defined for American schoolchildren as football, basketball, and wrestling. Basketball is popular with girls and women, and there have been few problems establishing separate teams and leagues for girls. Wrestling has presented more controversy because quite a few girls want to wrestle but rarely enough in one school to warrant their own team. Capable girls have been allowed to compete on boys' wrestling teams not because of Title IX but because the Fourteenth Amendment has been used to establish their right to wrestle on whatever team is available to them. Title IX, with its exception for contact sports, would not help girls who want to wrestle or play football unless there are enough of them to form their own teams. Less "major" contact sports are rugby and lacrosse, which are played by both sexes, usually on separate teams, and field hockey, which is primarily played by girls.

Baseball is not defined as a contact sport by Title IX. But since it was the first sport to be challenged by girls under the auspices of Title IX, baseball's first line of defense was to define itself as a contact sport. The first case went against the girl who wanted to play, because there were no enforcement mechanisms in place for Title IX and because there was no other legal precedent. Two months after Title IX became law, a second lawsuit was filed by the National Organization for Women (NOW) on behalf of eleven-year-old Maria Pepe against Little League Baseball, Inc.[3] The lawsuit was successful, but not because of Title IX.

Rather, the equal protection clause of the New Jersey constitution was used as the legal basis of mandating Little League Baseball to allow girls to play. The finding was not binding in any state except New Jersey, but it set legal precedents that emboldened girls to sue for the right to play youth baseball in other communities. What ultimately enabled girls to play nationwide was not federal legislation but congressional approval of Little League Baseball, Inc.'s changes in the language of its charter. There is no legislation nor any federal judicial finding that requires that girls be allowed to play baseball.

Little League and the Rights of Man

It has never actually been illegal for girls to play baseball, either. Neither federal nor state law keeps girls out of the game. Before Title IX, girls had been barred by local league bylaws and rules, often determined after a girl had unexpectedly proven she was athletically capable of playing. As Sarah Fields notes in *Women Gladiators*, "Generally, the rules against women's participation in the game were unwritten, until women tried to play. At that point rules intended to ensure that the American pastime remained a masculine one were written."[4] We have seen how this works, from the University of Pennsylvania woman who got the winning hit in a coed pickup game leading to the banning of women from baseball at Penn, to the success and exclusion of Margaret Gisolo from American Legion baseball in 1928, to Jackie Mitchell's voided minor league contract after she struck out Babe Ruth and Lou Gehrig in 1931. They are, obviously, not the only girls and women to be thrown out of baseball for being too good. But it's puzzling that three and a half decades after Title IX, girls still don't play baseball in sufficient numbers to be noticed.

Before Title IX was passed, the Fourteenth Amendment made it illegal to exclude girls. Yet there were no lawsuits. Not law but American culture discourages girls from playing. When the first lawsuits were brought against Little League Baseball, Inc., defenders of segregated youth baseball objected that a federal agency (the Office of Civil Rights) and a federal appellate court were dictating matters that should be left to local organizations. If a coach didn't want a girl on his team, that was his prerogative. When the Union, New Jersey, Little League was ordered to allow girls to try out in 1974, Wanda Stragalas, a mother of one of the boys who played, complained, "What I resent most . . . is the courts always telling us what we've got to do. 'You can't go to this school; you've got to go to that school. You've got to be bussed.'"[5] According to the *New York Times*, the Union Little League president Thomas Tedeschi "exploded" when ordered to allow girls to play baseball: "They talk about civil rights. Haven't men got civil rights? This country is in sad shape when a volunteer has no right to give his time as he wants to."[6] The federal government cannot change social prejudices against girls playing baseball. Without federal legal backing, girls who wanted to play hardball were at the mercy of individual leagues, the majority of whose leaders have proven that they find offensive the idea of allowing girls onto a baseball diamond.

When the first lawsuit to play Little League baseball was filed in 1973, rules to enforce Title IX were not yet in place. The parents of ten-year-old Pamela Magill sued the Avonworth Baseball Conference (ABC) in western Pennsylvania for violating her Fourteenth Amendment right to equal protection. However, the Fourteenth Amendment can only be used to aggrieve a "state actor." The Avonworth Baseball Conference claimed that it was a private organization and therefore had not violated the Fourteenth Amendment.[7] It also argued that it excluded girls for two reasons: girls would get hurt playing baseball and boys might quit. The federal court agreed. The initial response to girls playing baseball on the same teams as boys (nobody had yet attempted to put girls in a separate league) privileged the feelings of the hypothetical boys who might feel so indignant about playing baseball with girls that they would quit.

Pamela Magill lost her lawsuit because there was no precedent for taking it seriously, no enforcement provisions in place yet for Title IX, and because defenders of boys-only Little League baseball argued that baseball is a "contact sport," a highly debatable claim. The girls were to be protected for their own safety from the presumed violence of physical contact with boys said to occur regularly while playing baseball. The argument that baseball is a contact sport and that for their own safety girls shouldn't play with boys is a barely modified version of Albert Spalding's 1911 rhetoric that baseball is "too strenuous for womankind." As more girls joined the queue to sue for the right to play, baseball was left with only one legal defense: hardball was too rough for mixed-gender teams. From whom did the girls need to be protected? No doubt from the same sort of ballplayers that Jackie Robinson came in contact with when he first played with the Brooklyn Dodgers: players who would throw at him when he was batting, spike him with cleats when he was fielding, and spit at him when he was shaking their hand after a game. Jackie Robinson waited them out and won.

Maria Pepe of Hoboken, New Jersey, was the plaintiff in a second highly publicized lawsuit against Little League Baseball in 1973.[8] She was eleven when the suit was filed, and by the time the case was decided in her favor, she was thirteen and too old to benefit from the ruling. But her suit paved the way for younger girls to play in the future. Ironically, Maria had been allowed to play by

Maria Pepe, baseball player and dangerous feminist activist
(courtesy Little League Baseball, Inc.)

her local Little League organization, which was ordered to remove her or be dis-
enfranchised by the national Little League organization in Williamsport, Pennsylvania. The situation was exactly the reverse of the one that had so incensed
the Union Little League parents who complained that the federal government
was violating their individual rights as American citizens by telling them how
to run their local Little League. In Maria's case, her local Little League wanted
her. Only after she had played two games (without being injured in contact
with another ballplayer), did Little League Baseball, Inc., learn of her presence
and order the local team to get rid of her or lose its charter. One wonders what
the Union Little League parents and coaches would have advised the Hoboken
coaches to do in this situation.

Maria's parents decided not to take action against Little League. But this was
two months after President Nixon had signed Title IX into law, and the National
Organization for Women stepped up to the plate and brought a complaint before

the New Jersey Division on Civil Rights on behalf of girls age eight to twelve. During the testimony, Dr. Creighton J. Hale, a physiologist who was executive vice president of Little League Baseball, Inc., argued against girls playing ball because female bones were not as strong as male bones. He was hardly an impartial expert: as Little League Baseball's vice president, he had an obvious interest in the outcome of the case. His testimony was undermined because his evidence relied on a study that had been done on the bone density of cadavers of Japanese people who had died between the ages of eighteen and eighty. To counter his testimony, NOW called Dr. Joseph Torg, a pediatric orthopedic surgeon and a medical consultant to the Philadelphia Seventy-sixers basketball team. Dr. Torg testified that any disparity in bone strength was negligible between the ages of eight and twelve, and if anything, girls' bones tended to be more resistant to breakage than boys'.[9]

Attorneys for Little League Baseball also argued that injuries to the face and legs, which might result from the violent nature of baseball, would be more damaging to girls than boys if they caused permanent cosmetic disfigurement. They also expressed concern that girls would develop breast cancer if they were hit in the chest with a baseball. In its 1974 article on the legal battle, *Newsweek* reported:

> The debate centers around the girls' safety. Male officials claim that girls are inferior in bone and muscular strength and more susceptible to injuries. At the New Jersey hearing, one doctor asserted that "cancerous lesions may be produced by traumatic impact upon female breast tissue." He added that many baseball injuries were dental and therefore cosmetic, and girls had to be specially protected from facial injuries because of their social roles. Medical experts rejected the first claim as unproven hypothesis, and the hearing officer dismissed the second as gratuitous. But once the decision was handed down, it became apparent that the real "traumatic impact" in the case was on the adults.[10]

Frank Deford, in an article in *Sports Illustrated*, reported with bemusement the lengths to which Little League went to establish that girls should not be allowed to play baseball. "New Jersey officials were . . . horrified that vital parts might inadvertently be touched during, say, a close play at second base. And little girls might actually hear an obscenity. And what would happen to the hard and fast rule that catchers must wear cups and managers must hold catchers' cup inspection? And breast cancer. The Little League has been nearly obsessive in its concern that girls who get hit in the chest with a ball will suffer from breast cancer, despite the fact that a number of doctors say there is no medical evidence to support this contention."[11]

Little League vice president Hale, in his testimony against integrating Little League, was adamant: "It just wouldn't be proper for coaches to pat girls on the rear end the way they naturally do to boys. And suppose a girl gets hurt on the leg? Why that's just not going to go over, some grown man rubbing a little girl's leg."[12] A coach's right to pat boys on the rear was apparently more important than a girl's right to play baseball; girls were not seen as having any needs, rights, or voices with regard to the national game. Rather than obsessing about the sexual temptations girls would present to Little League coaches, about parents' sensitivity to male coaches touching their daughters, or the possible deprivation of something the coaches enjoyed doing to little boys, it would have been more protective of American youth had Little League taken measures to ensure that its coaches would not grope either boys or girls. But instead, Little League leaders fussed about the psychological consequences to girls of possible permanent cosmetic damage caused by baseball injuries, since a girl's appearance is vital to her future. Ray Platoni, a volunteer umpire with the Ridgefield, New Jersey, boys athletic organization, declared:

> Can't people understand? We've had boys getting broken noses, smashed teeth. Boys can get along real fine in that way, but girls are disfigured for life. And you feel like you're wasting your time with girls. They get to be thirteen or fourteen and they become amorous and lose interest. Now, we have nothing against little girls, but we set this program up for the boys all the way down the line. If we have to accept one girl it will degrade the whole program. What is it, what is it when a group of free men, supposedly free men, can't help the boys of their town. What has happened then?[13]

Besides his concern about cosmetic damage to girls, Platoni's belief that girls would lose interest in baseball at the onset of puberty disregards boys' similar distraction by girls when they reach their teens. Fine athletes of both sexes have always had to contend with the distractions of adolescence. Nonetheless, according to Platoni, girls had no future in the sport and would only deprive boys who might turn out to be major leaguers of their coaches' attention.

Finally, Little League Baseball, Inc., invoked the wording of its charter in defending itself against girls. That document defined its mission as instilling in American boys the qualities of "citizenship, sportsmanship, and manhood."[14] The language resembles the clause of the Fourteenth Amendment that associated citizenship with manhood and so worried the nineteenth-century women's rights advocates. The court ultimately found that "manhood" implied "adulthood," about which girls should also be taught. Rather than protect archaic language excluding girls from citizenship, the court reasoned, the language in the Little League charter could be easily amended to include girls. This would enable all children in the United States to be adults, rather than breeding a society of baseball-playing citizen men and overprotected civically uneducated women.

It is important to remember that the uproar about protecting little girls and breeding tough men concerned eight- to twelve-year-old children playing baseball together. In all youth sports, even those dedicated to building manliness, some effort is made to tailor the rules of the game to prevent serious injuries to young children. In Little League, base-stealing is forbidden, machine- or coach-pitching is used for several years before children face live pitching, batting helmets have been required for several decades, metal cleats are forbidden, and so on, all in an effort to protect children from serious injuries. Frequent injuries through collisions with other players, bats, and balls are no healthier for little boys than little girls, nor have the youngsters involved in such mishaps yet mastered the manly art of suppressing their normal response to pain. In spite of the truism that there is "no crying in baseball," anybody who has attended a Little League game can attest to the fact that boys as well as girls are still learning this baseball skill. Indeed, the tears of frustration, sadness, or embarrassment streaming down the face of a pitcher who has just given up a game-winning home run or a batter who has just struck out usually evoke sympathy and even admiration, indicating "desire." Far from being "girly," they are accepted as part of at least the children's version of baseball.

Robert H. Stirrat, a vice president of Little League Baseball, Inc., responded to the Office of Civil Rights' finding that the league must allow girls to play that he was "totally surprised" anyone would want to see boys and girls sharing the baseball diamond. "We always assumed baseball was a boys' sport. We think most people always have felt that way. We assume they've accepted baseball as a male prerogative of some sort."[15] Only one manager of a Little League baseball team in Tenafly, New Jersey, who asked to remain anonymous, said he thought the objection to girls' playing veiled concerns about machismo: "I think in most instances, the men are afraid the girls are going to play better than their sons, or compete better than the boys in general." He pointed out that one of the girls who was trying out among the 150 eight- and nine-year-olds had been the first draft pick by the coaches and managers in the league. "She was superior to all the boys," he said.[16]

The hearing officer for the New Jersey Division on Civil Rights deciding the Maria Pepe case was a woman named Sylvia Pressler, who found that Little League's prohibition against female players violated both state and federal antidiscrimination laws. "The institution of Little League is as American as the hot dog and apple pie. There's no reason why that part of Americana should be withheld from girls."[17] Little League Baseball appealed the decision to the Superior Court of New Jersey. Local leagues throughout the nation held their breath while awaiting the decision they knew would be precedent making, even though it was out of their jurisdiction. One Little League official in Houston explained that his league would wait to hear the outcome of the appeal because the initial finding had been handed down by a woman. He wanted a man's opinion: "It was a lady judge who ruled in favor of the girls. The case hasn't moved up to male judges yet."[18]

When the Supreme Court of New Jersey upheld the finding of lady judge Sylvia Pressler of the Office of Civil Rights, most New Jersey teams chose not to play at all rather than to allow girls to play on their teams. One Little League manager admitted, "What I'm afraid of is that if you have a girl who is good and plays more than some of the boys, it's bad for the boys. The kid's friends may get on him and say, 'Hey, how come a girl is playing more than you?'"[19] To prevent the possibility of such emotional damage to American boys, the two thousand teams in New Jersey's Little League suspended their season rather than allow girls to play. Some 150,000 boys lost their chance to play baseball that year because girls wanted to join them. Teaching American manhood to boys does not include lessons in acquiring the courage to risk being bested by a female. Conversely, teaching girls that they are toxic if they are more effective than boys at anything is acceptable. To teach a girl that her health, strength, and spirit are dangerous to boys and to her own well-being, and must be suppressed for the sake of the boys, is irresponsible and unforgivable. It is not far removed from the practice of female infanticide in cultures that we feel superior to. This attitude kills the soul and spirit of girls if not directly their bodies.

As a last-ditch effort to save their game from girls, the New Jersey Little League appealed to Governor Brendan Thomas Byrne. But Governor Byrne expressed approval of the ruling to allow girls to play: "I think that a qualified girl ought to be able to play baseball or whatever sport she can play. I know very few boys, including my own son, who would object to being beaten out by a better girl. Besides, I have more daughters than sons."[20]

The fear that boys would be traumatized by girls' success at baseball has been primarily an adult fear. When the Little League men got over their hissy fit and allowed girls to try out, the girls showed up in droves. At the very first tryout with girls in Tenafly, New Jersey, fifty girls joined one hundred and fifty boys for the tryouts. *New York Times* reporter Joseph Treaster was present to interview the ballplayers. Eight-year-old Johnny Pavsner had precociously absorbed the adult message. When asked how he liked having girls on the team, he responded, "Yeech. I don't like it. Most of the girls aren't so good." The majority of his teammates expressed satisfaction that girls had joined them. Johnny was cautioned by his teammate David Parisier, "One of the girls might become a pitcher and she might take you over. Some of them are pretty good." Another player, ten-year-old Tom Thornton, averred, "If they're good they won't get hurt. I think it's pretty good having them with us." One of the girls, Nicole Hottendorf, after hitting a home run, told Treaster she joined because she "just felt like playing baseball." She noted that her brothers were "always joining everything, but I didn't really join anything." While her ability to hit the long ball attested to the appropriateness of her presence on a baseball diamond, most important to her was her hope that playing baseball would make her a more desirable companion for her brothers. She told Treaster that before she joined the Little League, "the only thing my older brother [would] play with me is hide-and-go-seek and, really, I don't like that game." Adult Philip J. DeMarco, chairman of the hastily organized committee to Save Little League in Jersey, was unimpressed with either the largess of the boys or the skills and desire of the girls. He demanded, "Is this the American way? Our rights have been eroded."[21]

The finding of the Supreme Court of New Jersey could order Little League Baseball only in the state of New Jersey to integrate, but it set off a series of similar lawsuits in other states. The arguments were similar throughout: baseball was too rough a sport for girls, who are presumed to be physically more fragile than boys, and, contradictorily, boys would either quit if girls were allowed to play baseball with them or suffer psychological damage if they stayed and the girls were better than them. How these same fragile girls, kept off the nation's diamonds for their own protection, could manage to drive boys off the field and back to the bench by superior playing skills was not addressed. The courts were not convinced by the contradictory arguments either, ruling that there was insufficient medical and psychological evidence to prove either that girls were naturally weaker than boys between the ages of eight and twelve, or that American boyhood was threatened by the presence of girls in their midst while learning to play the national pastime. One court found that Little League's willingness to let physically disabled boys play undermined the argument that the same game was too dangerous for girls. Since there was no size or fitness requirement for the boys' play, there were no grounds for excluding girls as a class.

The last major baseball suit came in 1976, when a high school girl named JoAnn Carnes in Wartburg, Tennessee, tried out for and made her high school baseball team. The Tennessee Secondary School Athletic Association (TSSAA) told the school to remove her from the team because baseball was a contact sport. The district's athletic association was concerned, once again, with "protecting" girls from contact and also, it said, protecting girls' teams from being "taken over" by boys in the event that boys wanted to play on girls' teams. The judge in the case found that the school district's argument was overly broad, since some girls were likely to be fit to play and even the coach had found her sufficiently capable to pick her for the team. The judge also noted that the danger of boys unfairly dominating girls' teams was not an immanent threat, since there were no girls' teams to take over.[22]

Title IX's distinction between contact and noncontact sports has been called arbitrary. Thirty-five years after its passage, a few girls do play football and wrestle with boys on an advanced competitive level. But Little League Baseball seized the distinction as the basis for arguing against integrated baseball. The Fourteenth Amendment makes no such distinction, which is why it has been a more successful legal tool for establishing girls' equal right to play baseball or any other sport. The Fourteenth Amendment does not allow for the possible argument that girls as a class need protection from athletic contact with boys. If a girl is good enough to play any sport with boys, she has the right to try out for any team she wants.

The widespread local lawsuits begged for a federal response. When it came, the response was legislative rather than judicial. The U.S. Senate and not the Supreme Court made it federally mandatory for girls have the right to play youth baseball if they were qualified athletically. On December 17, 1974, the Senate passed a bill, sponsored by Senator Roman Hruska (R-Neb.), in which the word "boy" was replaced with the words "young people" each time it appeared in Little League Baseball's 1964 congressional charter, which had previously been signed into law by President Lyndon Johnson. The word "manhood" was dropped from the section of the charter that proclaimed that the purpose of Little League Baseball was to instill the qualities of "citizenship, sportsmanship and manhood." It was Little League Baseball itself that had requested the amendment to the charter, thereby avoiding any federal judicial precedent. It was passed by voice vote with no debate and sent on to President Gerald Ford for signature.[23]

Bobby Sox and Pony Tails

Baseball, or at least Little League baseball, was ordered to desegregate. Three and a half decades later, where are all the girls? Why aren't they progressing through the ranks of Little League baseball to Babe Ruth or Pony League, to high school and college baseball, and to the pros? Why haven't they emerged from children's baseball in the Little League to their own separate leagues?

One contributing factor to girls' absence from the game is Little League Baseball's creation in 1974 of Little League softball. The impulse to organize a separate girls' league is understandable, especially in the very beginning of what would become an era of rapid advances in girls' competitive athletics. But why didn't they organize separate girls' baseball? Before Little League was ordered to integrate, three mothers of girls banned from baseball in Wallkill, New York, organized a girls' baseball league and forty-five girls immediately expressed a desire to play. Fifty girls tried out to play with boys the first time it was legal in Hoboken, New Jersey.[24] It seems likely that if Little League hadn't offered a separate softball league, girls would have continued playing hardball.

Rather than offer baseball, either integrated or separated, eight- to twelve-year-old girls who did not want to play with boys were offered slow-pitch softball. The uniforms had shorts that were so short one caption on a photograph in a book chronicling the history of Little League states, "The short uniforms worn by girls during the 1975 Little League softball World Series make the players look more like Rockettes."[25] Also noteworthy in the picture is the absence of sliding pads. The picture shows a close play at third base with the base runner sliding with no protection for her legs, exposed from her buttocks to her knees. This is puzzling, given the arguments made in court by Little League Baseball that girls faced disfigurement if they played baseball with boys. How could men who had expressed so much concern about protecting the safety and beauty of American girls allow them to expose their legs to abrasions from sliding? The picture shows seven spectators sitting on the grassy hill behind the baseline, in sharp contrast to photos of the Little League baseball World Series in the book. The boys' championships are played on a multifield facility where the main playing field is a stadium with ten thousand permanent seats along the baselines and room for thousands more on grassy hills beyond the outfield fence. Little League baseball champions have been invited to play on the White House lawn and to meet the president. Most major league baseball players have come from the ranks of Little Leaguers. It's a serious business, with a pot of gold waiting at the end of the Little League rainbow. Tens of thousands of supporters are accommodated at the Little League baseball World Series, which is broadcast globally. While many more people now follow girls' and women's competitive softball seriously, the early message to the girls who chose to play the game was less than supportive.

Little League Baseball does not keep statistics on the number of girls play-ing in their leagues throughout the nation. Lance Van Auken, coauthor of *Play Ball! The Story of Little League Baseball,* explained since local leagues were not required to report how many girls play hardball, "We can only guess anecdot-ally that somewhere between 20,000 and 100,000 players are girls."[26] In 2005, according to Van Auken, 420,000 girls and 2.2 million boys participated in Little League's baseball and softball programs combined. It seems safe to guess the numbers are relatively sex-segregated.

James Glennie, president of the American Women's Baseball Federation and a man deeply committed to girls and women playing baseball, was not surprised that Little League did not know how many girls play baseball. He remarked, "I

Krissy Wendall of Brooklyn Center, Minnesota, in the 1994 Little League World Series (courtesy Little League Baseball, Inc.)

Girls in the 1975 Softball World Series wearing uniforms more appropriate for a chorus line (courtesy Little League Baseball, Inc.)

have never found [Little League Baseball, Inc.] willing to cooperate with anyone. Little League started a softball division and that has become the fastest growing division for them. They also started a softball division for boys to give the illusion of parity. However there are no boys' softball teams actively playing."[27] Glennie reiterated what he referred to as "no tightly-held secret" that girls are "simply shoved gently toward softball after Little League and many go there simply because they have a chance to continue playing through college."[28] And indeed, the number of women playing college baseball is infinitesimal. Glennie could only name one player, and he wasn't certain whether she was still playing. Glennie believes the only chance for women to break into baseball is with leagues of their own. He coaches an American women's baseball team that has toured in Japan, and he wryly noted, "Japan has developed many more opportunities for women in baseball. Go figure."[29]

Whether or not the invention of Little League softball represents a conscious effort on the part of Little League Baseball to discourage girls from playing baseball, it had that effect. The first girl who played in the Little League baseball World Series was Victoria Roche, an American, who in 1984 played on the European team from Brussels, Belgium. Only seven other girls have played on teams in the series since then. Meanwhile, the girls' softball program has over half a million players, almost entirely female. Statistics on how many girls play Little League hardball are not kept. But with the increasing "professionalization" of youth sports and the rewards of college scholarships waiting, it is likely that most girls will make the "sensible" choice of playing softball instead of baseball. Professional outlets for softball players don't exist. Professional opportunities for women who play baseball don't exist. Girls who like playing with balls and bats are stuck between a rock and a hard (ball) place. They can elect to play softball, a game with no professional future, in the hope that they will develop as players and be good enough to receive a college scholarship before being forced to give up playing the game on an elite organized level, or they can play baseball with boys if they're good enough to compete even as the boys are likely to grow bigger and stronger than them in adolescence, perhaps being the exception girl on a high school or minor college team, in a sport that also has no professional future for women and won't give out college scholarships, either. While it might be argued that any team sport is an unwise choice for a girl who wants to make enough income to support herself as an adult, avenues do exist (although on an incomparably more modest level than for men) for basketball and soccer players. Girls who love playing baseball and softball have no viable future in either sport.

No big league dreams are available for girls. An American girl has a better chance of growing up to be president than of taking the field in a major league baseball stadium. In the end, the hubbub over girls playing Little League hardly mattered.

NINE

Collegiate Women's Baseball

Culture Wars

Nothing remains of American law that enabled communities to prohibit girls from playing baseball. It's not legal anymore, anywhere in the United States. Nothing in NCAA regulations prevents college women from playing baseball. American girls and women decline to play the national pastime voluntarily. How is that possible? Girls and women have loved the game from the very beginning. Girls signed up for Little League baseball as soon as the path was legally cleared for them. But they were siphoned away from the game almost immediately with the creation of Little League softball. If kids don't play a sport when they're young, they're unlikely to play it when they get older. Not only do they lack the opportunity to develop the early love of the game childhood offers, but they never develop the skill to compete on progressively more difficult levels. If girls can be kept away from baseball between ages eight and twelve, they can probably be kept away for life. If girls have never played, when they grow to adulthood they lack the desire to teach their daughters. The absence of college baseball for women is the dead bolt in the door that has been locked against women trying to gain entry to baseball in the United States.

Most girls succumb to the pressure to play softball rather than baseball and are out of the national pastime by age twelve. Whether or not they actually prefer softball to baseball is a moot point. The struggle to "choose" baseball is too daunting to all but the most determined. The creation of organized softball was Little League's response to legal setbacks in their battle to exclude girls. It short-circuited girls' participation and prevented development of the requisite "interest and ability" in baseball. The absence of youth baseball for girls leads directly to the absence of high school girls' baseball. With these institutional inhibitions, women's baseball is unlikely to make an appearance among college sports, and even the few girls who play high school baseball have no place to go with it after their prep careers.

Title IX cannot be held responsible for failing to create a desire among girls to play baseball. It takes social encouragement for girls to be drawn into the game. MLB and Little League Baseball had the opportunity to bring the other half of the nation's children into the game when Title IX was passed and when girls indicated their strong desire to join. But organized baseball fought off the girls instead of courting them as future participants and consumers of the game. Preserving the masculine purity of baseball was more important to them than encouraging girls and women to love it, in spite of the fact that young people are drifting away from team sports in general. Currently, interest in baseball, along with organized team sports as a whole, is declining for both girls *and* boys, in comparison to their growing involvement in individual "extreme" action sports: snowboarding, skateboarding, wakeboarding, and the like. Harvey Lauer, president of American Sports Data, Inc., in a "Superstudy of Sports Participation," notes a "shifting landscape" in American youth involvement from traditional team sports to extreme sports. He observes,

> "The last decade of the 20th century has witnessed vast changes in American values and the popular culture. As part of a larger social and technological transformation, the thinking, lifestyles, and leisure behavior of children have been profoundly affected. . . . In the new millennium, Baseball, Basketball, and Football are still among the most popular participatory sports; but the number of people who participate in these activities is plummeting. . . . Traditional team sports . . . reflect traditional values: cooperation, teamwork, character-building, and healthy competition. Unlike traditional sports, the new genre of so-called 'extreme' sports (i.e. In-Line Skating,

Skateboarding, BMX, Snowboarding . . .) is rooted in a diametrically opposite set of values . . . fierce individualism, alienation, defiance, and inwardly-focused aggressive behavior."[1]

Baseball would rather lose half of their future fan base than encourage girls to play the game.

The financial power of athletics can be seen in every mall in America and many in Europe and Asia as well: football, baseball, and basketball jerseys, sweatshirts, hats, beanies, T-shirts, jackets, and so forth. America's major professional sports highlights are telecast globally. Collegiate athletics are following the same path as their professional big brothers. The omnipresence of American collegiate sports apparel worn by youth and adults throughout the world implies that sports fandom provides financial well-being for the universities that participate. Success at football and basketball brings big-time television exposure on ESPN, and now the coverage includes the telecast of the College World Series, which has given elite college baseball a higher profile. This generates more revenue and greater visibility that sells more jackets and jerseys, making major sports programs cost-effective. Alumni become excited about their school's winning football or men's basketball team and donate huge sums of money to improve athletic facilities and stadiums in order to enable their alma mater to compete with its rivals for top high school talent, to bring still more success, fame, and profits. Winning is profitable, or it appears to be.

But the wealth is an illusion for all but a handful of perennial athletic powerhouses. Football has the highest profile and brings out the biggest crowds, but even that most major of sports rarely pays for itself. Football is the indulged child at most universities, and it is a child with an obesity problem. Its dominance reflects a value that may be as fundamental to Americans as profit: the need to safeguard one version of masculinity.

College Football and Title IX

James L. Shulman's and William G. Bowen's detailed study *The Game of Life: College Sports and Educational Values* describes the University of Michigan's football program during a very good season.[2] During the 1998–1999 season, the Michigan football team shared the Big Ten title and won the Citrus Bowl, finishing its season ranked twelfth in the nation. Other Michigan sports, including men's ice hockey, men's gymnastics, and women's basketball did extremely well that year, too. "But when the fiscal year ended in June, the athletic department was projecting a deficit of $2 million. By September, when audited statements came out, the operating deficit had risen to $2.8 million; when capital expenditures and transfers are included, the shortfall was $3.8 million."[3] Shulman and Bowen ask how it was possible that a major athletic power could be that far in the red the same year the football team set a national attendance record, with an average of 110,965 fans attending six home games.

The simple answer is that while revenues were up, so were expenses. The success of the team and the national attention garnered made it necessary for the university to update the stadium, including installation of expensive luxury skyboxes for donors. The football program also needed a state-of-the art Web site. The basketball team, also successful, had lost key players who had elected to turn professional rather than finish their college careers. This meant basketball attendance, which contributed to the overall athletic budget and could have helped with football's expensive success, was down. In addition, the university took a fashion hit: the nation's youth had temporarily decided it was cooler to wear Tommy Hilfiger sweatshirts and jackets than university logo clothing. This vagary of fashion put a dent in the University of Michigan athletic budget. The point is that even the biggest, most successful football program in the nation did not turn a profit in a very good year. A postseason bowl or high-profile tournament appearance may temporarily balance a university's intercollegiate athletic budget, but that is nothing to bank on. Whether successful or not, most athletic programs are an expense for universities. "Only a very small number of schools that are committed to large outlays in these sports actually end up collecting revenues that can be said to justify the expenditures," state Shulman and Bowen.[4]

Most universities would rather have a successful football team, at almost any cost, than an unsuccessful one. But the argument that a good football team is financially worth the investment is bogus. It may earn its keep in terms of national prestige, which attracts prospective students and athletes, but it pays neither for itself nor for any of the smaller teams at its school. Still, a school that wants to compete for the best high school players in major sports must participate in an escalating game of expenditures to attract the prospective stars. The most promising high school football and basketball players in the nation are courted by many excellent programs and learn to expect the best coaches, first-rate facilities, no skimping on travel and other operating costs, and strong publicity and marketing efforts.

University of Nevada athletic director Cary Groth is one of the few female Division 1 athletic directors in the nation. She is a strong supporter of women's athletics, a former college tennis player and therefore sensitive to the needs of "minor" sports, but also realistic about the need of any university athletic program to defer to football and men's basketball. She knows that football doesn't make money even in the best of times and that basketball, if successful, will just manage to pay for itself with television revenues and so forth. Groth confirms that even in its best season in years, Nevada's football program will not bring in money. Yet football must be supported. "I think our culture plays a huge part. Our society loves college football. Football has to be a priority because of our culture. If you're not successful in men's basketball and football then it affects your conference affiliation, your NCAA status. Our society likes those sports, they judge us on those sports, the NCAA distributes revenue based on the success of those sports," says Groth.[5] Yet the more successful a football program becomes at a given school, the more that school is expected to compete with the most lavishly endowed competitors in terms of coaching salaries, facilities, and so forth. At major football powers, the coaches' salaries are several times as much as those of the university president. Groth believes, "It really is a train wreck waiting to happen. We [Nevada] can never afford to pay our basketball or football coach millions of dollars. Nor would I ever be a part of an institution that would think that was the right thing to do. But it's expected at a big time school."[6]

The expense of maintaining a football team will dominate a university's athletic budget. There are no women's football teams, and there are very few women who play college football. Since Title IX requires proportionality between men's and women's sports, if football requires a disproportionate part of the athletic budget, all of the other teams, both men's and women's, must divide the rest. The existence of a football program throws the entire athletic budget out of balance, and the men's and women's teams are left fighting over the remainder. The major American women's sports—basketball, volleyball, and softball—will be pitted against men's basketball and baseball. "Minor" sports, such as track and field, lacrosse, wrestling, crew, soccer, swimming, hockey, and whatever other interests might exist at a given college, must divide the table scraps left over from the men's and women's major sports, including football. In effect, the "minor" men's sports—although if lacrosse or wrestling has been your life's passion, it does not feel minor—are forced to compete with both football *and* women's sports.[7]

The ill will can be imagined, as men's track, wrestling, and soccer budgets are sacrificed in the name of women's basketball, volleyball, and softball. Title IX is more likely to be blamed for the men's teams' sacrifice than is football. When the wrestling team at Princeton was dropped in 1993 because of financial constraints, there was an uproar from alumni wrestlers as well as students who had intended to continue their wrestling careers at Princeton. It is difficult not to empathize with wrestlers who were deprived of their sport for the abstract goal of equity, but equally difficult not to acknowledge the reality that most girls and women have never been given the opportunity to pursue their sports at all. Shulman and Bowen comment that "women have not been welcome on campus *as students* for long enough to build their own myths, let alone to demonstrate conclusively their abiding interest in sports."[8]

Title IX is blamed for the injustices when in fact the imbalance created by football, and on some campuses men's basketball, is what creates the need to trim other teams. The football budget added to any other men's sport will almost always add up to a much larger expenditure than all the women's teams on campus combined. Fiscally trim men's teams see the savings generated by their spartan regimens plugged into the football program. Women's sports bear the blame and don't even benefit from cuts to men's minor sports budgets. Nevada's Groth believes that the vast majority of instances of men's programs dropped throughout the nation are casualties of football expenses rather than the result of Title IX forcing men's sports out. She states:

> Of all the cases of dropped programs around the country, nearly 90 percent of them have not been dropped because of Title IX. It's the finances. It's typically the pressure to have good football and good men's basketball programs and bigger and more buildings. Of those 90 percent of cases, those moneys did not go into women's programs. They were reinvested into football programs and so on. Case in point: [at one] school out west . . . when they cut a couple of their men's programs, they reinvested tens of thousands, even hundreds of thousands of dollars into cherrywood in the men's locker rooms and things like that. They just reinvested into the men's programs. And gave a little to the women's programs.[9]

They give so little to the women's programs that the softball team may be reduced to playing at a public park for lack of a softball stadium on campus, or the women's soccer team must play on the men's football field before a few hundred spectators whose cheers echo in a stadium built to hold fifty thousand. To highlight the discrepancy between the women's programs and the lavish funds spent on the men's major programs, Nevada assistant baseball coach Jay Uhlman muses, "Can you imagine a football program saying 'We've got a football program but we don't have a field for you. We don't have a stadium. Go play over there at the high school.' That would never happen."[10] Inadequate funding for women's and minor men's sports creates a cycle on a campus that builds on itself. It becomes impossible to recruit the nation's best athletes, who prefer to be treated decently at a wealthier university. The few rich programs grow from their devotion to football, and the poor schools languish in the shadow of the more prevalent football deficit. From this perspective, the major divide in college sports is not between men's and women's sports, but between the athletically rich and the athletically poor. Major athletic powers attract ever more wealth, and institutions that by necessity or choice have kept their athletic programs in balance with the educational mission of the university languish in ever deepening shadows.

Groth believes that this situation is concealed because the nation's athletic directors allow Title IX to be used as the scapegoat. The real culprit is football, which eats the portion of the budget that might have been used to fund smaller men's programs. "I blame athletic directors for the culture of Title IX because we stand up and say we are eliminating men's programs because of Title IX. The brave and the honest athletic directors will say we are eliminating these men's programs because we have to have competitive football and men's basketball programs and we have to put the resources in those programs so that those programs will be successful to help all the other programs, including the women's programs."[11]

College Baseball and Women Athletes

It is not my intention to analyze whether football should be central to college athletics; however, it does exemplify a more general reason why it is difficult to imagine girls playing college baseball. Division 1 intercollegiate athletics in general have become a training ground for professional athletes. This includes a cultural default for college football and to a lesser extent basketball, which has had impact on women's intercollegiate athletics and the ability to implement the intent of Title IX. That, in turn, has impact upon the ability of any college or university to foster a "new" women's sport such as baseball. A university's need to keep its teams winning in order to justify their existence makes it unlikely that the few girl high school baseball players in the nation will get a chance to play on a men's team in college. Why risk a losing season with an unknown factor in the lineup?

The most successful collegiate football and basketball programs act as training grounds for professional sports. Once a high school athlete signs with a Division 1 program, professional leagues are not allowed to offer him a contract before his junior year or before he is twenty-one years old. Football players are not allowed to sign with a professional team out of high school. A very few basketball prep superstars have signed to play with the NBA recently and been successful as teenage professionals. The NCAA has explicit regulations about when a college player can make him or herself available to the pros without compromising amateur status. It is no secret that the pros allow universities to give their players a few years of experience and seasoning before they are ready to move up, and there is some controversy over whether that metering is intended to benefit the finances of the professional leagues or the health of the young players. University athletic departments also benefit by delaying elite athletes' eligibility for the pros: it makes for higher-quality college games. Using university athletics in this way changes the meaning of collegiate amateur sports. In defense of this aspect of college athletics, it might be argued that universities train students for professional success in many areas: business, law, science, and even academia itself. Why should sports be any different?

Baseball doesn't follow the same model as football and basketball because professional baseball maintains its own active farm system. Professional baseball teams acquire and cultivate their talent out of high school, junior colleges, and four-year colleges, but the existence of a system of minor league teams owned by each major league franchise means that almost all major leaguers have spent some time in the minor leagues. An exceptional high school baseball player may choose to turn pro directly out of high school, spending a few years in the minor leagues before hopefully making it to the major leagues. He may also choose to play college ball first. If he chooses to play on a Division 1 college team and his professional baseball career doesn't work out, at least he has a college degree. Since baseball players have the option of signing professional contracts before college while football players do not, major collegiate baseball programs must stay competitive to attract those prospects for a few years. Because there is no future professional market for women baseball players, there is unlikely to be a place for them on a major men's university team. It would be regarded as a waste of precious resources.

But not all colleges and universities are major athletic powers. Might some of the smaller schools with smaller athletic budgets encourage women to play baseball? The NCAA has a hierarchy of divisions separating competition according to the size of the athletic constituency and resources at a given university. The larger colleges have a larger pool of athletes to draw from and are more competitive and higher profile than the small schools. These big schools comprise Division 1 of the NCAA, and the athletes they recruit are the top high school athletes in the nation, with the possibility of professional careers before them. A few of the Division 1 schools place so much emphasis on athletics that they have become perennial winners in all the major sports.[12] Some colleges have a tradition of excellence in baseball, but more often, the baseball programs at the major athletic universities are the beneficiaries of the successes of football and basketball.

Smaller, "mid-major" Division 1 schools have what some would regard as a saner balance between athletics and academics—less of an imbalance between, for example, the salaries of the football coach and the university president. These schools have more choices about where to put emphasis in their overall academic and athletic programs because generally a coach won't be fired for one losing season. Still, losing is less fun and profitable than winning, and even the coaches at these smaller Division 1 athletic programs must spend an enormous proportion of their time—between 50 and 80 percent, according to some sources—recruiting. Nevada baseball's Jay Uhlman remarked, "You can't win games without ballplayers. . . . It's fun when you get the guys that people didn't know were going to be good, and they end up being good . . . that sense of pride that comes with knowing, 'Hey, I found a guy that was kind of a sleeper.'"[13] Schools that aren't the nation's biggest athletic powerhouses are the ones that have the most opportunity to find and develop unrecognized talent. The major athletic powerhouses can lure the universally recognized "best players" with lavishness and reputation. The "best players" have been coached, packaged, and marketed from a very early age—a tremendous parental investment of time and money—and brought to the "showcases" that bring together elite high school players and college coaches. These showcases are invitational meat markets for prospective athletes and their doting parents. At that level, it is difficult to avoid the corruption wealth brings. The smaller or "mid-major" schools have the opportunity for a healthier athletic culture, where priorities are determined more by the culture of the school rather than the bottom line and how the rest of the athletic conference is doing.

Uhlman knows that most of his players come to the university to play baseball, hoping to continue with their sport professionally. But most of them will not make it to the big leagues simply because there are many more good college players than there are positions in major league baseball. These players get a college education, which is a good thing, and may discover career paths they didn't know about before they had an opportunity to go to college. Uhlman himself had hoped to play professional baseball when he arrived as an undergraduate at the University of Nevada. When it didn't work out according to plan, he found his calling in educational leadership, combining his love of athletics and education. While he believes that "You can't just have kids going to school for sports," he also knows sports often give a young athlete a future that he or she wouldn't have had without it.[14]

Uhlman is probably unusual among Division 1 athletic coaches in believing bigger is not necessarily better and that some balance should be struck between the value placed on fielding winning teams, on educating the athletes, and on rewarding coaches, university administrators, and professors. It is difficult for coaches and teenaged recruits to turn their backs on the perquisites that go with big money, especially when the coaching salaries at the smaller schools more closely resemble modest academic salaries than enticing professional salaries. Having closets full of shoes donated by Nike, or polo shirts, warm-ups, and fleece donated by athletic clothing manufacturers is alluring to both athletes and coaches, and it is just the tip of the iceberg. Little things such as complementary logo wear attracts new recruits and makes the coaching staff feel well-looked after. Financial logic thus dominates college athletics; the rich get richer, and even those individuals who place more value on educational balance than an obsession with winning are lured into the game.

It is certainly possible for people to resist the allure of wealth and stick to a more balanced perspective about college sports, but it's not the norm. In a *Sports Illustrated* interview with Matt Hasselbeck, the Seahawks' quarterback recalled his choice of Boston College over UCLA when he was being recruited out of high school: "When I went on my recruiting visit to UCLA in 1993, the big TV show was *Beverly Hills, 90210*, and some of the cast was at a party I attended that weekend. That's about as incriminating as I can get about my visit there, okay? When I visited BC, I got picked up by the strength coach in his beat-up car, dropped off at a player's dorm room, ate in the dining hall, slept on the floor. BC just felt more like me."[15] This is the sort of independent thinking that would be necessary on a large scale for changes to be made in the culture of collegiate sports. Conscious and vigilant resistance to the dominance of money and winning as the only goal of college athletics is a prerequisite to any program taking a chance on women's baseball. It is not likely to happen in Division 1.

There are also Division 2 and Division 3 NCAA programs. Division 3 consists primarily of small, academically elite colleges, and their model student athlete most closely resembles the old-school amateur athlete. In *Reclaiming the Game: College Sports and Educational Values*, however, William Bowen and Sarah Levin describe how the athletic culture overtaking Division 3 sports has begun to mirror what has happened at the Division 1 level in terms of devotion to winning and preprofessionalism. The ethos undermines the concept of the student athlete by creating an "academic-athletic divide" even at colleges and universities that are academically highly selective.[16] Bowen and Levin identify recruiting as the source of the problem and argue that coaches have excessive input about admission of student athletes, even at the Division 3 level. This results in the polarization of student athletes and academic students and under-mines the integration of athletics and academics as an educational ideal.

In spite of these problems, NCAA Division 3 is referred to as "the nerd division," implying that the students are smarter and not as athletically gifted as the Division 1 athletes. Unlike Divisions 1 and 2, NCAA regulations do not allow Division 3 schools to offer athletic scholarships, and there are strict rules for recruiting prospective athletes. In theory, students at these elite colleges should be able to gain admission academically. Athletics is an added bonus, both for the school and the student; it is not the admission ticket for an elite education. In other words, Division 3 schools represent the old approach to campus athletics.

It would seem that if there were a place in the American system of higher education for women to make an entrance into baseball, it would be the NCAA Division 3 schools. But the number of women playing Division 3 baseball is too small to count, and the explanation lies in all the factors discussed: no interest or ability at the college level because there is so little chance to nurture it in childhood: no Little League baseball, no high school baseball, therefore no college baseball. Division 3 schools are no more immune to the culture of winning than any other aspect of American life. It would take commitment and time to create a place for women in Division 3 baseball programs, first on men's teams because the numbers of women ballplayers would be small, and perhaps later on teams of their own. Few Division 3 men's baseball coaches are willing to "take a chance" on a woman, even one proven in high school varsity baseball. If a bigger, stronger man is available, he "looks" more like a baseball player, just as before the mid-twentieth century white men "looked" more like baseball players than men of color. This is certainly a prejudice that also plagues smaller men of any race who are fine ballplayers.[17] But while some small men make it, almost no women do. So long as most girls play softball, there are unlikely to be enough players to field a baseball team, much less a baseball league or conference, and women will continue to "look like" softball players rather than baseball players. It is also unlikely in the current economic climate that any university or college, even at the Division 3 level, will be in a position to add a new sport, especially a sport like baseball that so few women play. Organized softball also, of course, does not want to lose their potential pool of young players to baseball. Softball has no stake in encouraging girls' baseball to flourish. Western Michigan's athletic director Cathy Beauregard observes that with the current education budget situation, most athletic departments "are focusing on getting through tomorrow, let alone adding sports. Women's softball has been huge, girls have grown up with an opportunity. I think the Olympic years have been tremendous for softball. It's a mandatory sport in our conference."[18]

One possible avenue to women's college baseball is a more grassroots approach: club baseball. Club teams represent the school competitively against other schools but do not receive funding or coaching from the intercollegiate athletic budget. They are comprised of students who show up and suit up. Players are usually accomplished in their sport but may not want to devote the amount of time and energy called for by varsity sports. Club sports can be quite competitive: rugby, boxing, lacrosse, flag football, and Ultimate Frisbee are examples of club sports that are taken very seriously by students at individual colleges and universities. Club baseball could begin with mixed teams of men and women and slowly draw more women in. Former high school softball players and closeted female baseball players might be encouraged to try the game in the less intimidating club sport milieu. It would be a slow path, but along with more encouragement for girls to play youth baseball, a culture of women's baseball could be nurtured.

Professionalism and Women's College Sports

Bowen and Levin believe Title IX represents a missed opportunity to "recalibrate the entire athletics enterprise so that it would be more congruent with educational goals. This would have entailed reducing the emphasis on recruiting, spending less money on athletic scholarships (if not eliminating them altogether), and in other ways carefully considering the adoption of other aspects of the model of athletics that was pioneered and developed by the AIAW." Instead, Title IX was "in effect, superimposed on the pre-existing 'male model' of athletics."[19] It increased the scale of athletic recruitment and added pressure for national championships for women. The AIAW (Association of Intercollegiate Athletics for Women), governed women's intercollegiate athletics between 1971 and 1984, when it was folded into the NCAA, which would be the governing body for both men's and women's intercollegiate athletics. The AIAW had adhered to the early-twentieth-century model of sports for women that emphasized health, recreation, and inclusiveness rather than competition and athletic victory as first priorities. The values of the AIAW were eclipsed by the NCAA's more contemporary emphasis on winning at all costs.

The AIAW's amateur model was a throwback to an earlier age when college men and women of the nineteenth and early twentieth century were a privileged minority. In those days, being a "big man on campus" and a star athlete at college were icing on the cake of privilege: attractive, but not required to secure success in life. As the middle and working classes began to enter colleges and universities in great numbers, especially after World War II with the support of the GI Bill, the role of athletics in college life changed. Winning teams secured celebrity as major public universities challenged the Ivies for prestige. Public universities and middle-class students upset the established American hierarchy, spreading a new competitive ethos throughout every aspect of collegiate life. Now universities and colleges themselves have come to place value on numerically measured success rather than less tangible elements of academic life. They too are ranked, in a parody of athletic rankings. Which "top ten" school can attract the most academic "superstars"? How much will it cost for Princeton to be able to steal a Nobel Laureate from Harvard? And how will that "acquisition" affect its national rankings? How will marketing that purchase and other achievements increase the number of undergraduate applicants, so that the percentage of students admitted will decline and make the school appear more "selective"? How can a school manipulate its rankings? And who really cares about what goes on day to day at the university, so long as you can list your tenure there on your resume, like a won-lost record? Middle-class success has always been measured in a more product-oriented way than upper-class success. Winning, both athletically and academically, has become paramount. The professional is its product.

The AIAW model, emerging from the values of the women's physical education experts of the 1920s, reincarnated in the 1950s, and embodied in the first women's intercollegiate teams in the 1970s, represented a throwback. While men's athletics exploded into professionalism, gaining ever higher visibility with technological advances such as television and air travel, women's competitive athletics represented a model that was becoming outmoded: use sports to build the right sort of character and take nothing to a sweaty extreme. An overemphasis on competition was regarded as unseemly. To many people, this is still a desirable and balanced view of athletic competition. But it does not breed or attract elite athletes among the nation's girls and women, and it is out of pace with contemporary American culture. In view of the current commercialization of everything, including the corporatization of college sports as entertainment and athletes as celebrities, collegiate women's athletics would not have stood a chance had it not been willing to go the way of men's sports.

It is debatable whether this has helped women's athletics or contributed to what University of Nevada's Groth and authors Bowen and Levin regard as the "failed model" of male intercollegiate athletics. Uhlman's vision of the most desirable collegiate athletic program also places more emphasis on the balance between athletics and academics even at Division 1 programs. "To me that's what it's supposed to be to start with. Not overfunding, not overpaying. Funded right. Done right, with some dignity and class and values."

Can Women Play Baseball with Men?

If women are going to play college baseball, they will either have to play with men or on teams of their own. Since there are currently no women's collegiate baseball teams and the odds are against women's baseball becoming an NCAA sport in the near future, that means playing on mixed teams. But are women capable of playing baseball on men's teams? Cultural resistance would make a woman collegiate baseball player on any level an exception to the rule. It would take an extraordinarily committed, talented woman to survive the discouragement she would have to endure at each level of play with boys and men. It could be accomplished athletically. There are a few women who have played college ball with men. Julie Croteau and Ila Borders are two of the most well-known. Croteau was the first woman to play NCAA baseball, for Division 3 St. Mary's College of Maryland. She went on to become the first woman to coach Division 1 NCAA men's baseball at the University of Massachusetts. Borders, the daughter of a minor league pitcher, played on boys' teams from Little League through high school, and in 1993 earned a baseball scholarship to the University of Southern California at Costa Mesa. Neither Croteau nor Borders are unusually big women, and it is logical to surmise that there are other women out there with similar ability.

Jody Schwartz of Reno, Nevada, was a collegiate softball player at Creighton University, a member of the 1984 Olympic softball exhibition team, and more recently a member of the Reno Diamonds semiprofessional men's baseball team. She played Little League baseball in her hometown of Los Angeles as a girl, and then switched to softball because "I guess I didn't foresee myself going further with the baseball, and a lot of my friends were playing softball. So I switched over to softball and succeeded in softball in high school, which enabled me to get a scholarship to participate in college and get an education."[20] After college, Schwartz felt she was at the top of her game, but there wasn't anywhere to go with softball. "I felt like I wasn't through. Where I live, here in Reno, there wasn't a women's fast pitch team, so I started playing baseball. That's how I got into playing semipro baseball here with the Reno Diamonds. They put an ad in the paper, and I came to tryouts and made the team. I had the confidence knowing that physically I could compete, though I needed training with a wood bat, compared to using aluminum bats all my life."

Schwartz's male teammates were skeptical at first. She noted, "In the back of most men's minds, they think a girl should not be playing," but she won them over with her ability. Still, she remembers a time when she was traveling with her team in California and being continually thrown at by the opposing team. "Every time I got up [to bat], they would hit me." She just took it and got on base. At six feet, she is bigger than many women, but she doesn't think strength was an issue, nor does she think either baseball or softball is inherently a more difficult game. The challenges she faced were making adjustments from the game she had spent most of her life learning and having the self-confidence to play with men: "It's a sport; you take it for what it is. . . . The challenge of me going out there and playing with guys, showing and knowing that I can go out there and compete, I think it's a biggie for me. I think that most girls don't have the confidence. I think the guys will beat you up if you don't have the confidence."

Robert Conatser, certified athletic trainer and certified strength and conditioning specialist with a master's degree in athletic training (MA, ATL, CSCS), expressed some concerns about women competing with men in college and professional baseball, but he believes that training and experience would make it possible for some women to succeed at the integrated game. Conatser's concerns are twofold: as an athletic trainer and conditioning specialist, he and his colleagues are concerned with injury prevention, and the average size differential between men and women could possibly, although not necessarily, put women at greater risk of injury. He also raised issues about the role a coach or manager who put a woman on his team would have to play if the team wasn't immediately successful. Public objections to not winning immediately would likely turn to the "What were you thinking?" sort of outrage, blaming the coach and the female ballplayer for a lack of instant success. But that's a risk that any pioneer with a historic "first" has had to face, including Branch Rickey and Leo Durocher.

With regard to the greater risk of injury due to the size differential, Conatser mused, "Part of the resistance to letting women play with men is injury prevention. A female is going to face more chance of injury. She has a smaller size and frame, making it harder for women. If there's a collision at home plate, she's going to take a bigger hit if indeed she is smaller. From a preventative injury standpoint, if there is a collision, that female is going to hit somebody bigger than her and that injury potential is going to rise. She may be bigger than two or three [players on the team], but the other six or eight guys on the field most of the time are going to be bigger" than her.[21]

This problem concerns the "accidents" of baseball: collisions at home plate and on the base paths, pitches being hit right back at the pitcher, and so forth. The greater risks for women would be the result of their average smaller size: not endurance, not muscle mass, not bone density, according to Conatser. "If you took two people the same size, it would be equal."[22] Even if a woman were smaller than a man, if she were strong and well conditioned, her muscles would protect her bones in a collision just as a man's would. Breaking a bone is not a predictable event: it has much to do with the specifics of a hit, regardless of whether the player involved is a man or a woman. Again, this is assuming that contacts and collisions are not the norm in every baseball play, as they are in football and increasingly in basketball. And Conatser noted that it was just as dangerous for a baseball to be hit back at Roger Clemens as any other pitcher, male or female. The ability of a pitcher to avoid injury from a line drive streaming at him or her from sixty feet away is the result of training, reflexes, and luck, not gender.

With concern for size differentials factored in, Conatser believes that mixed teams are possible: "Could females be trained to play at that level . . . sure, why not?" The real differences in size and strength show up by the middle of high school, when boys and girls are fifteen or sixteen years old. "Early on a girl is more developed than a boy all the way until the last couple of years of high school. Strength comes along, and testosterone levels evolve. At that point, it becomes tougher for the girl. They have more work to do, but again there's no reason they can't compete. It's just can you find enough of them to push that hard, and put the effort in, and have a goal to play at that level."[23] There are performance differences between men and women that show up, for example, in speed trials: track events and marathons. "The best marathon or triathlon time of a man is better than that of a woman. In terms of baseball, it's a stat thing; it's not a race, not a timed event. Some of the baseball players are hitting two out of ten. Could a female hit three out of ten? Without a doubt."[24]

Baseball ability is the result of many factors, including interest, training, experience—and cultural encouragement. To say that certain groups of people, defined by race, nationality, or gender, are "built" for one sport or another is, according to Conatser, "baloney." He observed, "Culturally, Hispanics are given a soccer ball right away, and they just practice and practice and practice, and guess what? They're good at soccer. So to say some groups of people weren't made for a certain game is baloney."[25]

Colette Dowling describes the narrowing of "the strength gap" between men and women in *The Frailty Myth: Redefining the Physical Potential of Women and Girls*. She notes that on average, males are 10 to 15 percent larger in physical stature than women. But there are plenty of women who are larger than the average-sized man and there are plenty of men who are smaller than the average-sized woman. Dowling asks, "How big a power difference could really be legitimated by the fact that *some* men are larger than *some* women?" She finds that contemporary women are increasingly capable of competing at levels comparable to men, which has not resulted in welcoming them to "men's" sports but in creating new tactics for undermining women's accomplishments. Men's athletic institutions have responded by "deflecting attention from just *how* physically similar males and females actually are. One method has been to divide and conquer: keeping men's games separate from women's."[26] Baseball is certainly one such example.

Much athletic theory has been built by emphasizing differences in weight distribution, muscle mass, and center of gravity between male and female bodies. Dowling argues that differences in body types do not translate into ability in any given sport. To overemphasize these factors is to indulge in myth making—it is to regard every matchup as though it were an unathletic woman playing football against a professional football player. The similarities in body type also mean an unbalanced matchup is possible between an unathletic man and a Division 1 collegiate woman basketball player. To regard athletic ability as sexually determined—to believe that all males will be athletically superior to all females—is unrealistic. Different body types have different athletic advantages, but all male bodies are not endowed with a magic formula for elite athletic success any more than all female bodies are incapable of athletic excellence.

> On average, men can carry and use more oxygen. They tend to be heavier—an advantage in football—and taller: handy in basketball and volleyball. Men have more lean muscle mass, convenient in sports requiring explosive power. Less muscle-bound women generally have greater flexibility, useful in gymnastics, diving and skating. Their lower center of gravity helps in hockey, golf, tennis, baseball and even basketball. Women sweat better (less dripping, therefore better evaporation), which is critical, since bodies need to remain cool to function efficiently.[27]

Dowling's conclusion is much like Conatser's: ability in any given sport has as much to do with exposure, encouragement, training, and cultural context as it does with genetic endowment. Girls are capable of playing baseball with boys into and beyond adolescence, given sufficient cultural encouragement and a lifetime of athletic training like the boys get.

To provide perspective on the prejudice against women playing baseball on the same teams as men, in the next chapter I look at the roadblocks still in place that discourage American-born men of color from playing baseball.

TEN

The Invisibility of Bias

The Good Old Days

We have analyzed the history of girls' and women's participation in and exclusion from American baseball. We have considered the social and cultural structures that continue to bar them access to baseball at the youth level and the institutional barriers that keep them away from the college game. Now we turn to a discussion of recruitment and development practices that make it nearly impossible for women to play professional baseball, including the international business practices that have been used to develop Latin American ballplayers as inexpensively as possible. Outsourcing baseball's labor supply has had a negative impact on the number of African American even more than European American ballplayers in the game, and switched the dialogue from race and prejudice to economics: the need for a franchise to be profitable. The centrality and apparent undeniability of economic forces makes it difficult to see the persistence of racism. Even more occluded than racism is sexism. The exclusion of women still appears "natural." Physically, it is assumed, women cannot compete with men. Financially, it just doesn't pay to establish women's leagues. Whatever the rhetoric, the result is exclusion: a big sign on baseball's mythical clubhouse that reads "No Girls Allowed! Women Keep Out!" This chapter explores similarities between racial and sexual rationalizations for controlling access to American baseball.

Organized baseball has celebrated its racial "integration" and dated it from April 15, 1947, when Jackie Robinson first stepped onto a major league baseball field as a Brooklyn Dodger. Baseball believes that it solved the "problem" of excluding girls by creating Little League softball. But African American men and women of all races are a rarity in baseball, even in the twenty-first century. The reasons for this fall between overt prejudice, questionable scientific explanation, and benign neglect. The original ideology that excluded men who were not European-descended Christians is now easily recognizable as garden-variety bigotry. Yet similarly irrational "explanations" for the absence of girls and women from the game are sometimes still believed. Jackie Robinson had "too big" a neck to swing a bat properly. Women don't have *enough* upper body strength, they naturally "throw like girls," and their hips are set too wide to enable them to be fast enough fielders and base runners. The rationales used to exclude immigrant men in the early part of the twentieth century resemble the arguments that were used to exclude African American men and now women. Italians before Joe DiMaggio were also accused of throwing and running in an un-American way.[1] Hispanics, Asians, and Jews have been dismissed at one time or another as too small to play baseball, as have women. Contradictory justifications have been used to exclude men by race: blacks are too "big" for baseball, Jews are too small. The rhetoric has entertained unjustifiable generalizations while casting the few who succeed as exceptions: Joe DiMaggio was "surprisingly" good, even though he was Italian. So was Roy Campanella, who was small, like an Italian, *and* built like a wrestler, thick-necked, like an African American. (Campy had an African American mother and an Italian father, a double blessing for a professional baseball player in the 1950s.) The American public has also accepted arguments based upon exceptionalism to justify letting a few undeniably gifted members of racial minorities play baseball: Joe DiMaggio wasn't really like those other Italians because he didn't use grease on his hair and he enjoyed eating Chinese food; Hank Greenberg was an exceptional

Jew because he was as tall and strong as a gentile and Jews admired him all the more for his size; lighter skinned Cubans were not regarded as "colored" because they spoke Spanish, which could be used to establish their European rather than African pedigree.[2] This led some African American ballplayers to attempt to "pass" as European-descended Cubans. Nowadays most people would agree about the absurdity of these racialized rationalizations for exclusion and inclusion. However, few would regard the "reasons" for excluding women as equally absurd.

The arguments used to exclude men of racial minorities resemble arguments used to exclude women not only in their self-contradictory irrationality but because racial stereotypes usually involve a sexual dimension. The claim that a man is not acceptable by virtue of his race has historically implied that he isn't sufficiently manly.[3] Male victims of racial bigotry have been called "boys" or labeled sexual predators and savages, not self-controlled the way a rational man should be. When baseball insists that it is a manly game, its definition of manhood is Euro-American and middle class. The first ballplayers of any racial or religious minority were believed to be exceptional men for their ethnic groups. They took abuse in a "manly" way, the way a college fraternity pledge proves his manliness by taking physical and psychological abuse. When they survive the initiation and are talented and tough enough, baseball and America congratulates itself on its open-mindedness. But there is evidence that baseball is still overwhelmingly a game that excludes American-born men who are not white, whether African Americans, Hispanics, or Asian Americans. There are still disproportionately few Jewish major leaguers. As in the early twentieth century, when baseball found it more acceptable to be Cuban than African American, in the twenty-first century, the majority of darker-complexioned men who play professional baseball were born outside the United States. Perhaps understanding the dynamics that keep American men of color away from the game will enhance understanding of how women's exclusion is maintained and justified.

Outsourcing Baseball

The most simplistic explanation for women's exclusion from professional baseball goes something like, "There's no money in it. Nobody will pay to see women play baseball." The insistence on the unmarketability of women's athletic performance may disguise a cultural resistance to encouraging women to become the sort of athletes people will pay to see. Jackie Robinson's entrance into the most lucrative level of baseball signaled a weakening of the power of racism in American society. African American men can now become wealthy by excelling in any number of sports. But baseball has a persistent racial imbalance. While there was a sharp and steady increase in the number of African Americans playing major league baseball during the three decades immediately following Jackie Robinson's debut with the Dodgers, the trend peaked between 1975 and 1980 and then declined just as dramatically during the next two and a half decades. Now there are fewer African American professional baseball players than there are players from Latin America. In 1975, 25 percent of major league players were African American. In 1980, 19 percent of starters were African American and 10 percent were born in Latin America. In actual numbers, that was just over three African American players per team, and just under 1.5 Latin American players per team. Two decades later, in 2000, only 13 percent of major leaguers were African American, but 21 percent were Latin-born.[4]

Baseball as a business wants to maximize profitability and popularity, but baseball as a cultural icon seems unwilling to make itself inclusive enough to accomplish its goals. It is losing its fan base relative to football and basketball. Sociologist Alan M. Klein thinks MLB's biggest "marketing failure and cultural oversight" has been the loss of the African American community, a loss that is even more dramatic given the tremendous increases in the fan and player base for the NBA and NFL. The proportion of baseball's African American fans reached a low of 4.8 percent during the 1995–96 season.[5] Klein's study is focused on baseball's effort to increase its viability and profitability through an international base: globalization. He notes almost as an aside before addressing the intricacies of MLB's relationship with organized baseball in Latin America, Asia, South Africa, and Europe, "Major League Baseball, it can be argued, never really overcame its racial problems."[6] But he doesn't focus directly on race or racism. Rather, Klein addresses baseball's "problem" in economic terms, with reference to everything from the price of admission to a ballpark to the faster ascent to wealth and fame promised by professional basketball and football. Klein presents racial exclusion as a by-product of economic neglect rather than the result of a perhaps unconscious desire to keep the national game dominated by whites. Another perspective, however, suggests that prejudice, whether about race or sex, operates somewhat independently from pure economics. Exploring the globalization of baseball labor may shed light on underlying forces that maintain continued dominance of the game by white men.

Historian Adrian Burgos Jr. establishes in *Playing America's Game: Baseball, Latinos, and the Color Line* that Latin American men have been playing baseball in the United States (as have women) and in their home countries since the game's inception. Also like women in the United States, their ongoing presence in the game is unacknowledged, so the current preponderance of Latin American professional baseball players seems like a new phenomenon. Burgos argues that players who were sufficiently light-skinned to be credibly "Castillian" or "Spanish" were used by American baseball to expand the pool of available players without bringing African Americans into the professional game. While their presence in professional baseball was clearly profitable to owners and contributed to baseball's overall growth, white ballplayers' resistance to the Latin Americans' presence reveals a dimension that goes beyond economics. "Player productivity mattered little when it came to racial identification and job security. . . . The protests of white players demonstrated that when they retreated behind the wall of white privilege, merit and accomplishment mattered less than their claims of whiteness."[7]

Economics does play a huge role in the recruitment of Latin American baseball talent, however. Dominican and Salvadoran boys, often underage, uneducated, and the victims of contractual fraud, are paid a small salary to attend baseball "academies" and then abandoned if they are injured or don't pan out as major leaguers. The owners of professional baseball in the United States have sought talent in Latin America since the time when professional baseball players formed their first labor organization in 1885. But the profit motive and the ability to hire the best talent as inexpensively as possible are difficult to distinguish from racial considerations. Poverty and lack of education facilitate economic exploitation, and do not necessarily imply racial discrimination. The fact that poverty itself is often racialized, though, makes it difficult to ignore the possibility of a racist dimension in economic exploitation.[8]

The most recent incarnation of the battle between professional baseball labor and management was the institution of the major league draft and a system of labor market regulations that went into effect in 1965. The changes seem to be driven by pure economics, but they also disguise racial biases. Hidden racial biases in turn provide insight about how sexual prejudice is disguised as "economic reality." Before 1965, any professional team was free to contract with any high school player identified by their scouts. The 1965 player draft was an attempt to regulate the advantages in acquiring new players enjoyed by the richest teams; the draft ensures that the teams with the most money to invest in scouting and developing new players will not be able to dominate the hiring process entirely. Instead of individual teams contracting with individual players, all major league franchises must pick from a pool of prospects in the United States, in reverse order from their previous year's record—in other words, the least successful teams pick first. This is supposed to create more balance in the talent on each team, which makes for more competitive leagues, more compelling play, more fans, and more money for the sport as a whole. While this created some parity among professional baseball teams, it also meant that teams whose scouts had identified promising players at a very young age would no longer be able to reap the rewards of their efforts. A team with a lower finish the previous season would have a better chance of drafting the player no matter who first noticed him. In addition, if a high school player elected to attend college and play baseball there, he would not be eligible to be drafted until he was twenty-one years old.

Instituting these new rules effectively terminated the economics of the scouting system in professional baseball.[9] After the establishment of the draft, teams shifted large portions of their budgets for scouting and player development to Latin America, whose players aren't part of the draft pool; teams don't have to wait their turn to propose a contract. Most teams established more than one baseball academy throughout Latin America, resulting in a situation where "there's not a kid in the Caribbean who reaches his fourteenth birthday without being seen by the major-league teams."[10]

The major league draft does not apply outside of the U.S. because of professional baseball's own rules about player acquisition. Japan and Korea are sufficiently powerful nations to enforce their own regulations about how Americans may acquire their native baseball talent. Latin American countries allow thousands of boys desperate to escape poverty through American baseball to be treated as "free agents," signed however they can be by MLB. Obviously most of the young players are not talented enough or do not receive sufficiently high-level instruction to make it to the big leagues, and the numbers that can be brought to the United States as minor leaguers are limited by the numbers of visas granted by the U.S. government. Some commentators have suggested that a worldwide major league draft would put an end to the vulnerability and the abuses suffered by the young free agents. Burgos argues that the treatment of Latin American prospects goes beyond simple economics and reflects MLB's cultural biases: "Once they instituted an amateur draft in 1965, the major leagues effectively denied Latinos born outside of North America the same economic benefits and legal protections afforded players defined as draft eligible. Instead, the minimum eligible age for foreign-born Latinos to sign as undrafted amateur free agents was set at sixteen. These standards served as an initial marker of Latino difference within organized baseball; Latinos entered in a more vulnerable position not just because of their cultural difference but also due to the system created by organized baseball."[11]

Attorneys Arturo Marcano Guevara and David Fidler call the behavior of MLB toward their Latin American prospects "rapacious" child labor abuse. "Major league teams see these young children as commodities to appropriate (bring into academies and keep them away from other teams) and exploit (train them as cheaply as possible for maximum gain)."[12] If colonialism is the exploitation of people of "different" races for the profit of a powerful nation, then baseball colonialism accurately describes the relationship between MLB and the Latin American labor market. Marcano and Fidler preface their powerful story about Major League Baseball's abuse of young Latin American ballplayers with the warning that "understanding 'the globalization of baseball' requires seeing Major League Baseball as a business. The moniker 'national pastime' obscures the degree to which baseball has from its earliest days been a business designed to make money."[13] Latin American boys are regarded by MLB as so available and dispensable that they can be signed in droves to play minor league ball for a fraction of what it would cost to sign an American boy with the legal protections provided him in the United States.[14]

The poverty that makes Latin America an attractive source of inexpensive labor for many American businesses provides the same allure for Major League Baseball. Scouts from the big leagues can sign many young players cheaply, often in violation of their own rules about age restrictions, and then dump the ones who don't work out. Major league teams often pay a finders' fee to *buscones*, or local scouts, in Latin America to find them talent. The *buscones* are not regulated by Major League Baseball teams, and while some individuals may be more honorable than others, the system itself fosters abuse: it creates a stable of very young players, many uneducated, most with no knowledge of English to permit them to negotiate with team owners or even read a contract, and all desperate to escape poverty. The success of a few superstars who make it in the big leagues keeps the dreams of the impoverished youngsters alive, much as "hoop dreams" are nurtured among young African Americans in the nation's inner cities. But the success stories are bait, belying the casualties who never get that far. The wreckage involves not only shattered dreams but bodies destroyed by injuries and lack of proper medical and nutritional attention.

All the "children" in Marcano and Fidler's study of what they consider a minor league chattel system are boys. Baseball's global greed does not extend to girls. While Marcano and Fidler's concern about child labor abuse by baseball is well-founded, girls don't make baseball's radar screen at all. They are invisible to the teams, the scouts, and even the scholars and critics. Why would a Latin

American girl want to play baseball? The odds that a Latin American boy might escape poverty by playing a sport revered throughout his country are slim; for girls they are zero.

Outsourcing the baseball labor market to Latin America reveals the economic realities of the business of baseball, but it also serves to justify the continued exclusion of African American men and to shed light on why women can't break into the game. The system of scouting and sifting through large numbers of Latin Americans has contributed to the relative decline in the number of white U.S.-born professional ballplayers. But it hit African American ballplayers even harder. From 1980 to 2001, the number of African American professional ball-players declined 31 percent, compared to an 8 percent decrease for U.S. whites. The fact that U.S.-born players are now more highly protected, regulated, and expensive for Major League franchises to scout and hire means that they are also more expensive to produce. Without major league scouts turning up in neighborhood leagues or high schools, more effort must be spent attracting their attention. The result has been the privatization of youth baseball, with expensive traveling teams, showcases, and private coaches that are out of the financial reach of many families and are not held accountable to federal civil rights law precisely because they are private. This situation has contributed to the marginalization of poor boys and, of course, all girls.

The development of professional baseball's once intimate farm system into a corporatized global agribusiness reveals the expense of becoming a competitive baseball player. It offers perspective on the declining numbers of African American major league prospects, although the emphasis on economics may distract from any underlying racial bias against American-born men of color. It isn't necessary to accuse baseball of racial or gender prejudice if the sport is institutionally structured in a way that excludes a disproportionate number of American-born prospects who are not white and male. The early-twentieth-century "gentlemen's agreement" to exclude American-born men of color is now secured by economics. No personal responsibility for racial exclusion needs to be taken.

The Domestic Plantation

The absence of African American baseball players at the youth and collegiate level is the key to understanding their declining numbers in professional baseball, since overt prohibitions against African American men playing baseball no longer exist. The question is why the ballplayers who are there don't come to the attention of scouts.

Part of the difficulty in coming to the attention of scouts is actually being *seen* by them. Spotting a baseball player with potential to play at the NCAA Division 1 or professional level takes time. The "baseball body type" is not as clearly defined and easy to notice as a football or basketball body type, although even in those sports there are exceptions to the preference for big men. Here the privatization of the youth game is crucial: these specialized resources are how a player attracts the attention of MLB scouts. The first resource is likely to be a father who introduces his son to the game at a young age and gets involved in his early baseball education, coaching his Little League and youth teams, providing him with private coaching, and enrolling him at baseball camps and on tournament teams. The importance of these tournament teams is their access to college coaches and professional scouts. Since they are privately run teams, they are not required to adhere to civil rights law regarding equal access. They can invite anybody they want to play, frequently a small circle of youngsters known to the coach and his son, and they are very expensive because they involve frequent travel to cities and states that may or may not be nearby.

Access to these teams is limited for poor boys, minorities, and girls. It is difficult for a girl to gain a spot on a baseball tournament team, and there is virtually nothing she can do about it except, perhaps, convince one of her parents to organize and coach her own team of friends. Less affluent boys have similar difficulties, as do boys from economically or racially segregated neighborhoods who are not well-known to the men coaching the tournament teams. Undoubtedly some of those men would have no problem inviting a black or Hispanic or Asian boy to play on their teams. Undoubtedly also, some men *would* have trouble, if not on explicitly racial grounds, then with the excuse that it would be too difficult to integrate the outsider with his son's circle of more affluent friends in the familial environment of a traveling baseball team. The team chemistry would be "wrong." It would require taking "too great a risk." The teams don't exist to include unknown people. They exist to showcase the boys and perhaps to have a little fun playing ball.

This phenomenon has been called the "privatization of Little League baseball" by Ronnie McLellan of the LSU *Reveille*.[15] Baton Rouge parks and recreation sports director Marc Palmer observed, "I put the blame squarely on the parents. They take their kids to those leagues specifically for a purpose—put them in those situations where they want to win, win, win."[16] In Baton Rouge, there are two private baseball leagues that, as Palmer puts it, "snatch up most of the supportive parents in the community. Each league sponsors weekend tournaments that showcase up-and-coming talent, while developing a competitive atmosphere.

. . . Costs of these private leagues may exceed more than $1,000 per player [per season]. The children in the inner city cannot afford it and are left behind unless grant money providing equal programs exists." Such leagues are the invention of parents with athletic ambitions for their children, and, like many social institutions that arose in response to civil rights law, they avoid racial integration, intentionally or unintentionally, by creating a parallel private universe where federal and state civil rights law does not apply. Most working-class parents lack the money and the time to invest in weekend travel and frequent practices. Traveling youth teams are a wealthy white boys' phenomenon. Because they are private, they are immune to racial and gender integration.

The private little leagues feed directly into the college and professional recruiting networks. LSU athletic director and former baseball coach Skip Bertman noted, "Blue-chip recruiting that takes place in high school football and basketball is nearly impossible in baseball because of the game's nature. The mechanics of quality baseball players also take a while to observe. Unlike football and basketball, a coach cannot look at a videotape to judge a player's skills."[17] Instead, major Division 1 college coaches visit "Area Code" tournaments across the nation, which are designed specifically for recruiting. They are set up by professional baseball scouts, and only the best players are invited. However convenient this may be for coaches in the market for ballplayers, it is exclusionary, and it "discovers" self-fulfilling prophesies: the players who are invited are those who have been nurtured and brought along through Little League All-Stars and traveling teams, who have been coached by their fathers, attended skills camps and clinics, and played on the expensive traveling teams—players who are already on the scouts' radars. McLellan explains, "While Area Code Baseball may be a dream for college coaches, the opportunity to compete in such leagues proves difficult for players outside the scouts' scopes. The Area Code organization offers free camps to teach techniques, but tryouts are limited only to invited players. According to the organization's Web site, a player earns an invite with the recommendation of a scout."[18]

Here the arguments for excluding girls can be inferred from the arguments that were used to fight integration of girls into Little League Baseball thirty years earlier. Why waste a coach's time on a girl who can't get a college scholarship and can't go to the pros? Why waste a spot that could go to a talented boy with a future? But not inviting girls to private traveling teams and professionally coached clinics is not the *result* of the girls' lack of future in baseball. It is the *means* by which girls are deprived of a future in baseball. What is immediately at stake for the invited players is one of the 11.7 college scholarships per team that the NCAA allots.

Southern University baseball coach Roger Cador refuses to participate in the Area Code recruiting clinics. Southern University is the historically black university with a world-renowned marching band . . . but not a world-renowned baseball program. His school lacks the financial resources to compete with big-time university baseball programs, so he uses a series of contacts throughout the country to find "raw talents with great heart." Cador doesn't think he is taking risks by avoiding the most visibly celebrated players because to him, "college athletics is more than winning games." To call avoiding the private recruiting showcases "taking risks" is, he believes, a euphemism for racism. He will take both white and black ballplayers if they fit the profile he is looking for. "The risk thing is what people use when they don't want to give people an opportunity. . . . We're not going to be racist like some of those people and deny the kids opportunity. People will never make me believe there's not racism that plays a factor in why there haven't been more African Americans [in college baseball]. They will not take them because of the color of their skin."[19]

The issue of racial exclusion from the structure of amateur youth baseball is avoided by the privatization of the most competitive leagues and professionally sanctioned coaching opportunities, which limits access. Gender segregation is ensured by the same mechanism. Progressing through the ranks of baseball from T-ball to the major league draft requires membership in a tightly controlled old boys' club. Filial relationships thoroughly dominate the infrastructure of baseball. This institutionally sanctioned patriarchy goes beyond a father picking up a ball and a glove and inviting his son to play catch. That is a romanticized piece of the picture, sure enough, but it does not describe the closely guarded core of American youth baseball. Little League baseball, youth league baseball, and traveling team baseball prior to high school are dominated by the fathers whose sons play. While a few very talented boys may be recognized without their fathers' being coaches, the vast majority of boys who comprise the all-star teams and the expensive traveling teams that access nearly year-round experience playing baseball are there because their fathers introduced them to the game and coached the teams that enabled them to learn the finer nuances of the game. They are given coveted infield positions and allowed to play through slumps and learning curves. Boys without that sort of support, who are benched when they don't perform well and lack individual coaching, are also more likely to become discouraged and drop out when the going gets rough, the competition gets keen, and they're abandoned in the dugout rather than encouraged to work through difficulty. As for girls sticking to it in those discouraging and often humiliating conditions? Forget it.

Like any other business handed down from generation to generation, baseball skills and the love of the game passed from fathers to sons provide a foot in the door for those who want to pursue the game professionally. The baseball family names of major league fathers, sons, and brothers include Aaron, Alomar, Alou, Bonds, Boone, Brett, Clemens, DiMaggio, Giambi, Griffey, Gwynn, Krukow, Niekro, Ripkin, Sherry, and Torre.[20] Certainly the players who have made it to the pros have the talent to be there. But the frantic pursuit of that goal by thousands of men and boys who *don't* have what it takes to be professional baseball players has created a corrupt little club that keeps many other young ballplayers, no matter how talented, in their place: out.

There is nothing wrong with generations in a family passing along their love and expertise of any craft or profession. It's heartwarming, a throwback to an era when professions were learned that way and where knowledge was often strengthened as it was passed down through a family. But this is not simply learning an honorable trade from your old man. The closed baseball clubhouse teaches young men important lessons about who reaps the enormous rewards available to professional baseball players in our era. In an age of heightened intensity in the politics of institutionalized athletic competition, a family member in the game gives a tremendous political advantage. That's not necessarily corrupt. It's not exactly democratic, but it's not inherently corrupt. It does, however, court exclusion and provide a lesson in the unfairness of access to the expertise required to play baseball from Little League to the major leagues. The politics of Little League all-star selection mirror the politics of professional baseball selection. There are plenty of good ballplayers who don't make the cut, not because they're not as good as the ballplayers who do but because they lack membership in the fraternity, on whatever level they may be playing. Needless to say, the fraternity is all male. The fact that so many of the baseball families named above are African American does not change the systematic exclusion of the average black kid who likes baseball but finds everything in his world pushing him into basketball or football. The existence of a fraternity is exclusionary by definition. The doors to baseball are closely guarded, and the fact that a few American men of color have gained access does not change the nature of the club. It merely masks its exclusionary politics. In an age when girls follow their fathers into law, medicine, business, the military, professional basketball, and boxing, they are blocked from following their fathers onto even a Little League diamond.

Same Old Ball Game

Major League Baseball claims to be working to correct its recurring racial imbalance. Baseball's focus on the Caribbean labor pool makes financial "sense." It does not appear overtly racist since it grants entry to a racialized minority, most of whom would have been excluded in the Jim Crow era. Baseball's reliance on private showcases and camps to find future talent appears efficient, cost-effective, and scientific: so many eager prospects, so few slots in the pros. Coaches need a way to sift through the talent and they know what they're looking for with their lists of the five baseball "tools."[21] In an age where so many things are corporatized, professionalized, and specialized, risks must be minimized because mistakes can cost a team millions of dollars. Excluding players who don't make it onto the professional radar screens is the price to pay for the reliability of a proven system. It's not willful prejudice but an inevitable by-product of a scientific approach.

Still, some facts are difficult to ignore. One is the tiny number of African American college baseball players, and the fact that they continue to be subjected to racist abuse when they step onto a baseball diamond. Nine percent of Major League baseball players are African American. But only 4.5 percent of college players are. The *Los Angeles Times* reported, "Of 11 Division 1 baseball programs in Southern California, there are only 10 African Americans. That amounts to less than one per team with six teams, including former national champion USC, having no African Americans at all."[22] This is in sharp contrast to college basketball, in which 42 percent of the players are African American, and college football, where 32 percent of the players are African American. Basketball and football are overrepresented in relation to the national percentage of African Americans in the United States, and baseball is profoundly underrepresented.

Bill Plaschke of the *Los Angeles Times* interviewed Bobby Andrews, the centerfielder on the 2005 Cal State Fullerton baseball team. Andrews is the only African American player on the Fullerton team, where, in the twenty-first century, he must put up with racial taunts from the bleachers. This is not the Deep South in the 1950s; it's Southern California, with its reputation for open-mindedness toward diversity. "I try not to think about it, I just try to play baseball," Andrews said. "But it's hard not to notice . . . There's not many of us at any level of the sport." Plaschke notes, "The reason Andrews plays is the reason that many African Americans do not play. He grew up in a household where baseball was the passion. He grew up in a family that could afford his spot on traveling teams. He grew up thinking baseball was cool."[23] His buddies in the neighborhood chose basketball and football. Cal State Fullerton coach George Horton explains the lack of African Americans: "First, it's the socio-economic situation of some of these kids, it's just easier and cheaper to play basketball and football . . . Then, there's the major issue with scholarships." Baseball and softball must give equivalent numbers of scholarships because of Title IX. Because of the burden of football and men's basketball, which offer "countless full rides," the NCAA has mandated that a baseball team can only give 11.7 full rides while the softball team can give 13.

Not only are few baseball and softball scholarships available, but there are few scholarships in relation to the size of the team roster. Division 1 baseball rosters are now limited to fewer than thirty players, and softball, twenty players. If there aren't that many scholarships available, the NCAA dictates that they be divided up between players. The current rule is that each player must get at least 25 percent of a full scholarship. Horton continues, "You do the math . . . We can't give out full rides, kids can get a lot more money elsewhere so what do they do?"[24] That is, a young athlete who needs a scholarship to be able to attend college or who wants to use college as his path to professional sports will focus his energy on the sport that can pay his way. If African Americans on average are more financially disadvantaged than European Americans, they will be more likely to choose a scholarship sport from an early age. The players who pursue baseball in college are more likely to be able to afford college (they have already paid for the traveling teams and private coaching that allowed them to reach this level) without a full athletic scholarship. In the United States, playing at the elite levels of baseball is inaccessible for poor boys (and girls), and, to the extent that African Americans are more likely to have fewer economic resources than European Americans, they will have a more difficult time gaining access to the most competitive levels of the sport. This holds true for poor girls and softball, as well as all girls and baseball.

Beyond the math: in April 2005, Larry Cochell, the University of Oklahoma baseball coach, resigned for using the "N" word during an off-camera interview. Plaschke observes, "This wasn't a rookie backwater boss, but a man who had won a national championship in 1994. The most dangerous thing about that word was that it was spoken by an educator who was clearly comfortable using it."[25] Also beyond the math: Quinn Stewart, LSU's lone black baseball player, a left fielder, is subjected to taunts when his team plays the University of Ala-bama: "The crowd got into him at the start singing the 'Sanford and Son' theme song as he took the field for the first time. He shut them up a bit in the second inning as he started dancing to the music. 'I've always been pretty much the only black guy on my team,' he said as he glanced at the stand and at the white expanse of fans in the bleachers."[26] Reporter Ronnie McLellan notes, "Stewart is an anomaly in baseball. He is a black man playing what has become a nearly all-white game, college baseball . . . His singular status on LSU's forty-three-man roster says a lot about a sport that once boasted heroes like Willie Mays and Jackie Robinson."[27] Stewart became interested in baseball while growing up in a nearly all-white neighborhood in Southern California. His family moved to Dallas when his father, a career naval officer, was reassigned there. Stewart's love of baseball survived the move, but friends in his new, predominantly black neighborhood would ask, "Why are you playing baseball? Black people don't play baseball."[28]

There are probably ways to explain the absence of African Americans from baseball as being due to causes other than racism, just as there are ways to explain the exclusion of girls and women that appear rational. The most obvious explanations are the science of risk management (the expense of making a mistake on a multimillion-dollar investment, which is what a professional contract offer to an eighteen-year-old prospect is) and individual choice (African Americans prefer basketball and football). One way this thought has been expressed is that African Americans "prefer" faster games: baseball is too slow for them. This last "explanation" is very risky. The next thought in that sequence is that African Americans are physiologically "built" for basketball and football . . . just as women are "built" for softball. These rationales for the absence of women and African American men from baseball are close to flat-out prejudice.

David Ogden and Randall A. Rose, of the University of Nebraska at Omaha, look at institutional structures apart from baseball itself in order to explain the absence of African American baseball players.[29] They too note the dramatic decline in African American participation in baseball, from youth ball to college ball to professional ball. In addition to declining numbers of African Americans on the field, Ogden and Rose note the absence of African American faces in the grandstands of major league baseball and the absence of African American baseball stars in advertising. Compare baseball stars on television commercials to basketball and football celebrities, where the faces representing American corporations, from athletic shoes and hearty soups to sports drinks and soft drinks, are practically expected to be African American. If African Americans are in attendance at baseball games, few of them find their way onto the big-screen crowd shots.[30]

There is probably no conspiracy to keep African Americans out of the game. There is probably no conspiracy to keep Hispanics and Asian Americans out of the game either, but their numbers are very small when compared to both European American major leaguers and ballplayers born in Japan, Korea, and Latin America.[31] Major League Baseball does not keep statistics on the racial makeup of its teams any more than Little League Baseball keeps statistics on the number of girls playing Little League. But people quickly learn where they're not wanted.

Still No Girls Allowed

Is what keeps girls out of the game similar to what keeps out African Americans? It's close. It's the parallel that has always linked racism and sexism: the same problem with different victims. Racism is about one race thinking they're better than another and having the economic, political, and social power to enforce their unwarranted sense of superiority; sexism is about one gender believing they are in some way better than another. The differences between male and female bodies do not translate into innate or systematic superiority, or inability to do certain things other than the purely physiological. Baseball talent is not purely physiological. Baseball requires, among other skills, strength to throw long distances and pure speed. Hitting a home run is a beautiful aspect of the game but not required for the game to be played well. Nor is tremendous muscle mass and sheer size a guarantee of the ability to hit a home run, although ballplayers have in recent times availed themselves of medical technology to artificially manipulate their size for precisely that end.[32] But if the men think they can hit more home runs by taking artificial substances, women could accomplish that too. Elite women athletes are no more immune to the temptation to alter their bodies in the name of their sport than are elite male athletes. The consequences of such alteration crosses gender lines: both sexes run the risk of early death, heart disease, sexual dysfunction, and infertility, among other undesirable side effects.

Although under suspicion of steroid abuse himself, slugger Barry Bonds was absolutely correct when he said that muscle-enhancing substances cannot provide a ballplayer with quick wrists or the ability to see the ball required to hit a home run.[33] Pure baseball more importantly requires agility, the ability to think on one's feet, and a head for the game, none of which have been proven to reside in any specific type of person, wide-necked, wide-hipped, or otherwise. Using biological or sociopsychological rationalizations to exclude women from baseball makes no more sense than using biological or sociopsychological rationalizations to exclude men from baseball based on race.

Journalist Art Spander, in an article headlined "Fans Still Sing 'Take Me Out to the Ball Game,'" makes light of the problems baseball has managed to survive:

"Baseball will get past BALCO, the way it got past the Black Sox scandal, the way it got past the strike of '94. Our winter of discontent certainly will grow into a spring of anticipation . . . Baseball made it through world wars, corked bats, racism, spitballs and fixes. Baseball then will make it through steroids. Guaranteed."[34] Spander doesn't recognize that baseball will only survive by making accommodations to history, progress, and the need for inclusion. Too much exclusion will kill off anything, even baseball. Racism and sexism are problems of a different order than spitballs and corked bats. Baseball "made it through" the second world war by temporarily allowing women to play. It "made it through" the civil rights movement by temporarily encouraging African American men to play. "Making it through" should mean getting rid of discrimination, not surviving despite it.

Albert Goodwill Spalding's 1911 vision of baseball as a nationalistic sport controlled by white American men has proven resilient. The contemporary exclusion of girls and women and the marginalization or exploitation of men of color mirrors Spalding's description of an international baseball empire. Major League Baseball has demonstrated neither the willingness nor ability to move beyond its history of entitlement for the few, and a century after *America's National Game* was written, half of the nation is still discouraged from playing the game on any level. Perhaps it is time to acknowledge that a new millennium has arrived.

What Does Equality Look Like?

The Underground

Not much has changed during the past century of women's baseball. A handful of girls play with boys; a few stand out and are noticed by the media for a while. Then they disappear. The Colorado Silver Bullets, a women's professional team that survived from 1994 to 1997, was one recent incarnation of an elite American women's baseball team. But a more careful look reveals the existence of an underground. Girls' and women's teams play each other and occasionally men's minor league teams and semiprofessional teams. You have to look hard to find them. You won't find them in the sports pages of the major newspapers or covered by the evening news or ESPN as a regular feature. Perhaps women's baseball organizations have learned, after a century and a half of being beaten and battered into oblivion, to keep a low profile. These baseball players don't get paid, they don't get noticed, and the institutions that guard the entrances to American baseball are still actively staving them off. Girls and women play locally in a multitude of small leagues of their own in the Northeast, the West Coast, the upper Midwest, and Florida. There are also several American and Canadian associations or consortiums that organize tournaments and publicize events, although there is no formal administrative body. The American Women's Baseball Federation, the Women's Baseball League, the North American Women's Baseball League, and various regional baseball leagues make it their business to keep women's baseball in the United States and Canada alive. USA Baseball sponsors the women's national team, which has played in an international Women's World Cup Tournament every two years in recent years. There are also women's baseball leagues in Canada, Australia, Japan, Korea, China, Taiwan, Hong Kong, India, and Cuba.[1] The long-term goals for the Americans involved in women's baseball are an Olympic women's baseball team, annual international competitions, and institutional growth of girls' baseball in the United States.

The ages of the women who play competitive baseball in the United States range from the late teens to thirties and even forties, just like men who play professionally. Some have played on teams with boys in high school, in youth leagues, and rarely as the only girl on traveling teams. Little League Baseball, Inc., does not keep data on how many of its baseball players are girls, but there are no all-girl Little League teams. Nor are there all-girl traveling teams anywhere in the United States. The visibility accorded to the boys' traveling baseball circuit with showcases and Area Code tournaments that bring out the college and pro scouts are off limits to girls. But there is no crying in baseball, and if the baseball establishment continues to have its way, no girls, either. Some girls stick with baseball for as long as they can in Little League and youth league ball, and then in high school switch to softball with an eye toward a college scholarship. Some leave boys' youth and high school baseball for other college sports entirely. One former high school baseball player is now a javelin thrower at her Division III college, and another is now a collegiate golfer. The appeal of those two substitute sports can be readily understood: throwing something as far as you can, and hitting a little white ball with a stick into a big green field are undisguised aspects of baseball. But it is heartbreakingly obvious that these two athletes are making the best of the fact that they have been driven out of their sport of choice.

The girls and women who comprise this baseball underground are experienced and talented ballplayers. They have survived in their sport against stiff odds. Former baseball players, both men and women, are the administrators of this underground organization. Most have the same ideas about why women's baseball has had to be revived over and over again in the United States while amateur women's baseball leagues flourish with year-round programs in Japan, Cuba, Australia, Canada, and China. The consensus about this bizarre reversal is that American men don't want women to play baseball, and Major League Baseball doesn't help the effort with either financing or publicity. Pretty simple, pretty straightforward.

The biennial moment that brings American ballplayers and their supporters together is the formation of a national team to compete against teams from Japan, Cuba, Korea, China, Canada, Australia, and India in a tournament that has been held every two years since 1994. The international organization overseeing the tournament is the International Baseball Federation. The American administrative unit is USA Baseball, the same outfit that fielded the American men's team in spring 2006 to enormous fanfare. The big controversy of that tournament was that Cuba was allowed to play for the first time. USA Baseball sponsors a women's team under its auspices only because it is legally required to do so by the *international* organization's bylaws. If it were up to the American baseball establishment, there would be no American women's team. Of all the teams who compete in the women's baseball World Cup competition, the American team struggles with the most paltry infrastructure. Canada supports more baseball leagues for girls at all levels than the United States. In Australia, women's baseball leagues developed right alongside men's, and the consequence is that women play at a very competitive level there. The Cuban women play all year, and Japan is the perennial powerhouse, with twenty college women's baseball teams, two hundred high school teams, and an effective feeder system in the form of countless recreational youth leagues. The Japanese national team is deep, with forty to fifty players who practice together five days a week all year long. How is it that those traditionally patriarchal societies, one steeped in a tradition of Latin machismo, the other of samurai warriors, are unthreatened by women's baseball?

The American women's team has done well enough, given that its capacity to put together an effective playing unit is, as one veteran player of the All American Girls' Professional Baseball League put it, "mission impossible." The major obstacles to be surmounted fall into two categories: development and recruitment. Open tryouts must be publicized nationally, with no assistance from Major League Baseball and minimal financial help from USA Baseball, to attract as many prospects as possible. The thirty best players are identified at three open regional tryouts held in 2006 in Arizona, Florida, and New Jersey, winnowed down to eighteen players at a second national invitational tryout, and molded into a team that can compete with the best women players in the world, all in one month. This happens with no financial backing whatsoever from any professional men's baseball organization. To put this task in perspective, imagine a team of male baseball players finding each other, coaches, and sufficient funding to enable them to form a team to bring to international competition. They must accomplish this in the absence of Little League, Babe Ruth and Pony League, and collegiate baseball, and without any professional baseball whatsoever: no minor leagues and no major leagues. It sounds like a game on reality TV, with the prize at the end of the elaborate challenge being not money but a trip to a foreign country to play baseball for a week. The fact that American women ballplayers have brought a high quality of play and had reasonable success at the international tournament is testimony to their grit and tenacity.

American boys who reach this level of competition in baseball are invited to expense-paid tryouts, often with their families' travel and lodging included. Major League Baseball's only contribution to international women's baseball has been to forbid the women to use the title "Women's World Series" for their tournament. Paradoxically, the women's tournament really *is* a world competition, compared to the American men's professional World Series or the College World Series.

Meager finances aside, the team must identify players and build a competitive team on extremely short notice in the absence of a reliable feeder system. How can girls be encouraged to take a chance on playing baseball during their crucial developmental years between twelve and eighteen when there is no college baseball, no Olympic team, and virtually nothing to encourage them to take a chance on this sport except pure love of the game? Most people involved in women's baseball agree that girls can and should play Little League baseball with boys, and be welcomed to play in Little League, at least up to age twelve. After that, there should be girls' baseball leagues developed, to give girl Little Leaguers a place to continue to develop into high school and college players. If they have the size, talent, and desire, they should be able to play with boys in high school or college. If they aren't big enough to compete with the older boys and young men, they shouldn't be expected to: they should be able to play with ballplayers of their own size and skill level. If they can't play on a professional level or sufficient public interest to support women's professional baseball is lacking, Jim Glennie, president of the American Women's Baseball Federation says, "So what? Why can't they play ball anyway?"[2] Why does the possibility of turning pro have to determine what youth and amateur sports are available to anybody in the United

States? How can the American public allow Canada, Australia, Japan, and Cuba to outdo them in their support of girls' and women's baseball?

Coach Hideki Yamaguchi of the Japan women's baseball team asked Glennie why American girls play softball when "the ball doesn't even fit their hand." Glennie answered, "American men really don't want girls playing baseball." Glennie believes that women's baseball in the United States will not succeed without a major goal on which young girls can set their sights. He hopes for a women's Olympic baseball team. Girls play softball because there is the possibility that they can play at the collegiate level. Until recently, Olympic softball was also a possibility. Boys play baseball because they dream of one day being like their big league heroes. There is no baseball dream for little girls. The message that there is no future in baseball for girls is cruel, a deprivation of passion and potential. Glennie says, "Baseball is in your soul. It doesn't matter if you're a girl or a boy." And that soul craves a goal.

Some suggest that the baselines should be shortened to 80 feet, with the pitcher's rubber 55 feet from home plate. That would speed up the game, advocates argue. But most people interested in advancing the women's game believe that shrinking the infield would undermine progress. It would be admitting that girls can't play the game as it is, once again using a smaller field to signify women's "weakness." It would also make it nearly impossible to find baseball fields for girls to use as they develop their skills. Keeping the same field dimensions enables girls and women's leagues to use the fields already in existence and used by boys and men. Today's women athletes are more than capable of running 90 feet and throwing the ball major league distances if they trained for those dimensions throughout their lives. Besides, the baseball that people love is played on a field with 90–foot base paths and 60 feet, 6 inches between the pitcher and batter. Meddling with those dimensions might anger the baseball gods.

Baseball Girls

A handful of the old veterans of the All American Girls' Professional Baseball League were in attendance at the Team USA tryouts in Scottsdale, Arizona, on June 17 and 18, 2006. They were invited to watch approximately fifty girls, ages sixteen to thirty-five, try out for the team and give feedback to Julie Croteau, the coach who would be picking the traveling team. Two other tryouts, one in Florida and one in New Jersey, were held the same weekend. Over one hundred young women attended the three tryouts. The final thirty were invited to Scottsdale where the team of eighteen players to play in the Women's World Cup tournament in Taipei would be selected.

Shirley Burkovich played on the Muskegon Lassies and the Rockford Peaches from 1949 to 1951.[3] She had a coveted speaking part at the end of the movie *A League of Their Own*, posing in the final scene in Cooperstown with Geena Davis, Madonna, and Rosie O'Donnell as one of the Rockford Peaches. Shirley was born in Pittsburg, and raised in Swissvale, Pennsylvania, and grew up in the 1940s playing baseball with boys. She said, "Like most girls in my era, we played with boys. Baseball in vacant lots and in the alleys. No organization, no Little League. Not even for the boys. But for the girls, nothing. Even at school, if we wanted to play basketball in the gym, we had to play at lunchtime when the boys weren't using it." In 1949, an ad in a newspaper for a girls' professional team caught her brother's eye. Shirley, who was a sixteen-year-old high school student at the time, didn't think it was a possibility, but her brother took a day off work and told her, "Come on. We'll just go sit in the stands and watch." They went, sat in the stands, and her brother urged her to go down to the field and try out, assuring her, "You can play as good as those girls." Shirley went down, and somebody threw her a glove and asked, "What position do you play?" She replied, "What position do you have?" Playing with her brother and his friends, she had taken whatever position the boys didn't want. She always got last choice and learned to play every position. The tryout took three or four days. "There were lots and lots of girls," she remembered. In a couple of weeks she received a telegram to report to spring training in West Baden, Indiana. After convincing her mother and the high school administration to allow her to complete the year's schoolwork by mail, Shirley joined the team and became a professional baseball player. I asked her if it was hard to leave her family for the first time at such a young age, and Shirley was unequivocal: "Was that hard? For me? No! I got a uniform. I got a glove, shoes! For me, it was a dream come true. When I joined the League, that was my career. I didn't even think of anything else. I was sixteen. I thought I had another twenty years. I started out at $55 a week. I ended up making $75 dollars a week."

But after a couple of years, it became clear to Shirley that the league wasn't going to last. Teams were moving around, not making enough money in the cities. Attendance was declining by 1951. "I just had to make a decision. I knew the league wasn't lasting, and I knew I was going to eventually have to get a job. That League never should have folded. But anyway it did. You move on." She took a job with the phone company for $42 dollars a week, a pay cut of nearly 50 percent and no more baseball.

I asked her what it would take to get American girls to play baseball in sufficient numbers, and she responded, "We need to start these girls out not at this age [sixteen to thirty-five, the women who were trying out for Team USA] but like the boys do, and then we'll have girls who can play. When we have a girls' Little League and bring these girls up through the ranks, bring them up like the boys do, and condition them to this position, then we'll have [women's baseball].

"I don't know what it is [why women don't play more baseball]. . . . whether [men are] intimidated by the women being as good as some men. In baseball, I would say that younger girls could compete with boys. When they get to that level when boys start to mature and get stronger, that's when the girls need their own league. Then they can compete on their own level and not have to worry about competing against a man. Major League Baseball is not a big help to us. They more support women's softball."

Karen Violetta Kunkel was a catcher and utility player during the early 1950s for the Grand Rapids Chicks of the All American Girls' Professional Baseball League. She later became athletic director at Northern Michigan State University and director of the United States Olympic Education Center. She was the technical advisor to *A League of Their Own*. Like Burkovich, Kunkel was a young woman who needed to make a living. She was a freshman at Michigan State University when she was approached by a coach to try out for a women's professional baseball team. She was trying to work her way through college by playing professional basketball with a Texas team, a difficult commute from Lansing, Michigan. "I was a freshman at Michigan State University, and I was recruited by a coach who happened to be on campus for men's sports. He saw me, and said he scouted for women's pro baseball teams, and he asked 'Would you be interested?' And I needed a way to work my way through college. I'm a poor girl. I had a contract with the Texas Cowgirls basketball team that used to travel all over the country. But that was in the wintertime, and it was hard to go on tour and go to school. I had to get work. I had an opportunity to go for the tryouts for the All Americans, and I made it. That was summer, that was easier [than playing winter basketball on the road], and it was good money. It was near the end of the league, and when the league split up and went on tour in '54, I didn't want to do that."

Like Burkovich, Kunkel had to give up baseball to make a living. She didn't question the alternatives. "So many of us, we played, we did it, left it and that was it, went on with life. Never gave it a single thought. My husband and I were married two years before he found out that I was catcher and he had come down to watch ball games. We had never talked about it."

I asked Kunkel about the tryouts for Team USA 2006, and she responded, "This is almost 'mission impossible' here. We've been struggling to get a better feeder system and to get more playing time. I was in Japan watching the Japanese system, and they're awesome. We have players in this country, but we've just got to find the right combinations. They have to play together so they know each other. Outfielders, for example, have to know how far that person that they're playing next to can run. What they can and can't handle and when they have to try to take over. Just knowing how each one handles her position. That's hard to come by: you have to play together for a long time. In Japan, they do that five days a week, twelve months out of the year. Their national team is forty to fifty players, twelve years old up to thirty-five-year-olds, mentors. In this country, baseball is a male game. Simple as that."

Kunkel believes that girls will play baseball in the United States, but it will take girls playing with boys when they're young and in their own leagues when they reach adolescence. Some young women will have to continue to play baseball with men and incorporate what they learn into their own skills as ballplayers. Gradually, she believes, women will play baseball in America. "A lot of girls have to have a lot of courage to go out and play on a boys' team. That's the only way right now, because there is no real volume of girls coming up from Little League. They say women shouldn't play with men. Well, take Annika Sorenstam or Michelle Wie. They went and played with the men because the men play it differently. Whatever the game is, the men have different strengths and speeds. You learn from them how they approach certain situations. You take that back and you've raised your game. Girls have to play Little League and be readily acceptable in Little League as an option rather than softball. That's all. It's simple. There's no reason why a woman can't throw a baseball. They [critics] always bring up 'the shoulder situation' and 'the shoulder muscles' and so forth. Aw, come on! You get on a weight program. It's just so totally absurd. And they say women can't play baseball because it's too strenuous. It's certainly a whole lot easier to catch a small ball in a regular-size glove than catch a bigger ball in a regular-size glove. It's a whole lot easier when you can get your hand around a baseball compared to getting your hand around a softball."

Kunkel said, "It just takes patience, education, understanding the law. Being politically astute and working through the system. You can cry and whine and scream, but that's not going to get the job done. Patience. Handle the rejection, find another way. Sometimes you have to be tough. Some men don't want women to play. But the only problem is that our baseball Hall of Fame is the National Baseball Hall of Fame. It's not the National Men's Hall of Fame nor the National Major League Baseball Hall of Fame. We just unveiled a statue there. It's absolutely gorgeous. It's of a woman in a skirt and batting. And they

Ball players from AAGBL at 2006 Team USA trials, Scottsdale, Arizona (courtesy of the author)

Lilly Jacobson warms up in the bullpen for Wooster High School, Reno, Nevada, 2006 (courtesy of the author)

The four Boden sisters of the Chicago Pioneers after winning the fifteen and under division championship at the Roy Hobbs tournament, Ft. Myers, Florida, October 2007 (courtesy Jim Glennie, American Women's Baseball Federation)

Stacy Piagno, high school pitcher from St. Augustine, Florida, pitching for the Chicago Pioneers at the Roy Hobbs tournament, Ft. Myers, Florida, October 2007 (courtesy Jim Glennie, American Women's Baseball Federation)

Team USA after winning the gold medal at the Women's World Cup, Taipei, Taiwan, 2006 (courtesy of the author)

put it right with the men's statues. And they're going to put Satchel Paige right next to them. We're making progress. But some people get impatient."

A Fair Game

My daughter Lilly is trying out for the American team that will travel to Taiwan in August for a six-day tournament against international competition. I'm in the stands watching her, as usual. I'm profoundly curious about the other hundred or so girls who want to play baseball for the United States. About fifty are attending the western regional tryouts in Scottsdale at the Oakland Athletics spring training facility, Phoenix Municipal Stadium. Lilly and I arrive a day early, and the first thing she wants to do is look at the ballpark. We drive to the stadium and park our rented car in the players' parking lot. Two groundskeepers painting the foul lines and preparing the infield smile and invite us to take a look around. It suddenly dawns on me that they are preparing the field for the *women* who will try out during the next three days; the A's are in the middle of the regular season in Oakland. When I see the familiar green and yellow Athletics insignia and circular A's logo on top of the dugout, it is all I can do to keep from screaming and running around the field like a little kid. I feel like I am in a dreamworld as I walk down the right field foul line to home plate. Lilly is frozen in deep right field, where she has entered. She yells, "Do NOT walk onto the mound!" But I already know that. It's sacred, no place for a civilian. Tomorrow she'll warm up in the bullpen and walk onto the same mound that her hometown heroes have thrown from.

"Barry Zito and Huston Street were here!" she suddenly yells, as though she has just realized where she is.

"Yeah, and probably Dennis Eckersly too!" I shout back, not sure if that ancient history means anything to her. She is still standing in right field and I am now behind home plate, but neither of us dares to step onto the dirt. I'm thinking, "I'm nuts. I'm really nuts. What *is* it about this game?" I am swooning, although the 112 degree heat may be contributing a little.

The next day, Lilly is as nervous as I have ever seen her. I try to calm her down by reminding her that she is undoubtedly one of the few girls in the nation who have played 4A varsity baseball, but it's useless: she's a wreck. And then I begin wondering, "Who *are* these girls, and how good are they?" The head coach, who will make the final selection, is Julie Croteau, who sued her high school for the right to play and was the first woman in the nation to play NCAA Division 3 men's baseball in college. She also coached baseball at the University of Massachusetts, a Division 1 school. I have read about her in every women's baseball book I know of but have never met her. Croteau is young, smart, and now living in Los Angeles, the mother of two young children. She invited the former players from the All American Girls' Professional Baseball League to watch the tryouts and give input. She also enlisted help from Brian Bright, who coached with her at U Mass; Jim Glennie, president of the American Women's Baseball Federaton; Ed Kurakazu, a baseball coach at a Phoenix high school and involved in Area Code scouting; and some former players on the Colorado Silver Bullets, the professional women's baseball team that had a short life in the 1990s. The five All American ballplayers are in their seventies, silver haired, perched on the top of the dugout bench wearing baseball hats, T-shirts, and shorts. They keep up a stream of wisecracks, try to put the young players at ease, and are a vision of how to have fun while aging gracefully.

I climb to a shady seat in the nearly empty stands, one thermos of ice water and another of iced sports drink with me. The heat, even at eight in the morning, is unimaginable. Major league teams that play in Arizona and Florida have air-conditioned stadiums for their regular seasons. On the field, fifty young women in cleats, long socks, baseball pants, T-shirts, and hats are warming up, stretching, running wind sprints, playing catch. Croteau and the other coaches are clustered near home plate, organizing the first of the two-day tryouts. I sit with my usual cohort, the dads. The chatter is similar in some ways to what I'm used to. The men talk about the season their daughters have had, and they evaluate, in the all-knowing way of baseball dads everywhere, the other players on the field, finding this or that fault with speed, strength, mechanics, and so forth. But as the day wears on, I begin to hear an additional dialogue, more like what's been going on in my own head for the last ten years. "You know, they pay the boys and their families to come to tryouts like this." "Has your daughter always been a baseball player, or has she played softball too?" "Have you been able to find a traveling team for her? I looked, and there's nothing for girls. Couldn't even find one online, nowhere." "Mine plays on a boys' traveling team." "They ought to have all-girl traveling leagues." "Hey! Check that girl out . . . did you see that? She just hit it to the warning track! Wow! Look at that . . . she bounced it out of the park!"

It's different from anything I've ever heard before at a baseball park. I begin to relax in a way that I never have been able to achieve while watching Lilly play. I don't know if she will make the cut for this team, and that is oddly comforting. It's not at all comforting to Lilly, but it is unprecedented for me to think that there might be other girls as accomplished and talented at baseball as she is. She might not be the victim of injustice this time; if she is cut, it might still be fair. Some of the girls on the field are clearly softball players, having difficulty adjusting to the distances on a baseball diamond. It shows in the rainbows they throw from catcher to second, from shortstop to first, and in their outfielding, which is slow. But some of the girls are really good and look as much like baseball players as Lilly does. If she doesn't make this team, it will be because other girls are better than her, not because so few men are capable of seeing, much less acknowledging, her skill. Then I realize one more thing. In all my years of watching baseball, I have never seen girls play together. In all Lilly's years of baseball, she has never played with girls. Not one. Maybe that explains why she is so nervous. This is a test of her baseball ability unlike any other she has faced. For this one moment, the field is level, and the tryout is about sheer ability. I wonder how it is possible that in my half century of life, and in her dozen and a half years, neither of us has ever seen this many girls on a baseball diamond.

Postscript

Lilly made Team USA. She and seventeen other women, along with Coach Croteau, three assistants, and a representative from USA Baseball, traveled to Taipei, Taiwan, from July 29 to August 6, 2006. With less than one week's practice together as a team, they won the gold medal at the Women's World Cup at Tienmu Stadium. They accomplished "mission impossible." There was no American press at the tournament, no ESPN, and the tournament itself was never even mentioned in *Sports Illustrated*. The Japanese team had a television crew traveling with them, and the tournament was covered live on Taiwanese television. The *Reno Gazette-Journal* and local Reno television stations covered the tournament daily, out of respect for and interest in their local baseball girl. A few of the other members of the American team were also covered by their local media. But the team did not warrant national attention. Imagine how good these ballplayers could be if they received the same support and attention lavished on American boys.

Notes

Prologue: Entitlement and Its Absence

1. Doug Bukowski, "Softball by Gender, Baseball by Choice," *Elysian Fields Quarterly* 22, no. 3 (Summer 2005): 24.

2. Ibid., 23.

3. David A. Andelman, "In the Suburbs, Little League Is More Than Just a Game," *New York Times*, June 2, 1973, 66.

4. Bukowski, "Softball by Gender, Baseball by Choice," 23.

Chapter 1. A Quick and Dirty History of Baseball

1. Richard Crepeau, *America's Diamond Mind* (Lincoln: University of Nebraska Press, 2000), 161.

2. Kenneth Burns, *Baseball: Inning 1, Our Game, 1840–1900*. Washington, D.C.: Public Broadcasting Service, VHS, 1986.

3. Gai Berlage, *Women in Baseball* (Westport, Conn.: Praeger, 1994), 75.

4. Crepeau, *America's Diamond Mind*, 161.

5. Ibid.

6. Crepeau, *America's Diamond Mind*, 160.

7. "Throwing Her Best Stuff, Pitcher Battled Rejection," *New York Times*, May 10, 1998.

8. Albert Goodwill Spalding, *America's National Game* (1911; reprint, Lincoln: University of Nebraska Press, 1992).

9. Tim Wiles, introduction to *Baseball Before We Knew It: A Search for the Roots of the Game*, by David Block (Lincoln: University of Nebraska Press, 2005), xiv.

10. Block, *Baseball Before We Knew It*, 1.

11. Ibid., 3.

12. Ibid., 6.

13. Ibid., 7.

14. Ibid., 17.

15. Ibid., 18.

16. Robert Henderson, *Baseball: Notes and Materials on Its Origin* (New York: New York Public Library, 1941).

17. Block, *Baseball Before We Knew It*, 28.

18. Ibid., 30.

19. Ibid., 75.

20. Joel Zoss and John Bowman, *Diamonds in the Rough: The Untold History of Baseball* (Chicago: Contemporary Books, 1996), 45.

21. Harold Seymour, *Baseball: The People's Game* (New York: Oxford University Press, 1990), 454.

22. Zoss and Bowman, *Diamonds in the Rough*, 199.

23. Ibid., 200.

24. Seymour, *Baseball: The People's Game*, 454.

25. Ibid., 455.

26. Ibid., 454.

27. Adrian Burgos Jr., *Playing America's Game: Baseball, Latinos, and the Color Line* (Berkeley: University of California Press, 2007).

28. Jules Tygiel, *Baseball's Great Experiment* (New York: Oxford University Press, 1997), 76; Jules Tygiel, *Extra Bases: Reflections on Jackie Robinson, Race, and Baseball History* (Lincoln: University of Nebraska Press, 2002); Robert Peterson, *Only the Ball Was White: A History of Legendary Black Players and All-Black Professional Teams* (New York: Oxford University Press, 1970); Allen Guttmann, *A Whole New Ball Game: An Interpretation of American Sports* (Chapel Hill: University of North Carolina Press, 1988); Michael A. Messner and Donald F. Sabo, editors, *Sport, Men, and the Gender Order: Critical Feminist Perspectives* (Champaign, Ill.: Human Kinetics Press, 1990), particulary chapter 8, Richard Majors, "Cool Pose: Black Masculinity and Sports," and chapter 15, Susan Birrell, "Women of Color, Critical Autobiography, and Sport"; Zoss and Bowman, *Diamonds in the Rough*, particularly chapters 5–7, "Don't Look Back," "Robinsonia," and "Women and the Game."

Chapter 2. The Girls' Game

1. Block, *Baseball Before We Knew It*, 77.

2. Ibid., 82–93.

3. Seymour, *Baseball: The People's Game*, 5; Block, *Baseball Before We Knew It*, 178–79.

4. Todd Avery, "The Girls in Europe Is Nuts over Ball Players: Ring Lardner and Virginia Woolf," *Nine: Journal of Baseball History and Culture* (2005): 31. Also see Jane Austen, *Northanger Abbey* (New York: Cambridge University Press, 2006).

5. Dr. Sonia Kruks, personal correspondence, April 2003.

6. Zoss and Bowman, *Diamonds in the Rough*, 204.

7. See chapter 5 for a more in-depth discussion of the parallels between women's baseball and the American women's suffrage movement.

8. Seymour, *Baseball: The People's Game*, 463.

9. Ibid., 464.

10. Gai Ingham Berlage, *Women in Baseball: The Forgotten History* (Westport, Conn.: Praeger/Greenwood Publishing Group, 1994), 18, and *Vassarion*, volumes 1900–1925, Vassar College Library.

11. Berlage, *Women in Baseball*, 18.

12. Ibid., 18.

13. Ibid., 26.

14. Ibid., 27.

15. "Games were usually played between classes or between faculty and students for the sheer fun of the game rather than as hard-nosed competition. Any girl who wanted to participate could. In most instances games were a private, intramural affair played on the women's campus and the public was not invited" (Berlage, *Women in Baseball*, 19).

16. Seymour, *Baseball: The People's Game*, 469.

17. University of Missouri, *Savitar* (1915).

18. University of Indiana, *Arbutus* (1917): 173.

19. University of Indiana, *Indiana Daily Student*, May 18, 1917, 3:2.

20. Ibid., May 19, 1917, 3:4.

21. University of Indiana, *Arbutus* (1921): 112–13, 173.

22. *Chicago Defender*, October 16, 1920. Also see Susan Cahn, *Coming On Strong: Gender and Sexuality in Twentieth-Century Women's Sport* (Cambridge: Harvard University Press, 2000), 38.

23. Lawrence Ritter, *The Glory of Their Times: The Story of the Early Days of Baseball Told by the Men Who Played It* (New York: MacMillan, 1966), 148–49.

24. Berlage, *Women in Baseball*, 63.

25. Ibid., 81.

Chapter 3. A. G. Spalding and America's Needs

1. Peter Levine, *A. G. Spalding and the Rise of Baseball* (New York: Oxford University Press:1985), 4.

2. Ibid.

3. Ibid.

4. Ibid., 5.

5. Ibid., 6.

6. Some scholars suggest that parts of *America's National Game* were actually ghostwritten by Henry Chadwick.

7. Block, *Baseball Before We Knew It*, 34.

8. Albert G. Spalding, *America's National Game: Historic Facts Concerning the Beginning Evolution, Development and Popularity of Base Ball with Personal Reminiscences of Its*

vicissitudes, its victories, and its votaries (1911; revised edition, San Francisco: Halo Books, 1991).

9. Ibid., 3.

10. Ibid., 4–5.

11. Ibid., 5.

12. Ibid., 6.

13. Ibid., 7.

14. Ibid., 9.

15. Ibid., 11.

16. Ibid., 14.

17. Ibid., 29.

18. Ibid., 31.

19. Ibid., 533.

20. Gail Bederman, *Manliness and Civilization: A Cultural History of Gender and Race in the United States, 1880–1917* (Chicago: University of Chicago Press, 1996); Michael S. Kimmel, *The History of Men: Essays on the History of American and British Masculinities* (Albany: State University of New York Press, 2005). See chapter 6 of this volume for fuller discussion.

Chapter 4. Enter Softball

1. Paul Dickson, *The Worth Book of Softball: A Celebration of America's True National Pastime* (New York: Facts on File, 1994), 48.

2. Ibid., 52.

3. Ibid., 51.

4. Ibid.

5. Ibid.

6. Other fine discussions in addition to Berlage, Seymour, and Zoss and Bowman are found in Susan Cahn, *Coming on Strong: Gender and Sexuality in Twentieth-Century Women's Sport* (Cambridge: Harvard University Press, 1994); Susan E. Johnson, *When Women Played Hardball* (Seattle: Seal Press, 1994); Jonathan Fraser Light, *The Cultural Encyclopedia of Baseball* (Jefferson, N.C.: McFarland, 1997); and Lisa Smith, *Nike Is a Goddess: The History of Women in Sports* (New York: Atlantic Monthly Press, 1998).

7. As president of the American Women's Baseball Federation, involved with organizing international women's baseball tournaments, James Glennie was asked by one of the coaches of the Japanese team, "Why do American women play softball? The ball doesn't even fit in their hand!" (personal correspondence with author, March 27, 2006).

8. Berlage, *Women in Baseball*, 103, 105.

9. Harold Seymour, *Baseball: The Golden Age* (Oxford University Press, 1989), 4.

10. Ibid., 445.

11. Dudley and Kellor, *Athletic Games in the Education of Women*, 6.

12. Ibid., 27.

13. Ibid.

14. Ibid., 31.

15. Ibid., 33–34.

16. Dudley and Kellor write, "Development of moral qualities necessarily means control of the emotions. Here games have an especial advantage for girls, for many are abnormally sensitive, introspective or morbid and live too subjective a life. . . . Games are largely objective and afford little opportunity for analysis of feeling or consciousness of the process. The attention is centered upon the thing to be done and not upon the process of doing it" (36).

17. Ibid., 151.

18. Ibid., 212.

19. Ibid.

20. Ibid., 213.

Chapter 5. How Baseball Became Manly and White

1. *Chicago Defender*, October 16, 1920. See also Susan Cahn, *Coming On Strong: Gender and Sexuality in Twentieth-Century Women's Sport* (Cambridge: Harvard University Press, 2000), 38.

2. Todd Crosset, "Masculinity, Sexuality, and the Development of Early Modern Sport," in Michael A. Messner and Donald F. Sabo, eds., *Sport, Men, and the Gender Order: Critical Feminist Perspectives* (Champaign, Ill.: Human Kinetics Books, 1990), 46.

3. Ibid.

4. Ibid., 51.

5. David Whitson, "Sport in the Construction of Masculinity," in Messner and Sabo, *Sport, Men, and the Gender Order*, 22.

6. Anne Fausto-Sterling, *Sexing the Body: Gender Politics and the Construction of Sexuality* (New York: Basic Books, 2000), 151.

7. Messner and Sabo, *Sport, Men, and the Gender Order*, 22.

8. Cahn, *Coming On Strong*, 12.

9. See multiple works by bell hooks, including *Ain't I a Woman: Black Women and Feminism* (Boston: South End Press, 1981); Patricia Hill Collins, *Black Feminist Thought: Knowledge, Consciousness, and the Politics of Empowerment* (New York: Routledge, 2000); Paula Giddings, *Where and When I Enter: The Impact of Black Women and Race and Sex in America* (New York: Perennial, Harper Collins, 2001); Angela Davis, *Women, Race, and Class* (New York: Random House, 1983); Jacqueline Jones, *Labor of Love, Labor of Sorrow: Black Women and the Family from Slavery to the Present* (New York: Random House, 1985).

10. See David R. Roediger, *Working toward Whiteness: How America's Immigrants Became White* (New York: Basic Books, 2005); Matthew Frye Jacobson, *Whiteness of a Different Color: European Immigrants and the Alchemy of Race* (Cambridge: Harvard University Press, 1998); Ian Haney Lopez, *White by Law* (New York: New York University Press, 2006); Karen Brodkin, *How Jews Became White Folks and What That Says about Race in America* (New Brunswick: Rutgers University Press, 1998); Michael Ignatiev, *How the Irish Became White* (New York: Routledge, 1995).

11. Jean Baker Miller, *Toward a New Psychology of Women* (Boston: Beacon Press, 1983) quoted in William Pollack, *Real Boys: Rescuing Our Sons from the Myths of Boyhood* (New York: Henry Holt, 1998), 345.

12. Warren Goldstein, *Playing for Keeps: A History of Early Baseball* (Ithaca, N.Y.: Cornell University Press, 1998), 45.

13. Ibid., 31.

14. Adrian Burgos Jr., *Playing America's Game: Baseball, Latinos, and the Color Line* (Berkeley: University of California Press, 2007), 27.

15. Ibid., 29.

16. Ibid., 64.

17. Burgos writes, "The Brotherhood's emphasis on big-league players' status as white, highly skilled professionals addressed an audience experiencing the alienating conditions of wage work within the emergent industrial order. . . . Baseball's color line allowed players who were recent European arrivals or first-generation European Americans to assert a *white* American identity by objecting to the presence of blacks on the professional diamond. Race-based exclusion thus created a professional arena where white players could validate their demand for higher salaries precisely because they were white and not black" (65).

18. Pollack, *Real Boys*, 24.

19. Ibid., 345.

20. Goldstein, *Playing for Keeps*, 20.

21. Jules Tygiel, *Past Time: Baseball as History* (New York: Oxford University Press, 2001), 16.

22. Goldstein, *Playing for Keeps*, 19.

23. Ibid.

24. Tygiel, *Past Time*, 17.

25. Ibid., 19.

26. Ibid., 22.

27. Ibid., 25.

28. Ibid.

29. Ibid., 31.

30. Darryl Brock, *If I Never Get Back* (Berkeley: Frog Books, 2007), 88.

31. Goldstein, *Playing for Keeps*, 48.

32. Ibid., 49.

Chapter 6. American Womanhood and Athletics

1. Judith Butler, *Gender Trouble: Feminism and the Subversion of Identity* (New York: Routledge, 1990), 19.

2. See Anne Fausto-Sterling, *Sexing the Body* (New York: Basic Books, 2000), for a thorough discussion of reasons why genes and hormones may not be solely responsible for creating differences between biological maleness and femaleness, either. That is, current ideas about sex, as well as gender, may be socially constructed: "While male and female stand on the extreme ends of a biological continuum, there are many other bodies . . . that evidently mix together anatomical components conventionally attributed to both males and females. The implications of my argument for a sexual continuum are profound. If nature really offers us more than two sexes, then it follows that our current notions of masculin-

ity and femininity are cultural conceits. Reconceptualizing the category of 'sex' challenges cherished aspects of European and American social organization" (31).

3. Susan Cahn, *Coming On Strong: Gender and Sexuality in Twentieth-Century Women's Sports* (Cambridge: Harvard University Press, 1998), 29. See also Mariah Burton Nelson, Lissa Smith, and Lucy Danziger, *Nike Is a Goddess: The History of Women in Sports* (New York: Atlantic Monthly Press, 2000); Patt Griffen, *Strong Women, Deep Closets: Lesbians and Homophobia in Sport* (Champaign, Ill.: Human Kinetics Press, 1999); and Colette Dowling, *The Frailty Myth: Redefining the Physical Potential of Women and Girls* (New York: Random House, 2000).

4. Cahn, *Coming On Strong*, 26.

5. Grantland Rice, *Collier's Magazine*, April 6, 1929.

6. Ibid., 28.

7. Ibid., 47.

8. Ibid., 53.

9. Ibid., 122.

10. Ibid., 70.

11. Ibid., 123.

12. Ibid.

13. Ibid., 85.

14. Lynne Emery, "The First Intercollegiate Contest for Women: Basketball, April 4, 1896"; Reet Howell, *Her Story in Sport: A Historical Anthology of Women in Sports* (New York: Leisure Press, 1982), 417–23.

15. "Waterloo for Berkeley Girls," *San Francisco Examiner*, April 5, 1896.

16. Ibid.

17. Ibid.

18. Pamela Grundy, *Shattering the Glass: The Dazzling History of Women's Basketball from the Turn of the Century to the Present* (New York: New Press, 2005); Joan Hult, *A Century of Women's Basketball: From Frailty to Final Four* (National Association for Girls & Women in Sport, 1991).

Chapter 7. Cricket

1. Nancy Joy, *Maiden Over: A Short History of Women's Cricket and a Diary of the 1948–1949 Test Tour to Australia* (London: Sporting Handbooks, 1950), 14.

2. Jennifer Hargreaves, *Sporting Females: Critical Issues in the History and Sociology of Women's Sports* (London: Routledge, 1994), 277.

3. Rachael Heyhoe Flint and Netta Rheinberg, *Fair Play* (Melbourne: Angus and Robertson, 1976), 13.

4. Joy, *Maiden Over*, 14.

5. *Morning Post*, January 22, 1778, quoted in Joy, *Maiden Over*, 19.

6. Joy, *Maiden Over*, 15.

7. Ibid., 16.

8. Ibid.

9. Ibid.

10. Ibid.

11. Heyhoe Flint and Rheinberg, *Fair Play*, 14.

12. *Nottingham Review*, 4 October, 1833, quoted in Flint and Heyhoe, *Fair Play*, 20.

13. For an illuminating discussion of male wisecracks about women in sports, see Marilyn Constanzo, "One Can't Shake Off the Women: Images of Sport and Gender in Punch, 1901–1910," *International Journal of the History of Sport* 19, no. 1 (March 2002): 31–56.

14. *Ladies and Gentlemen's Magazine*, August 1777 as quoted in Joy, *Maiden Over*, 19.

15. Joy, *Maiden Over*, 21.

16. Ibid., 26.

17. Ibid., 27.

18. Flint and Rheinberg, *Fair Play*, 28.

19. Joy, *Maiden Over*, 29.

20. Flint and Rheinberg, *Fair Play*, 29.

21. Joy, *Maiden Over*, 28.

22. Ibid., 23.

23. Flint and Rheinberg, *Fair Play*, 31.

24. Ibid., 39.

25. Ibid., 37.

26. See chapter 9 for a more thorough discussion of the issues surrounding sexually integrated versus segregated athletic associations.

27. Jennifer Hargreaves, *Sporting Females: Critical Issues in the History and Sociology of Sports* (New York: Routledge, 1994), 277.

28. "Modernisers Stumped in MCC Vote," *BBC News*, February 24, 1998, http://news.bbc.co.uk/.

29. Alexander MacLeod, "It's a Sticky Wicket as Women Aim to Join Old Boys," *Christian Science Monitor* 90, no. 201 (September 10, 1998): 90. Of the 18,000 members in the club, only 12,000 voted: 6,969 members voted to admit women, and 5,538 voted against.

30. "Modernisers Stumped In MCC Vote."

31. MacLeod, "It's a Sticky Wicket," 90.

32. Darcus Howe, "To Enter Lord's a Girl Must Know Her Googlies," *New Statesman* 127, no. 4405 (October 2, 1998): 24.

33. Stephen J. Bull, "Reflections on a 5–Year Consultancy Program with the England Women's Cricket Team," *Sport Psychologist* (1995): 149.

34. Howe, "To Enter Lord's a Girl Must Know Her Googlies."

35. Bull, "Reflections," 149.

36. J. Hargreaves, *Sporting Females: Critical Issues* (London: Routledge, 1994), 277.

37. Celia Roblin and Roz Tritton (Oxford Women's Cricket Club, Oxford University), conversation with author, August, 2004.

38. Block, *Baseball Before We Knew It*, 156.

Chapter 8. Stolen Bases

1. United States Constitution, Fourteenth Amendment.

2. Kathryn M. Reith, *Playing Fair: A Women's Sports Foundation Guide to Title IX in High School and College Sports*, Fourth Edition, 2004, 12–16.

3. *National Organization for Women v. Little League Baseball, Inc.*, 318. A.2d 33 (N.J. Spr. Ct. AppDiv. 1974).

4. Sarah K. Fields, *Female Gladiators: Gender, Law and Contact Sports in America* (Champaign-Urbana: University of Illinois Press, 2005), 19.

5. Joseph Treaster, "Town's Little League Reluctantly Signs Three Girls," *New York Times*, 27 April, 1974, 66.

6. Joan Cook, "Jersey Bids Little League Let Girls Play on Teams," *New York Times*, November 8, 1973, 51.

7. *Magill v. Avonworth Baseball Conference*, 516 F.2d 1328 (3d Cir. 1975).

8. *National Organization for Women v. Little League Baseball, Inc.*, 1974.

9. Cook, "Jersey Bids Little League Let Girls Play on Teams."

10. "Cathy at the Bat?" *Newsweek* April 1, 1974, 53.

11. Frank Deford, "Now Georgy-Porgy Runs Away," *Sports Illustrated* (April 22, 1974): 26.

12. Ibid., 28.

13. Ibid.

14. The official motto of Little League was "From the ranks of boys who stand now on the morning side of the hill will come the leaders, the future strength and the character of the nation," followed by a statement of goals which included the desire to "assist . . . boys in developing the qualities of citizenship, sportsmanship, and manhood" (*This Is Little League Baseball* [Williamsport, Pa.: Little League Baseball, Inc., 1969], back cover).

15. Joseph Treaster, "Girls a Hit in Debut on Diamond," *New York Times*, March 25, 1974, 35.

16. "Cathy at the Bat?" 53.

17. "Little League in Jersey Ordered to Allow Girls to Play on Teams," *New York Times*, Nov. 8, 1973.

18. Fields, *Female Gladiators*, 23.

19. Robert W. Peterson, "You Really Hit That One, Man," *New York Times*, May 19, 1974.

20. Walter H. Waggoners, "Byrne Declares 'Qualified' Girls Should Play Little League Ball," *New York Times*, March 28, 1974, 81.

21. Treaster, "Girls a Hit in Debut on Diamond," 67.

22. Fields, *Female Gladiators*, 27.

23. "Senators Vote to Allow Girls to Play Little League Baseball," *New York Times*, December 17, 1974, 20.

24. Richard Phalon, "50 Girls Join 175 Boys at Tryout for Little League," *New York Times*, March 28, 1974, 83.

25. Lance and Robin Van Auken, *Play Ball! The Story of Little League Baseball* (University Park: Pennsylvania State University Press, 2001), 159.

26. Lance Van Auken e-mail correspondence with Leah Lin Jones, November 3, 2005.

27. Jim Glennie, personal conversation with author, March 27, 2006.

28. Ibid.

29. Ibid.

Chapter 9. Collegiate Women's Baseball

1. Harvey Lauer, "Superstudy of Sports Participation" (North Palm Beach, FL: American Sports Data, Inc., 2002), sponsored by the Sporting Goods Manufacturers Association of North Palm Beach, Florida, http://www.americansportsdata.com.

2. James L. Shulman and William G. Bowen, *The Game of Life: College Sports and Educational Values* (Princeton: Princeton University Press, 2001), xxiii.

3. Ibid.

4. Ibid., 234.

5. Cary Groth (director of athletics, University of Nevada, Reno) discussion with author, October 17, 2005.

6. Western Michigan University athletic director Cathy Beauregard commented that the "train wreck" Groth anticipates reflects "where our world is headed . . . and it's not just in football." The problem of escalating Division 1 athletic budgets and the mandate to stay competitive by paying coaches and their programs disproportionately to academic salaries also involves men's and women's basketball. "Most of the salaries that we are seeing that are large . . . are coming from private dollar resources, boosters, endowments or other ways to enhance salaries for those coaches. . . . That's a way to get 3 million for a coach that does not come directly from the university general fund" (phone interview with Beauregard, April 19, 2007).

7. For detailed statistics on NCAA expenditures at all levels, see *The National Collegiate Athletic Association Gender Equity Report* (Indianapolis, IN: NCAA, 1999–2000), http://ncaa.org. See also *Playing Fair: A Women's Sports Foundation Guide to Title IX* (Women's Sports Foundation, 2004), and Valerie Bonnette, *The Title IX Athletics Investigator's Manual* (Office of Civil Rights, 1990).

8. Shulman and Bowen, *The Game of Life,* 116.

9. Groth, discussion with author, October 17, 2005.

10. Jay Uhlman (assistant baseball coach, University of Nevada, Reno), discussion with author, December 21, 2005.

11. Groth, discussion with author, October 17, 2005.

12. For an excellent report on this phenomenon, see L. Jon Wertham, "Ohio State: The Program. Big Wins, Big Money, Big Spirit," *Sports Illustrated* (March 5, 2007): 54–69.

13. Uhlman, discussion with author, December 21, 2005.

14. Uhlman, discussion with author, December 21, 2005.

15. Peter King, "First Person with Matt Hasselbeck," *Sports Illustrated* (January 10, 2006): 29.

16. William G. Bowen and Sarah A. Levin, *Reclaiming the Game: College Sports and Educational Values* (Princeton: Princeton University Press, 2003).

17. David Eckstein, the diminutive St. Louis Cardinals shortstop, was not recruited by a single college to play baseball out of high school. He was a walk-on at Florida State who ultimately became a major league star on the Angels and Cardinals. He has two World Series rings and was the 2006 World Series MVP. Dustin Pedroia isn't much bigger than Eckstein, and won a World Series ring with the 2007 Boston Red Sox. The vast majority of bigger men in the history of major league baseball don't have anything close to that sort of recognition and success.

18. Beauregard, phone interview with author, April 19, 2007.

19. Bowen and Levin, *Reclaiming the Game*, 214.

20. Jody Schwartz, interview with author, April 10, 2007.

21. Robert Conaster, interview with author, January 18, 2006.

22. Ibid.

23. Ibid.

24. Ibid.

25. Ibid.

26. Colette Dowling, *The Frailty Myth: Redefining the Physical Potential of Women and Girls* (New York: Random House, 2000), 192–93.

27. Ibid., 206.

Chapter 10. The Invisibility of Bias

1. Joel Zoss and John Bowman, in *Diamonds in the Rough: The Untold History of Baseball* (New York: MacMillan, 1989), especially chapter 4, "The Ballpark as Melting Pot," describe the racial and cultural stereotypes prevalent in the United States that have been used to rationalize the exclusion of various groups from baseball. E.g., "Italian boys were too small to play against the big boys, Italians stuck together in a few city neighborhoods and weren't exposed to the game" (123). Another journalist wrote about a Polish American catcher in the 1930s, "It is not the impression of the writer that Glenn [born Gurzensky] will ever develop into a real great catcher. He hasn't sufficient speed afoot and it may be that around the slag piles on the wrong side of the tracks Joe's schooling was neglected" (123). A *Life* magazine story of May 1, 1939 described the young Joe DiMaggio: "Italians, bad at war, are well-suited to milder competitions. . . . like heavyweight champion Joe Louis, DiMaggio is lazy, shy and inarticulate" (124). Bob Feller described Jackie Robinson in the sports pages this way: "He has football shoulders and couldn't hit an inside pitch to save his neck. If he were a white man I doubt they would consider him big league material" (Jules Tygiel, *Baseball's Great Experiment* [New York: Oxford University Press, 1997], 76).

2. Zoss and Bowman quote *Life* magazine: "Instead of olive oil or smelly bear grease [DiMaggio] keeps his hair slick with water. He never reeks of garlic and prefers chicken chow mein to spaghetti" (*Diamonds in the Rough*, 124). See Adrian Burgos Jr., *Playing America's Game: Baseball, Latinos, and the Color Line* (Berkeley: University of California Press, 2007) for an excellent detailed history of professional baseball's extraordinary efforts

to delineate which Latin Americans were sufficiently European-descended to play baseball without undermining the color line that excluded African-descended men. As early as the 1880s, for example, "The process of clearing such individuals for participation in organized baseball would involve differentiating them from blacks by emphasizing Spanish or some other European ancestry" (35). African American Bud Fowler told *Sporting Life* in 1895, "My skin is against me. If I had not been quite so black, I might have caught on as a Spaniard or something of that kind" (Burgos, 66).

3. George L. Mosse wrote, "Depiction of sexual 'degenerates' was transferred almost intact to the 'inferior races,' who inspired the same fears. These races, too, were said to display a lack of morality and a general absence of self-discipline. Blacks, and then Jews, were endowed with excessive sexuality, with a so-called female sensuousness that transformed love into lust. They lack all manliness. Jews as a group were said to exhibit female traits, just as homosexuals were generally considered effeminate" (*Nationalism and Sexuality: Middle-Class Morality and Sexual Norms in Modern Europe* [Madison: University of Wisconsin Press, 1985], 36).

4. Joanna M. Shepherd and George B. Shepherd, "U.S. Labor Market Regulation and the Export of Employment: Major League Baseball Replaces African-Americans with Latins," Emory Law and Economics Research Paper No. 7 (2002): 1, and Alan Klein, *Growing the Game: The Globalization of Major League Baseball* (New Haven: Yale University Press, 2006), 19.

5. Alan M. Klein, *Growing the Game*, 16.

6. Ibid., 22.

7. Burgos, *Playing America's Game*, 59.

8. Ibid., 63.

9. Arturo J. Marcano Guevara and David P. Fidler, *Stealing Lives: The Globalization of Baseball and the Tragic Story of Alexis Quiroz* (Bloomington: Indiana University Press, 2002), 26.

10. Angel Vargas, "The Globalization of Baseball: A Latin American Perspective," *Indiana Journal of Global Legal Studies* 8 (Fall 2000): 21–36, quote is from 24.

11. Burgos, *Playing America's Game*, 236.

12. Marcano and Fidler, *Stealing Lives*, 9.

13. Ibid.

14. See Marcano and Fidler for a discussion of legal protections afforded U.S.-born players seeking to sign with MLB as compared to Latin Americans. E.g., "The draft also empowers amateur ballplayers in their dealings with major league teams because it provides opportunities for many ballplayers to retain agents to help them in negotiations with teams that draft them. . . . baseball prospects typically arrive in the majors through formal and organized systems, from Little League through high school into college. . . . private and public regulatory regimes protect baseball prospects from unscrupulous agents. The NCAA imposes rules on its member universities that regulate student-athlete contact with agents and professional teams" (*Stealing Lives*, 22, 28).

15. Ronnie McLellan, *Reveille*, LSU, May 5, 2005. See also Aaron Kuriloff, "Baseball Is Striking Out in the City," *New Orleans Times-Picayune*, March 19, 2000; Eric Fisher,

"Baseball Asks, 'Where Are the Kids?'" *Washington Times*, May 22, 2004; Rick Hummel, "Baseball No Longer Is Attracting Many Young Black Players," *St. Louis Post-Dispatch*, April 13, 2003; Dave McKibben, "Where Have All the Little Leaguers Gone?" http:// www.sportsbusinessnews.com (The Daily Dose), August 14, 2004 (originally published in the *Los Angeles Times*).

16. McLellan, *Reveille*, May 5, 2005.

17. Ibid.

18. Ibid.

19. Ibid.

20. Peter Gammons, *The ESPN Baseball Encyclopedia*, 4th ed. (New York: Sterling Publishers, 2007).

21. The five tools are batting for power, batting for average, running, throwing, and fielding.

22. Bill Plaschke, "Andrews Is in the Minority on College Baseball Fields," *Los Angeles Times* June 5, 2005, 1D.

23. Plaschke, "Andrews Is in the Minority."

24. Ibid.

25. Ibid.

26. Ibid.

27. McLellan, *Reveille*, May 5, 2005.

28. Ibid.

29. David Ogden and Randall A. Rose, "Using Giddens's Structuration Theory to Examine the Waning Participation of African Americans in Baseball," *Journal of Black Studies* 34, no. 4 (2005): 225–45.

30. Ogden and Rose quoted in T. Boyd and K. L. Shropshire, eds., *Basketball Jones* (New York: New York University Press, 2000), 27–50. Not only are there few black baseball players portrayed on TV, there are also few blacks portrayed as spectators. "In an analysis of crowd shots during televised major league games, only 2 percent of such shots focused solely on black spectators in the stands. Where 12 percent of the shots showed a racially mixed crowd in the stands, 85 percent focused exclusively on white spectators. The crowd shots give the impression that few African Americans spend leisure time at baseball parks, giving credence to studies that show African Americans feel welcome and accepted in some leisure places but not in others."

31. The racial profile for college baseball players is, if anything, more skewed toward European Americans, and the exclusion of American-born men from racial minority groups is dramatic. According to Richard Lapchick's "2004 Racial and Gender Report Card" for college sports (College of Business Administration, University of Central Florida, June 2, 2005), the percentage of Latino Division 1 baseball players was 2.9 percent, Asian-Americans was 1.2 percent, and American Indian/Alaskan Natives was 0.3 percent. Compare these figures to the percentage of whites, 83.8 percent, and the percentage of African Americans, 6.1 percent.

32. See, for example, the *New York Times* sports section Sunday, April 24, 2005: "Senior for

Dons makes the most of what he has. Fukuroku is 5 feet 3 inches tall and is tied for the team lead in home runs." The article described Royce Fukuroku, the senior second baseman for the University of San Francisco, a Division 1 school.

33. On the subject of steroid abuse, crime in general, and an unbalanced focus on black athletes, see Richard E. Lapchick, "Race, Athletes, and Crime," Northeastern University Institute for Sport in Society, http://www.sportinsociety.org; and Howard W. Rosenberg, "Finding Cure for the Evils of Baseball," *Houston Chronicle*, August 14, 2005, sports section, pg. 1.

34. Art Spander, *Marin Independent Journal*, "Giants" special section, April 5, 2004.

Epilogue: What Does Equality Look Like?

1. The American Women's Baseball Federation (http://www.womensbaseball.com), the Women's Baseball League (http://www.baseballglory.com), North American Women's Baseball League (http://www.nawbl.com), regional U.S. women's baseball leagues, the Women's International Baseball Association (http://www.wiba.com), and women's baseball leagues from Canada, Australia, New Zealand, Japan, Korea, China, and India. I know of no data kept about how many American girls and women play in these leagues as a whole, or how many play high school varsity baseball. The number of American women collegiate baseball players can be counted on one hand at any given time.

2. Jim Glennie, conversation with author, June 18, 2006.

3. Interviews with author conducted at USA Baseball western regional team trials, Phoenix, Arizona, June 17, 2006.

Index

JENNIFER RING is professor of political science and former director of women's studies at the University of Nevada at Reno. She is the author of *The Political Consequences of Thinking: Gender and Judaism in the Work of Hannah Arendt; Modern Political Theory and Contemporary Feminism: A Dialectical Analysis*; and articles and chapters on political theory, feminist epistemology, race, identity, and sports and gender, which have appeared in scholarly and popular publications.

The University of Illinois Press
is a founding member of the
Association of American University Presses.

Composed in 11/13.5 Fournier
with Aachen and Avenir display
by Jim Proefrock
at the University of Illinois Press
Designed by Kelly Gray
Manufactured by Sheridan Books, Inc.

University of Illinois Press
1325 South Oak Street
Champaign, IL 61820-6903
www.press.uillinois.edu